SOUTH CAROLINA POLITICS AND GOVERNMENT

BY COLE BLEASE GRAHAM JR. AND WILLIAM V. MOORE

South Carolina Politics & Government

UNIVERSITY OF NEBRASKA PRESS
LINCOLN & LONDON

The paper in this book
meets the minimum requirements of
American National Standard
for Information Sciences–Permanence of
Paper for Printed Library Materials,
ANSI Z39.48-1984.

Library of Congress
Cataloging-in-Publication Data
Graham, Cole Blease.
South Carolina politics and government /
by Cole Blease Graham Jr.
and William V. Moore.
p.   cm.—(Politics and governments
of the American states)
Includes bibliographical references and index.
ISBN 0-8032-2136-3 (cloth). —
ISBN 0-8032-7043-7 (pbk.)
1. South Carolina—Politics and government.
I. Moore, William V.
II. Title.
III. Series.
JK4216.G73   1994
320.4757—dc20
94-8616   CIP

To Blease, Cammie, Laura, and Mark

CONTENTS

List of Tables and Maps, ix

Series Preface by John Kincaid, xi

Acknowledgments, xiii

Series Introduction by Daniel J. Elazar, xv

ONE
Themes and Issues in Political Culture, 3

TWO
Traditionalistic Culture and Constitutional Responses, 21

THREE
Intergovernmental Relations: Nation and State, 46

FOUR
Political Parties and the Electorate, 64

FIVE
Recent Elections and Their Outcomes, 79

SIX
Lobbyists and Interest Groups, 100

SEVEN
The South Carolina Legislature, 119

EIGHT
The Governor, 138

NINE
Government and Policy Implementation, 156

TEN
The Judiciary, 182

ELEVEN
State and Local Government, 198

TWELVE
Epilogue, 217

THIRTEEN
Suggestions for Further Reading, 228

Notes, 243

Index, 271

TABLES AND MAPS

TABLES

1. South Carolina: A Thumbnail History, 22
2. Significant Historical Questions and Constitutional Responses, 28
3. Partisan Self-Perception, 1980, 1985, 1990, 70
4. Distribution of Party Identification of South Carolinians by Age Cohort, 71
5. South Carolina Party Chairs' Self-Perception of Ideology, 1989, 73
6. Voter Turnout for Presidential Elections, 75
7. Presidential Voting Outcomes in South Carolina, 1948–1992, 80
8. South Carolina Republican Presidential Primary, 1988, 85
9. Contested Senatorial Elections in South Carolina, 86
10. South Carolina Congressional Elections, 1948–1992, 90
11. Contested Gubernatorial Elections in South Carolina, 1966–1990, 93
12. Selected Counties in the Statewide Gubernatorial Election, 1986, 96
13. Characteristics of Members, South Carolina House of Representatives, 1971–1993, 122
14. Characteristics of Members, South Carolina Senate, 1971–1993, 123
15. Legislative Turnover Service Record of Legislators, 125
16. Seniority in the General Assembly, 126
17. Record of Bills, Acts, and Length of Session, 131
18. Evolving Measures of the South Carolina Governor's Power, 139
19. Significant Twentieth-Century Milestones in South Carolina Public Education (Prior to *Brown*), 165

MAPS

1. Geological Regions of South Carolina, 8
2. Counties by General Sociocultural-Political Characteristics, 17

JOHN KINCAID

Series Preface

The purpose of this series is to provide intelligent and interesting books on the politics and governments of the fifty American states, books that are of value not only to the student of government but also to the general citizens who want greater insight into the past and present civic life of their own states and of other states in the federal union. The role of the states in governing America is among the least known of all the 83,217 governments in the United States. The national media focus attention on the federal government in Washington, D.C., and local media focus attention on local government. Meanwhile, except when there is a scandal or a proposed tax increase, the workings of state government remain something of a mystery to many citizens—out of sight, out of mind.

In many respects, however, the states have been, and continue to be, the most important governments in the American political system. They are the main building blocks and chief organizing governments of the whole system. The states are the constituent governments of the federal union, and it is through the states that citizens gain representation in the national government. The national government is one of limited, delegated powers; all other powers are possessed by the states and their citizens. At the same time, the states are the empowering governments for the nation's 83,166 local governments—counties, municipalities, townships, school districts, and special districts. As such, states provide for one of the most essential and ancient elements of freedom and democracy, the right of local self-government.

Although for many citizens the most visible aspects of state government are state universities, some of which are the most prestigious in the world, and state highway patrol officers, with their radar guns and handy ticket books, state governments provide for nearly all domestic public services.

Whether elements of those services are enacted or partly funded by the federal government and actually carried out by local governments, it is state government that has the ultimate responsibility for ensuring that Americans are well served by all their governments. In so doing, all of the American states are more democratic, more prosperous, and better governed than most of the world's nation-states.

This is a particularly timely period in which to publish a series of books on the governments and politics of each of the fifty states. Once viewed as the "fallen arches" of the federal system, states today are increasingly seen as energetic, innovative, and fiscally responsible. Some states, of course, perform better than others, but that is to be expected in a federal system. Each state is unique in its own right. It is our hope that this series will shed light on the public life of each state and that, taken together, the books will contribute to a better, more informed understanding of the states themselves and of their often pivotal roles in the world's first and oldest continental-size federal democracy.

Acknowledgments

We have accumulated debts of gratitude to the many people who have shaped our understanding of South Carolina's government and politics. We are especially indebted to the editors of the Center for the Study of Federalism and University of Nebraska Press Series, Politics and Governments of the American States. Daniel Elazar gave us intellectual challenges and insights and John Kincaid provided constant encouragement and evaluation. Joan Dee at the College of Charleston and Rosa Thorn at the University of South Carolina ably assisted in the preparation of the manuscript.

We have explored South Carolina and its politics with many professional colleagues and practitioners over the years. To mention some is to leave out many, but those who come especially to mind as we think back are Lee Bandy, Thad Beyle, Earl Black, Merle Black, Ann Bowman, Glen Broach, L. Fred Carter, Walter Edgar, Don Fowler, Phil Grose, Charles Kovacik, Bill Kreml, David Mann, Alan Stokes, Charlie Tyer, Kenny Whitby, and John Winberry. Discussions with members of the General Assembly, especially senators Glenn McConnell and Theo Mitchell and representatives Robert Barber and Ron Fulmer, with former governors Robert McNair, John West, James Edwards, and Richard Riley, and with Judge Alex Sanders, president of the College of Charleston, were informative and helpful. Bill Moore is grateful to Russell Atkinson and Kathy Heape for their unique insights into South Carolina politics.

Factual or interpretive errors belong solely to the authors.

DANIEL J. ELAZAR

Series Introduction

The more-than-continental stretch of the American domain is given form and character as a federal union of fifty different states whose institutions order the American landscape. The existence of these states made possible the emergence of a continental nation where liberty, not despotism, reigns and self-government is the first principle of order. The great American republic was born in its states, as its very name signifies. America's first founding was repeated on thirteen separate occasions over 125 years, from Virginia in 1607 to Georgia in 1732, each giving birth to a colony that became a self-governing commonwealth. Its revolution and second founding was made by those commonwealths, now states, acting in congress, and its constitution was written together and adopted separately. As the American tide rolled westward from the Atlantic coast, it absorbed new territories by organizing thirty-seven more states over the next 169 years.

The American states exist because each is a unique civil society within their common American culture. They were first given political form and then acquired their other characteristics. Each has its own constitution, its own political culture, its own relationship to the federal union and to its section. These in turn have given each its own law and history; the longer that history, the more distinctive the state.

It is in and through the states, no less than the nation, that the great themes of American life play themselves out. The advancing frontier and the continuing experience of Americans as a frontier people, the drama of American ethnic blending, the tragedy of slavery and racial discrimination, the political struggle for expanding the right to vote—all found, and find, their expression in the states.

The changing character of government, from an all-embracing concern with every aspect of civil and religious behavior to a limited concern with maintaining law and order to a concern with providing the social benefits of the contemporary welfare state, has been felt in the states even more than in the federal government. Some states began as commonwealths devoted to establishing model societies based on a religiously informed vision (Massachusetts—less so in its Maine district—Connecticut, Rhode Island). At the other end of the spectrum, Hawaii is a transformed polytheistic monarchy. At least three were independent for a significant period of time (Hawaii, Texas, and Vermont). Others were created from nothing by hardly more than a stroke of the pen (the Dakotas, Idaho, Nevada). Several are permanently bilingual (California, Louisiana, and New Mexico).

Each has its own landscape and geographic configuration that time and history transform into a specific geo-historical location. In short, the diversity of the American people is expressed in no small measure through their states, the politics and government of each of which have their own fascination.

South Carolina Politics and Government is the twelfth book in the Center for the Study of Federalism and University of Nebraska Press Series, Politics and Governments of the American States. The aim of the series is to provide books on the politics and government of the individual states of the United States that will appeal to three audiences: political scientists, their students, and the wider public in each state. Each volume in the series examines the specific character of one of the fifty states, looking at the state as a polity—its political culture, traditions and practices, constituencies and interest groups, constitutional and institutional frameworks.

Each book in the series reviews the political development of the state to demonstrate how the state's political institutions and characteristics have evolved from the first settlement to current times, presenting the state in the context of the nation and section of which it is a part, and reviewing the roles and relations of the state vis-à-vis its sister states and the federal government. The state's constitutional history, its traditions of constitution-making and constitutional change, are examined and related to the workings of the state's political institutions and processes. State-local relations, local government, and community politics are studied. Finally, each volume reviews the state's policy concerns and their implementation from the budgetary process to particular substantive policies. Each book concludes by summarizing the principal themes and findings to draw conclusions about the current state of the state, its continuing traditions, and emerging issues. Each volume also contains a bibliographic survey of the existing literature on the state and a guide to the use of that literature and state government documents in learning more about the state and its political system.

Although the books in the series are not expected to be uniform, they do focus on the common themes of federalism, constitutionalism, political culture, and the continuing American frontier, to provide a framework within which to consider the institutions, routines, and processes of state government and politics.

FEDERALISM

Both the greatest conflicts of American history and the day-to-day operations of American government are closely intertwined with American federalism—the form of American government (in the eighteenth-century sense of the term, which includes both structure and process). American federalism has been characterized by several basic tensions. One is between state sovereignty—the view that in a proper federal system, authority and power over most domestic affairs should be in the hands of the states—and national supremacy—the view that the federal government has a significant role to play in domestic matters affecting the national interest. The other tension is between dual federalism—the idea that a federal system functions best when the federal government and the states function as separately as possible, each in its own sphere—and cooperative federalism—the view that federalism works best when the federal government and the states, while preserving their own institutions, cooperate closely on the implementation of joint or shared programs.

During its political heyday in the eighteenth and nineteenth centuries, South Carolina was noted for being the center of opposition to the federal government and even to what became the standard American theory of federalism. Indeed, its leaders, led by John C. Calhoun, proposed an opposite theory as an alternative, understanding the building blocks of political society to be the states as organic polities that grew up naturally through the accepted processes of human evolution and understanding the federal union to be a product of a compact among those organic states—derivative, artificial, and thereby secondary. On the basis of this theory South Carolina fought the war of the revolution for independence as part of these new United States but then went into opposition, developing the doctrines of nullification and secession as natural outgrowths of the theory of the constitution as a political compact between organic polities whereby each polity of necessity must retain its own ability to control its fate regardless of the stance of others.

South Carolina's ideology and politics of federalism were so dominant that it is difficult even to view its intergovernmental relations from any other perspective. While it benefited from certain forms of federal activity in the field of coastal and harbor improvements and defense installations before the Civil War, it also abstained from certain commonly accepted benefits because of that ideology and politics. All this dissipated after the Civil War, and South Carolina's primary relationship with the federal government was as an active member of the "Solid South," whereby its white elites, restored to power, used the political process to safeguard increasing segregation and disfranchisement of blacks. It was not until the Woodrow Wilson administration that a new dimension of intergovernmental relations was added, whereby South Carolina became one of the southern states able to secure more than the average share of federal assistance, a pattern that persisted, reaching its high point in the years between 1933 and 1968 when the Democratic-led New Deal and Great Society rested so heavily on senior Southern senators and representatives who dominated Congress.

After the breakdown of the old congressional seniority system, in the wake of the civil rights revolution and the upheavals of the 1960s, South Carolina's ability to mobilize more than an average share of federal aid diminished somewhat, although the state, because of its own political system and culture, was able to maintain much more of the old seniority system than many of its southern sisters. At the same time, South Carolina became more of a two-party state as the solid South crumbled and the Republicans seemed to be more in sympathy with maintaining established interests or those of the new business community than Democrats. The race issue moved off the center stage of South Carolina's politics of federalism and indeed has virtually ceased to exist as a federalism issue.

Today, South Carolina relates to the federal government and the federal system as any other medium-size state, having its own interests to be sure, no longer racial but more topocratic (that is to say, having to do with the spatial location of the state and the character of its ruling coalition). For the first time in its relatively long history (for an American state), race is no longer the focal point of its politics.

CONSTITUTIONALISM

American constitutionalism had its beginning in New England. Representatives of the Connecticut River valley towns of Hartford, Windsor, and Wethersfield met in January 1639 to draft a constitution. That document, the Fundamental Orders, established a federal union to be known as Connecticut and inaugurated the American practice of constitution-making as a popular act and responsibility, ushering in the era of modern constitutionalism.

The American constitutional tradition grows out of the Whig understanding that civil societies are founded by political covenant, entered into by the first founders and reaffirmed by subsequent generations, through which the powers of government are delineated and limited and the rights of the constituting members clearly proclaimed in such a way as to provide moral and practical restraints on governmental institutions. That constitutional tradition was modified by the federalists, who accepted its fundamental principles but strengthened the institutional framework designed to provide energy in government while maintaining the checks and balances they saw as needed to preserve liberty and republican government. At the same time, they turned nonbinding declarations of rights into enforceable constitutional articles.

American state constitutions reflect a melding of these two traditions. Under the U.S. Constitution, each state is free to adopt its own constitution, provided that it establishes a republican form of government. Some states have adopted highly succinct constitutions, such as the Vermont Constitution of 1793 with 6,600 words that is still in effect with only fifty-two amendments. Others are just the opposite—for example, Georgia's Ninth Constitution, adopted in 1976, which has 583,000 words.

State constitutions are potentially far more comprehensive than the federal constitution, which is one of limited, delegated powers. Because states are plenary governments, they automatically possess all powers not specifically denied them by the U.S. Constitution or their citizens. Consequently, a state constitution must be explicit about limiting and defining the scope of governmental powers, especially on behalf of individual liberty. So state constitutions normally include an explicit declaration of rights, almost invariably broader than the first ten amendments to the U.S. Constitution.

The detailed specificity of state constitutions affects the way they shape each state's governmental system and patterns of political behavior. Unlike the open-endedness and ambiguity of many portions of the U.S. Constitution, which allow for considerable interpretive development, state organs, including state supreme courts, generally hew closely to the letter of their constitutions because they must. This means that formal change of the constitutional document occurs more frequently, through constitutional amendment, whether initiated by the legislature, special constitutional commissions, constitutional conventions, or direct action by the voters, and, in a number of states, through the periodic writing of new constitutions. As a result, state constitutions have come to reflect quite explicitly the changing conceptions of government that have developed over the course of American history.

Overall, six different state constitutional patterns have developed. One is the commonwealth pattern, developed in New England, which emphasizes Whig ideas of the constitution as a philosophic document designed first and foremost to set a direction for civil society and to express and institutionalize a theory of republican government. A second is the constitutional pattern of the commercial republic. The constitutions fitting this pattern reflect a series of compromises required by the conflict of many strong ethnic groups and commercial interests generated by the flow of heterogeneous streams of migrants into particular states and the early development of large commercial and industrial cities in those states.

The third, found in the South, can be described as the southern contractual pattern. Southern state constitutions are used as instruments to set explicit terms governing the relationship between polity and society, such as those that protected slavery or racial segregation or sought to diffuse the formal allocation of authority in order to accommodate the swings between oligarchy and factionalism characteristic of southern state politics. Of all the southern states, only Louisiana stands somewhat outside this pattern, since its legal system was based on the French civil code. Louisiana's constitutions have been codes—long, highly explicit documents that form a fourth pattern in and of themselves.

A fifth pattern is that found frequently in the states of the Far West, where the state constitution is first and foremost a frame of government explicitly reflecting the republican and democratic principles dominant in the nation in the late nineteenth century, but emphasizing the structure of state government and the distribution of powers within that structure in a direct, businesslike manner. Finally, the two newest states, Alaska and Hawaii, have adopted constitutions following the managerial pattern developed and promoted by twentieth-century constitutional reform movements in the United States. Those constitutions are characterized by conciseness, broad grants of power to the executive branch, and relatively few structural restrictions on the legislature. They emphasize natural resource conservation and social legislation.

Because South Carolina's polity was different from those of the other states, even those of its neighbors in the South, its constitution was also different. Even though it fits within the southern contractual pattern, it has consistently had much less democracy built in, even as it has moved to become more democratic as the country has changed. The state constitution was designed to preserve control by the state's locally based oligarchies, and it did not shy away from providing for state intervention into the economy for development purposes on behalf of those oligarchies. Following the southern pattern, it went through the many changes of the Civil War period, from union to secession to reunion to reconstruction to Bourbon restoration within the space of a generation. While in the twentieth century South Carolina became increasingly Democratic, it managed to find ways to retain as much of its old oligarchic ways as it could, given the spirit of the times and the decisions of the U.S. Supreme Court.

THE CONTINUING AMERICAN FRONTIER

For Americans, the very word *frontier* conjures up images of the rural-land frontier of yesteryear—of explorers and mountaineers, of brave pioneers pushing their way west in the face of natural obstacles. Later, Americans' picture of the frontier was expanded to include the inventors, the railroad builders, and the captains of industry who created the urban-industrial frontier. Recently television has begun to celebrate the entrepreneurial ventures of the automobile and oil industries, portraying the magnates of those industries and their families in the same larger-than-life frame as once was done for the heroes of that first frontier.

As is so often the case, the media responsible for determining and catering to popular taste tell us a great deal about ourselves. The United States was founded with a rural-land frontier that persisted more or less until World War I, spreading farms, ranches, mines, and towns across the land. Early in the nineteenth century, the rural-land frontier generated the urban frontier based on industrial development. The creation of new wealth through industrialization transformed cities from mere regional service centers into generators of wealth in their own right. That frontier persisted for more than a hundred years as a major force in American society as a whole and perhaps another sixty years as a major force in various parts of the country. The population movements and attendant growth on the urban-industrial frontier brought about the effective settlement of the United States in freestanding cities from coast to coast.

Between the world wars, the urban-industrial frontier gave birth in turn to a third frontier stage, one based on the new technologies of electronic communication, the internal combustion engine, the airplane, synthetics, and petrochemicals. These new technologies transformed every aspect of life and turned urbanization into metropolitanization. This third frontier stage generated a third settlement of the United States, this time in metropolitan regions from coast to coast, involving a mass migration of tens of millions of Americans in search of opportunity on the suburban frontier.

In the 1970s, the first post–World War II generation came to a close. Many Americans were speaking of the "limits of growth." Yet despite that antifrontier rhetoric, there was every sign that a fourth frontier stage was beginning in the form of the rurban,[1] or city belt–cybernetic, frontier generated by the metropolitan-technological frontier just as the latter had been generated by its predecessor.

The rurban-cybernetic frontier first emerged, as did its predecessors, along the Atlantic coast as the East Coast metropolitan regions merged into one another to form a six-hundred-mile-long megalopolis (the term in this usage is Jean Gottman's)—a matrix of urban and suburban settlements in which the older central cities came to yield importance if not prominence to smaller ones, extended by new loci of settlement in medium-size and small cities and in the rural interstices of the megalopolis and immediately beyond.

Computer technology is the most direct manifestation of the cybernetic tools that have made such citybelts possible. Countrywide, there was a shifting of population growth into rural areas. Both phenomena are as much a product of direct dialing as they are of the older American longing for small-town or country living. Both reflect the rurbanization of the American way of life no matter what lifestyle is practiced, or where.

Although the Northeast was first, the new rurban-cybernetic frontier, like its predecessors, is finding its true form in the South and West, where these citybelt matrices are not being built on the collapse of earlier forms but are developing as an original form. The present sunbelt frontier—strung out along the Gulf Coast, the southwestern desert, and the fringes of the California mountains—is classically megalopolitan in citybelt form and cybernetic with its aerospace-related industries and sunbelt living made possible by air conditioning and the new telecommunications.

The continuing American frontier has all the characteristics of a chain reaction. In a land of great opportunity, each frontier, once opened, has generated its successor and, in turn, has been replaced by it. Each frontier has created a new America with new opportunities, new patterns of settlement, new occupations, new challenges, and new problems. As a result, the central political problem of growth is not simply how to handle the physical changes brought by each frontier, real as they are. The challenge is how to accommodate newness, population turnover, and transience as a way of life.

South Carolina began its land frontier stage pointed in two directions: one, the more common rural plantation-dominated society and economy of the southern land frontier, and the other, as the commercial entrepôt for trade with the Caribbean, including slave trade. Thus Charleston became a city early on, one with a sophisticated and relatively complex life as an eighteenth-century urban center of continental importance, very unlike the situation in the other southern colonies.

In addition, in the early years of its settlement Charleston had attracted many Huguenots fleeing from the oppressive actions of the French Catholic monarchy. These Huguenots, many if not most of whom were from aristocratic families in the old country, brought with them a special sophistication and tone. They also brought a higher level of intellectualism than that found in other parts of the South, an intellectualism that formed early on, perhaps two generations before that of Virginia, which is much better known because its products were so much involved in the establishment of the United States and the writing of its basic constitutional documents. The Huguenot intellectuals of South Carolina, who were joined by Scotch-Irish settlers or their children, partook of the intellectualism of the Protestant Reformed Church, but in consideration of their economic and commercial interests, turned it in the defense of slavery and their particular version of a slave-based civil society.

Thus, South Carolina took on the intellectual leadership of the South very early, by the end of the seventeenth century. Moreover, with the exception of that brief flowering of the Virginia nationalists during the Revolutionary War period, it kept that leadership until after the Civil War. We see it in the works of Calhoun and some of his associates.

That particular combination of agricultural and commercial interests also kept South Carolina from generating the next frontier stage until after the Civil War. Then, at least, the piedmont region of the state was the site of the development of that particularly southern synthesis of an industrial base organized along the lines of a plantation society, which typified the first stages of southern industrialization and has been portrayed so well by W. J. Cash. This was with difficulty an urban-industrial frontier. It did give birth to some small cities in the piedmont region, but so much of the industrial plant was absentee-owned, by northerners at that, that its transformatory effect on South Carolina society was limited and mostly negative. Thus, South Carolina populism was more closely tied to white racism than to progressivism.

The first stirrings of a frontier rebirth came after World War II in the emergence of the metropolitan-technological frontier, which slowly reached

South Carolina, where its impact was much less than on other southern states. South Carolina remained predominately rural until relatively late, more like Mississippi than like Georgia. Its metropolitan centers were medium-size cities and they became medium-size metropolitan areas, skipping the large-city phenomenon that we associate with metropolitanism in the Northeast, the Midwest, or the West Coast.

The frontier that has really found an outlet for itself in South Carolina is the rurban-cybernetic frontier. South Carolina's land, climate, and culture were just made for rural crossroads settlements and for their expansion, and the size of the state meant that people could live in these crossroads and work almost anywhere else, or work in one crossroads and live anywhere, even before the onset of the cybernetic-based technological revolution. So in this fourth frontier stage South Carolina may be moving back toward center stage in the American historical experience.

THE PERSISTENCE OF SECTIONALISM

Sectionalism—the expression of social, economic, and especially political differences along geographic lines—is part and parcel of American political life. The more-or-less permanent political ties that link groups of contiguous states together as sections reflect the ways in which local conditions and differences in political culture modify the impact of the frontier. This overall sectional pattern reflects the interaction of those three basic factors. The original sections were produced by the variations in the impact of the rural-land frontier on different geographic segments of the country. They, in turn, have been modified by the pressures generated by the first and subsequent frontier stages. As a result, sectionalism is not the same as regionalism. The latter is essentially a phenomenon—often transient—that brings adjacent state, substate, or interstate areas together because of immediate and specific common interests. The sections are not homogeneous socioeconomic units sharing a common character across state lines but are complex entities combining highly diverse states and communities with common political interests that generally complement one another socially and economically.

In many respects South Carolina is a quintessential state of its section. At one time its inhabitants even thought of it as *the* quintessential state, especially in the years when it was the intellectual and political leader of the secessionist movement. In that respect it stands in great contrast with Virginia, whose culture and society were rooted in a rural environment and whose intellectual expressions took their greatest form as expressions of American nationalism. In South Carolina those expressions were as urban as rural and stood for southern particularism.

In a sense South Carolina has always been the most extreme expression of southern sectionalism: secessionist when the rest of the South was trying to remold the Union in its image, Bourbon restorationist when the rest of the South was trying to find an accommodation between the antebellum and postbellum worlds, militantly segregationist when all but the most retrograde southern states were seeking to accommodate themselves to new winds (often with the minimum amount of change but still to accommodate). Today, now that the South has turned, one might say that South Carolina remains as quintessentially southern in the way that it has turned.

Intrasectional conflicts often exist, but they do not detract from the long-term sectional community of interest. More important for our purposes, certain common sectional bonds give the states of each section a special relationship to national politics. This is particularly true in connection with those specific political issues that are of sectional importance, such as the race issue in the South, the problems of the megalopolis in the Northeast, and the problems of agriculture and agribusiness in the Northwest.

The nation's sectional alignments are rooted in the three great historical, cultural, and economic spheres into which the country is divided: the greater Northeast, the greater South, and the greater West. Following state lines, the greater Northeast includes all those states north of the Ohio and Potomac Rivers and east of Lake Michigan. The greater South includes the states below that line but east of the Mississippi plus Missouri, Arkansas, Louisiana, Oklahoma, and Texas. All the rest of the states compose the greater West. Within that framework, there are eight sections: New England, Middle Atlantic, Near West, Upper South, Lower South, Western South, Northwest, and Far West.

From the New Deal years through the 1960s, Americans' understanding of sectionalism was submerged by their concern with urban-oriented socioeconomic categories, such as the struggle between labor and management or between the haves and have-nots in the big cities. Even the racial issue, once the hallmark of the greater South, began to be perceived in nonsectional terms as a result of African American immigration northward. This is not to say that sectionalism ceased to exist as a vital force, only that it was little noted in those years.

Beginning in the 1970s, however, there was a resurgence of sectional feeling as economic social cleavages increasingly came to follow sectional lines. The sunbelt-frostbelt contribution is the prime example of this new sectionalism. *Sunbelt* is the new code word for the Lower South, Western South, and Far West; *frostbelt,* later replaced by *rust belt,* is the code word for the New England, Middle Atlantic, and Great Lakes (Near Western) states. Sectionalism promises to be a major force in national politics, closely linked to the rurban-cybernetic frontier.

A perennial problem of the states, hardly less important than that of direct federal-state relationships, is how to bend sectional and regional demands to fit their own needs for self-maintenance as political systems. One of the ways in which the states are able to overcome this problem is through the use of their formal political institutions, since no problems can be handled governmentally without making use of those formal institutions.

Some would argue that the use of formal political institutions to deflect sectional patterns on behalf of the states is "artificial" interference with the "natural" flow of the nation's social and economic system. Partisans of the states would respond not only by questioning the naturalness of a socio-economic system that was created by people who migrated freely across the landscape as individuals in search of opportunity, but by arguing that the history of civilization is the record of human efforts to harness their environment by means of their inventions, all artificial in the literal and real sense of the term. It need not be pointed out that political institutions are among the foremost of those inventions.

THE VITAL ROLE OF POLITICAL CULTURE

The United States as a whole shares a general political culture rooted in two contrasting conceptions of the American political order that can be traced back to the earliest settlement of the country. In the first, the polity is conceived as a marketplace in which the primary public relationships are products of bargaining among individuals and groups acting out of self-interest. In the second, the political order is conceived to be a commonwealth—a polity in which the whole people have an undivided interest—in which the citizens cooperate in an effort to create and maintain the best government in order to implement certain shared moral principles. These two conceptions have exercised an influence on government and politics throughout American history, sometimes in conflict and sometimes complementing each other.

The national political culture is a synthesis of three major political subcultures. All three are of nationwide proportions, having spread, in the course of time, from coast to coast. At the same time each subculture is strongly tied to specific sections of the country, reflecting the streams and currents of migration that have carried people of different origins and back-grounds across the continent in more-or-less orderly patterns. Considering their central characteristics, the three may be called *individualistic, moralistic,* and *traditionalistic.* Each of the three reflects its own particular synthesis of the marketplace and the commonwealth.

The *individualistic political culture* emphasizes the democratic order as a marketplace in which government is instituted for strictly utilitarian reasons, to handle those functions demanded by the people it is created to serve. Beyond the commitment to an open market, a government need not have any direct concern with questions of the good society, except insofar as it may be used to advance some common view formulated outside the political arena just as it serves other functions. Since the individualistic political culture emphasizes the centrality of private concerns, it places a premium on limiting community intervention—whether governmental or nongovernmental—into private activities to the minimum necessary to keep the marketplace in proper working order.

The character of political participation in the individualistic political culture reflects this outlook. Politics is just another means by which individuals may improve themselves socially and economically. In this sense politics is a business like any other, competing for talent and offering rewards to those who take it up as a career. Those individuals who choose political careers may rise by providing the governmental services demanded of them and, in return, may expect to be adequately compensated for their efforts. Interpretations of officeholders' obligations under this arrangement vary. Where the norms are high, such people are expected to provide high-quality public services in return for appropriate rewards. In other cases, an officeholder's primary responsibility is to serve himself and those who have supported him directly, favoring them even at the expense of the public.

Political life within the individualistic political culture is based on a system of mutual obligations rooted in personal relationships. In the United States, political parties serve as the vehicles for maintaining the obligational network. Party regularity is indispensable in the individualistic political culture because it is the means for coordinating individual enterprise in the political arena and is the one way of preventing individualism in politics from running wild. Such a political culture encourages the maintenance of a party system that is competitive, but not overly so, in the pursuit of office.

Since the individualistic political culture eschews ideological concerns in its businesslike conception of politics, both politicians and citizens look upon political activity as a specialized one, essentially the province of professionals, of minimum and passing concern to the lay public, and with no place for amateurs to play an active role. Furthermore, there is a strong tendency among the public to believe that politics is a dirty—if necessary—business, better left to those who are willing to soil themselves by engaging in it. In practice, then, where the individualistic political culture is dominant, there is likely to be an easy attitude toward the limits of the professionals' perquisites. Since a fair amount of corruption is expected in the normal course of things, there is relatively little popular excitement when any is found, unless it is of an extraordinary character. It is as if the public is willing to pay a surcharge for services rendered and rebels only when it feels the surcharge has become too heavy. (Of course, the judgments as to what is normal and what is extraordinary are themselves subjective and culturally conditioned.)

Public officials, committed to giving the public what it wants, normally will initiate new programs only when they perceive an overwhelming public demand for them to act. The individualistic political culture is ambivalent about the place of bureaucracy in the political order. Bureaucratic methods of operation fly in the face of the favor system, yet organizational efficiency can be used by those seeking to master the market.

To the extent that the marketplace provides the model for public relationships in American civil society, all Americans share some of the attitudes that are of first importance in the individualistic political culture. At the same time, substantial segments of the American people operate politically within the framework of two other political cultures.

The *moralistic political culture* emphasizes the commonwealth conception as the basis for democratic government. Politics, in the moralistic political culture, is considered one of the great activities of humanity in its search for the good society—a struggle for power, it is true, but also an effort to exercise power for the betterment of the commonwealth. Consequently, both the general public and the politicians conceive of politics as a public activity centered on some notion of the public good and properly devoted to the advancement of the public interest.

In the moralistic political culture, there is a general commitment to utilizing communal—preferably nongovernmental, but governmental if necessary—power to intervene in the sphere of private activities when necessary for the public good or the well-being of the community. Accordingly, issues have an important place in the moralistic style of politics, functioning to set the tone for political concern. Government is considered a positive instrument with a responsibility to promote the general welfare, though definitions of what its positive role should be may vary considerably from era to era.

Politics is ideally a matter of concern for every citizen. Government service is public service, placing moral obligations on those who serve in government that are more demanding than those of the marketplace. Politics is not considered a legitimate realm for private economic enrichment; a politician is not expected to profit from political activity and in fact is held suspect if he or she does.

The concept of serving the commonwealth is at the core of all political relationships, and politicians are expected to adhere to it even at the expense of individual loyalties and political friendships. Political parties are considered useful political devices but are not valued for their own sake. Regular party ties can be abandoned with relative impunity for third parties, special local parties, nonpartisan systems, or the opposition party if such changes are believed helpful in gaining larger political goals.

In practice, where the moralistic political culture is dominant today, there is considerably more amateur participation in politics. There is also much less of what Americans consider corruption in government and less tolerance of those actions that are considered corrupt, so politics does not have the taint it so often bears in the individualistic environment.

By virtue of its fundamental outlook, the moralistic political culture creates a greater commitment to active government intervention in the economic and social life of the community. At the same time, its strong commitment to communitarianism tends to keep government intervention local wherever possible. Public officials will themselves initiate new government activities in an effort to come to grips with problems as yet unperceived by a majority of the citizenry.

The moralistic political culture's major difficulty with bureaucracy lies in the potential conflict between communitarian principles and large-scale organization. Otherwise, the notion of a politically neutral administrative system is attractive. Where merit systems are instituted, they tend to be rigidly maintained.

The *traditionalistic political culture* is rooted in an ambivalent attitude toward the marketplace, coupled with a paternalistic and elitist conception of the commonwealth. It reflects an older, precommercial attitude that accepts a substantially hierarchical society as part of the ordered nature of things, authorizing and expecting those at the top of the social structure to take a special and dominant role in government. Like its moralistic counterpart, the traditionalistic political culture accepts government as an actor with a positive role in the community, but it tries to limit that role to securing the continued maintenance of the existing social order. To do so, it functions to confine real political power to a relatively small and self-perpetuating group

drawn from an established elite who often inherit their right to govern
through family ties or social position. Social and family ties are even more
important in a traditionalistic political culture than personal ties in the individualistic, where, after all is said and done, one's first responsibility is to
oneself. At the same time, those who do not have a definite role to play in
politics are not expected to be even minimally active as citizens. In many
cases, they are not even expected to vote. As in the individualistic political
culture, those active in politics are expected to benefit personally from their
activity, although not necessarily by direct pecuniary gain.

Political parties are not important in traditionalistic political cultures because they encourage a degree of openness that goes against the grain of an
elitist political order. Political competition is expressed through factions, an
extension of the personal politics characteristic of the system. Hence political systems within the culture tend to have loose one-party systems if they
have political parties at all. Political leaders play conservative and custodial
rather than initiatory roles unless pressed strongly from the outside.

Traditionalistic political cultures tend to be antibureaucratic. Bureaucracy by its very nature interferes with the fine web of social relationships
that lies at the root of the political system. Where bureaucracy is introduced,
it is generally confined to ministerial functions under the aegis of the established power holders.

South Carolina may well be the most traditionalistic state in the Union.
This is one of the ways in which it is quintessentially southern. More than
that, from the earliest years of its settlement it was built around the maintenance of traditional patterns of rule and institutions to support them. Its oligarchy not only used subtle means to discourage ordinary people from voting but included the most stringent franchise restrictions possible. It not only
developed informal ways to manage incipient democratic trends but institutionalized limits on democratic participation in decision making. Moreover,
it is hard to read the more recent changes in South Carolinian civil society as
being other than traditionalistic accommodation. While the state is certainly
more progressive than it has ever been, its progressivism is also within the
traditionalistic frame and does not require its exponents to step outside of
that frame.

LIVING WITH A DIFFERENT POLITICAL TRADITION IN AMERICA

It is hard for most Americans to conceive of South Carolina, today a mid-
dling state in almost every respect, as it was in the past, the intellectual cut-

ting edge of the South, not only a major center of the "slave power," as northerners referred to the southern way of life in the antebellum years, but its intellectual home. South Carolina was the only southern society that produced a serious effort to academically and philosophically justify that way of life, slaves and all. It generated works of such intellectual power that they have become part of the mainstream American political tradition despite the distaste of a majority of Americans then and all but the smallest handful of Americans now for the institution they defended. The Civil War not only destroyed South Carolina's economy and reputation but actually removed it or discredited it from its position of intellectual preeminence in the Union and in its own section as well. It remained a part of the South: poor, backward, and solidly Democratic, making headlines only through acts of populist racism, while other states, especially Virginia, reaped whatever benefits were to be found in the glories of the lost cause. Leadership in industrial progress was vested in Georgia and the sense of elegance in lifestyle passed to Louisiana. Texas acquired the replacement myth of the Southwest and Florida became the image of the new frontier.

It was not until the 1960s and 1970s, a full century later, that South Carolina began visibly to climb back. That climb is now in progress as the state responds to the latest frontiers of commerce and industry but without any parallel repositioning in the world of ideas. Still very much part of its section, South Carolina has never resumed its leadership in the South but now, perhaps for the first time in centuries, is becoming part of the American mainstream.

The sum and substance of all this is that within the American Union, South Carolina does indeed march to a different drummer, one whose drumbeats are not applauded. Perhaps had South Carolina not had the intellectual strength necessary to articulate its special drumbeat in earlier times and thus to better entrench it so it could survive less favorable climes, the state would have begun moving toward the American mainstream much earlier and lost much of its distinctiveness, but it did not. Even after its intellectual strength had been dissipated and then destroyed as a result of a lost war, the residue of that strength continued to influence South Carolina's polity and civil society.

Unfortunately, South Carolina's intellectual heritage, which so shaped its politics, has been lost to sight. Despite its many weaknesses and the fact that many parts of it would rightly be rejected today, it still remains worth understanding, to better understand not only South Carolina but the contemporary United States and why it is the way it is. For students of contemporary South Carolina government and politics, however, it may be enough.

SOUTH CAROLINA POLITICS AND GOVERNMENT

Themes and Issues
in Political Culture

Political culture is the unifying theme of this book. Chapter 1 introduces the major types of political culture. From its beginning, South Carolina has had a traditionalistic political culture. However, recent social and economic changes suggest more diversity in the sociocultural political life of the state today.

TYPES OF POLITICAL CULTURE

Daniel J. Elazar defines political culture as "the particular pattern of orientation to political action in which each political system is imbedded."[1] The three major types of American political culture are traditionalistic, moralistic, and individualistic. Each type originated in unique sectional, ethnic, and religious affiliations of colonial settlers. Each culture type was then carried and adapted to new conditions as people moved around the country.[2]

The types of political culture reflect important perspectives and developments in American political life. Elazar theorizes that the three distinct types have spread, in varying degrees and combinations, throughout the American political landscape. South Carolina and the changes it is undergoing afford an interesting opportunity to explore Elazar's concepts in a specific state setting.

The concept of political culture suggests that the underlying values of citizens influence political outcomes in various settings. In a study of American cities, for example, John Kincaid found that cities with moralistic cultures scored higher on quality-of-life measures than traditionalistic cities; individualistic cities scored in between.[3]

Traditionalistic Political Culture

Traditionalistic political culture is often directly associated with the South. It emphasizes social hierarchy with an economic, social, and political elite at the top to which ordinary citizens routinely defer. Early planters in the southern coastal and tidewater regions symbolized the top of the hierarchy and offered "honorable, generous, and patronizing" consideration for the ranks below. Such aristocratic conduct, often associated with elite status, wealth, and rank, is at the heart of the traditionalistic social structure.

South Carolina may be the original model for the traditionalistic type. From its founding in 1670, Charleston became the intellectual center of South Carolina and the antebellum South.[4] Widespread interest in slavery and agriculture allowed South Carolina's aristocracy to grow by incorporating new families. The extended aristocracy was not restricted to a specific religious background or a uniform religious establishment, despite the prominence of the Anglican Church in colonial South Carolina.[5]

South Carolinians developed extensive and scholarly justifications and defenses of slavery and, ultimately, of secession. Their distinctive erudition gave the state's civilization a unique component. Other southern states, including Virginia, did not duplicate the extent and intensity of South Carolina's studious devotion to slavery and secession.

Preservation and extension of the established social structure and traditionalistic political culture, especially from 1820 to 1860, is defined by an agricultural economy. The plantation and slave economy, so essential to colonial prosperity, had spread throughout most of the state by the start of armed conflict with the Union. The traditionalistic political culture was perpetuated during Reconstruction through the eventual transformation of the plantation aristocracy into a small town–based banker/merchant/farmer class as the dominant elite. The subordination of many people through the crop-lien system and the renewed importance of personalized, local government offices are additional examples of traditionalistic political culture that were highlighted by late nineteenth-century economic and political developments.[6] These traditionalistic conditions changed little well into the twentieth century in South Carolina and dominated its social and political culture.

Moralistic Political Culture

The moralistic political culture originated in New England. It emphasizes attitudes and actions that reflect the citizenry's sense of civic obligation and commonwealth. From this view, broad citizen participation should advance the public interest through an active government that emphasizes common moral principles and a public agreement to pursue the common good.

Significant moralistic elements developed along with South Carolina's traditionalistic core. French Huguenots were an early example in the Carolina colony. They offer a good illustration of how different political cultures uniquely blend into a state society that is distinctive in the South. The Huguenots were Reformed Protestants who could be moved to action by noble ideas, but they were also aristocrats, and South Carolina offered them a tantalizing opportunity for studious rationalization of moralistic ideals in support of slavery.

The Scotch-Irish, among others, moved into the South Carolina foothills from Pennsylvania and gave their settlements names such as Chester, Lancaster, and York. They could also be aroused by moralistic values, as illustrated by the Great Awakening.[7] German and Swiss Protestants who inhabited the mid–eighteenth century South Carolina townships in the middle and lower sections also established focused, moralistic communities. Following the bridges established by the Huguenots, these groups gradually either moved into the social system of a ruling, slave-owning aristocracy or chose not to challenge such a system.

A primary source of moralistic culture for the nation was the Congregationalists from New England, who spread moralistic social and political ideals westward. Congregationalists were present in South Carolina as well; New Englanders from Dorchester, Massachusetts, settled on the Ashley River in 1696 and established a Congregational church in Charleston. Accompanied by cotton traders from Philadelphia and New York, they were numerous enough to form a New England Society by 1819, but not numerous enough to transform the state's established traditionalistic political culture.

Today, a professional wave of educators, managers, and entrepreneurs, many trained in major universities across the United States, has moved into the state from different parts of the country. They imitate the separate political culture of the early moralists in South Carolina by often advocating a statewide public interest over narrow local interests. However, it is an overstatement to characterize them as the basis for a new, moralistic political culture. The new, educated professionals reflect a difference between "cosmopolitans" and "locals" as they attempt to define the public interest.[8] Nevertheless, some of them show moralistic strains as they speak out against social laxness or corruption, self-service in government, and the "ol' boy" network.[9]

Individualistic Political Culture

The third type of political culture is individualistic. Stemming from the middle colonies, including Pennsylvania and parts of New York, this culture views the political process as a marketplace where public values and re-sources are allocated according to their merits. Industrialization is a primary support for a merit-based and market-oriented political culture. Competition among individuals, between tradition and modernization, and between fa-miliarity and mobility generates breaks from the past. New social, business, and governing structures develop within which individual purpose and drive are more important than traditions or a specific moral code.

Usually, individualistic cultures are introduced by outsiders who are de-tached from local traditions and who are not moralistically bound to the de-fined local way of life. However, the individualistic political culture is fully indigenous to the areas north of South Carolina. Given that South Carolina had few mineral deposits and little marketable timber or other natural re-sources to exploit, it did not attract individualists intent on creating competi-tive markets. Neither did its relatively closed society attract or preserve en-during groups of moralists from outside the state.

CHALLENGES TO TRADITIONALISTIC POLITICAL CULTURE

By contrast, the current and projected growth of today's service economy, plus rapid real estate development, attracts new entrepreneurs to South Car-olina. The state's geographic characteristics that so long supported agricul-ture now more frequently give way to urbanization, industrialization, and tourism. Changes in one-crop agriculture, one-industry textiles, and white supremacy have unfolded, not fast enough or soon enough for many people, but more and more—especially when economic development began to speed up after the 1940s. Far-reaching economic changes are inducing differ-ent social and political attitudes within the population. These changes and at-titudes also advance racial harmony and sustain the state's aristocratic aver-sion to overt racial animosity.

Economic changes and different social and political attitudes have cre-ated more variety in South Carolina's political culture today, challenging the traditionalistic political culture of the past. The new South Carolina has em-phasized more spending for educating and training its citizens. Despite other pressing spending needs (such as for prisons), the public schools, technical colleges, and higher education institutions are long-term beneficiaries of state budgets. The population today is more educated, more skilled, and less rural than before.

Today, assorted political values compete with the historically traditional-istic culture in areas such as the newer suburbs along the interstate highways. With a modern infrastructure, including highways and communications, the physical features that once underpinned the agricultural society are now capable of supporting a greater variety of economic pursuits and social styles.

New patterns of geographic use and improvements, population growth, economic development, and emerging social diversity have steadily challenged the old traditionalistic culture, along with its political values and its governing framework.

Geographic and Geological Qualities

South Carolina's geographic and geological features encouraged the statewide development of large-scale agriculture. Early colonization established a coastal aristocracy centered in Charleston. The many rivers emptying into the ocean along the coastline provided transportation to the interior for aristocratic social values and economic interests. The absence of significant mountains presented no physical barriers to the regular pattern of large-scale agricultural development.

To turn the state's extensive flatlands, river valleys, and low-lying hills into cultivated fields before the advent of modern machinery required labor-intensive tree clearing, stump grubbing, and terracing, ditching, and draining. Cheap labor was the key to the profitability of these improvements. Thus, South Carolina's geography encouraged agricultural practices dependent on slavery. At the same time, geology furnished fragile soils that limited the long-term conditions under which successful large-scale agriculture could work.

The state is customarily described as having two major geographic and geological regions: a Low Country, or coastal plain and sandhills section, and an Up-Country, or piedmont section. The geological variations in regional land surfaces and soils have influenced population movements, land-use patterns, and political choices.[10] The two regions are often defined by a fall line that bisects the state from northeast to southwest—a separation of plains and hills that is evident even to a casual observer from such points as atop Williams-Brice Stadium in Columbia. The fall line resulted when an ancient seabed shifted upward to form the coastal plain in front of low-lying hills. As shown in map 1, the two general sections may be further defined by specific physical differences within each.[11]

The Low Country Sandhills and Coastal Plain. The Low Country is more varied and larger than the Up-Country. It contains three major types of land surface and accounts for about two-thirds of the state's total area. The land surface at or near sea level is a coastal region of sea islands, with salt marsh

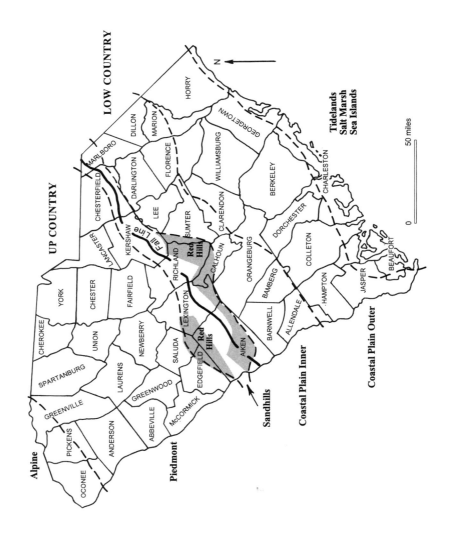

Map 1. Geological Regions of South Carolina.

and tidelands on the mainland. Next, stretching inland toward the west, is the coastal plain. The coastal plain is one of the largest flatland regions in the United States, and South Carolina's section is just a slice of it. Above the coastal plain along the fall line are gently rolling hills composed primarily of sandy soils with some scattering of red clay soils. This part of the Low Country land surface, the sandhills, resembles the Up-Country despite the difference in soils.

The sea islands are a string of low, sandy barrier islands that were originally covered with coastal grass and scrub and dotted with pines and palmettoes. South Carolina's nickname, the Palmetto State, is derived in modern times from the extensive use of the tough, cannonball-resistant, palm-tree-like palmetto to protect early settlements and to build Revolutionary War fortifications. The sea islands were the location of extensive plantations that became noted for the production of long-staple cotton for foreign export. Today, many of the sea islands house vacation resorts as well as productive farms. The islands north of Charleston were hit especially hard by Hurricane Hugo in 1989.

The tidelands are a narrow belt of land, often several miles wide, that runs along the state's entire coast. Rich tideland soil was developed to establish rice and indigo plantations early in the colonial period. The many wide bays and rivers that cross the tidelands kept the coastal counties relatively isolated until the twentieth century, when permanent highway bridges were built to replace outdated ferries.

The coastal plain is a broad belt of rich to medium-rich agricultural land that stretches more than seventy miles inland. Where the trees have been cut and the fields are open, the panorama resembles an expansive view in the Great Plains or in an agricultural valley of Texas or California. The outer coastal plain stretches from the tidal backwaters to an elevation of about one hundred fifty feet. It was the area of later colonial expansion into rice plantations. The "long-leaf" or loblolly pine is its characteristic tree. This area is low enough to be flooded by clear, freshwater rivers at high tide, and it is poorly drained. The swampy, water-filled inland areas in the coastal plain are named "Carolina Bays" after the bay trees that often grow along their edges.[12] Extensive slave labor made it possible to drain them and to convert these former swamps into excellent farmland.

The lower plain is tied to the coastal shore by an abundance of creeks, streams, and rivers, such as the Coosawhatchie (koo za hat ́chee), the Santee, and the Black. Many of these coastal streams begin below the fall line. They are slow running, and the water is often murky or "black." Swamps are the sources of most of these rivers, and the decaying organic materials in the swamps give the unique color to the water. Some black-water rivers are connected to longer river systems that are clear, fast-running streams beginning above the fall line. The Low Country black-water river network was the primary means of early travel. As travel and commerce became more extensive, settlements and business centers developed on the unflooded bluffs close by the rivers as South Carolina's next wave of settlements after Charleston.

Moving farther inland and westward to elevations above 150 feet to about 300 feet, the coastal plain begins to look more and more like the Up-Country. The long-leaf pines become mixed with many kinds of hardwood trees such as oak and poplar. Farming areas appear less expansive and are more often limited to river-bottom lands that are separated by rolling hills. This inner coastal plain is about twenty miles wide. Upper parts of the inner coastal plain rise from 300 feet to elevations of about 600–700 feet among the sandhills.

The sandhills are a band of rolling hills with gentle slopes about 600–700 feet above sea level. They lie both above and below the fall line, though mostly below it. Despite the fact that they are more than a hundred miles from today's coastline, the sandhills actually are extensive sand dunes formed by the action of an early ocean. The old sand dunes and beach ridges become noticeable when highway routes are cut through the rolling hills. The area has been described as a miserable stretch of stubby blackjacks and gnarled pines, especially by military recruits who have taken their basic infantry training at Fort Jackson in Richland County. Because sandhills make poor farmland, destitute farmers inhabited the area for a long time. Today, with modern agricultural practices, some of the sandhill areas profitably support productive orchards and managed forests.

The Low Country's red hills are scattered in parts of Aiken, Edgefield, Calhoun, Orangeburg, and Sumter counties. They are different from the sandhills because they have better soils for agriculture and much good farmland. The High Hills of Santee on the east banks of the Wateree River are significant hills that resemble low-lying mountains. They were popular resorts during colonial times.

The Up-Country Piedmont. The piedmont, or foothills, is a belt more than one hundred miles wide from the fall-line sandhills to the Blue Ridge Mountains. It accounts for about one-third of the state's total area. Only a small area in the northwestern portion of the state is actually mountainous. This alpine Blue Ridge section resembles the typical Appalachian Mountain topography. Sharp slopes and rough land surfaces are common because elevations change rapidly and range widely from nine hundred to thirty-five hundred feet. The land surface is too uneven and good soil too scarce for large row-crop operations to have ever developed here. Today, there are some orchards mixed in with real estate, tourism, and industrial developments.

Moving from the mountainous northwest toward the east, the foothills gradually change from extremely hilly to rolling hills to gentle hills at the fall line. The highest hills are about twelve hundred feet. At the fall line, the foothills have an altitude of only about four hundred feet, but they seem higher because the expansive coastal plain appears to spring forth directly beneath them. The piedmont foothills typically have broad tops and are often separated by deep valleys or "bottoms" in which a creek or river often runs.

Piedmont soils are distinguished by rapid runoff and high erosion risk. Many formerly rich piedmont surface lands were long ago ruined by intensive cotton farming. Nevertheless, large areas were under heavy row-crop cultivation, mainly cotton, as recently at the late 1940s. Planned forests, home subdivisions, or industrial sites have replaced many row-crop farms.

Now, nearly two-thirds of the piedmont is in managed forest or naturally regenerated woodlands. From an aerial survey, piedmont agricultural areas appear as groups of islands scattered across an ocean of trees. Farming is still practiced on the broad-topped hills and in the river or creek "bottoms." Stands of pines and hardwoods often grow on the steeper slopes that are more difficult to work with modern farm machinery. The falling rivers and streams of the piedmont have readily available water power from extensive rainfall and broad watersheds. This made them a magnet for relocation of the nineteenth-century textile industry from New England.

Throughout the twentieth century, significant numbers of people in all parts of the state have moved away from agricultural pursuits, and the unique dominance of the textile industry has declined.

The Population Challenge

The population density of South Carolina climbed 31 percent between 1960 and 1980 to 103 persons per square mile. In 1990, the population density was 115 persons, an increase of more than 10 percent over 1980. Between 1975 and 1980 more than 90,000 people, or about 3 percent of the total population, migrated into the state. Population has steadily increased—by 8.7 percent in the 1960s, by 20.5 percent in the 1970s, and by 11.7 percent in the

1980s—to a 1990 total of 3,486,703.[13] Current projections estimate population growth during the 1990s at more than 13 percent to almost 4 million people by July 1, 2000.[14] In terms of 1990 population, South Carolina ranks twenty-fifth nationally, just ahead of Colorado (twenty-sixth) and just behind Arizona (twenty-fourth).[15]

The African American population of the state has also changed in number and distribution: from a majority of over 60 percent in 1880, the proportion has slipped to about 30 percent today. Many African American citizens live in rural counties where they are the majority population, such as Allendale (68.0%), Williamsburg (64.2%), Lee (62.5%), and Jasper (57.4%).[16] Minority voter registration rates improved significantly in the 1960s, so that some counties with a majority African American population also had a registered African American voting majority.[17] African Americans were a majority of the registered voters in ten South Carolina counties at the beginning of 1992.[18]

The urban population increased from about one-third in 1950 to over one-half in 1980 to almost 55 percent in 1990.[19] South Carolina still has a noteworthy proportion of rural population and rural influences on public decision making. However, the rural influences will steadily diminish if the recent increases in the rate of urbanization continue.

In 1990, 58 percent of the population lived in Metropolitan Statistical Areas (MSAS), compared to 75.8 percent nationally.[20] Today, the state's MSAS include sixteen of its forty-six counties. Four counties (Cherokee, Edgefield, Sumter, and Horry) were added by the United States Census Bureau in 1993, increasing the proportion of the state's population in MSAS to 65.7 percent. The four newly designated MSAS counties represent about 9 percent of the total population. Horry and Sumter are single-county MSAS, as is Florence. Horry County has 144,053 citizens, and its largest city, Myrtle Beach, has a population of 24,848. Sumter County's population is 102,637, including 41,943 residents in the city of Sumter.

In the 1990 census, no South Carolina municipality had more than 100,000 residents. Columbia was the largest city in the state with an official population of 98,052, down from its count of 101,202 in 1980. Only three other cities had populations over 50,000 in 1990: Charleston (80,414), North Charleston (70,218), and Greenville (58,282).[21] City populations are low because the formal boundaries of cities are smaller than the surrounding urbanized areas. South Carolina has very complex annexation procedures that usually fail to be approved by voters. Reform efforts to extend city limits have resulted in recent legislative adoption of general procedures for city-county consolidation but no significant changes in the annexation laws.

The metropolitan settlements are near the crossroads of the interstate highways. The older centers, including their surrounding surburban counties—Charleston (Charleston, Berkeley, and Dorchester counties), Columbia (Richland and Lexington counties), Greenville (Greenville and Pickens counties), and Spartanburg (Spartanburg and Union counties)—align east to west along I-26, a major interstate route. The nine I-26 corridor counties contain 1.3 million people, or 37 percent of the state's population. Greenville County has the highest population of any South Carolina county at 320,167 persons.[22]

Today, interstate highways, not rivers, connect Charleston and the rest of the state, the nation, and the world. State Ports Authority officials trace the growth of export shipping from major port operations at Charleston to the interstate highway system. Highway I-26 begins in Charleston and crosses I-95 about fifty miles west. I-26 continues westward to connect with I-20 and I-77 at Columbia and I-85 at Spartanburg. I-385 runs from Clinton, about sixty-five miles west of Columbia, and intersects with I-85 at Greenville.

The state is literally crisscrossed with other interstate routes. I-85 passes through Cherokee, Spartanburg, Greenville, and Anderson counties on the route between Charlotte and Atlanta; I-77 links Charlotte to Columbia through a growing York County that is part of the Charlotte–Gastonia–Rock Hill, North Carolina–South Carolina MSA. I-20 starts at Florence, where it connects with I-95, the principal north-south highway along the east coast. I-20 moves across the state through Columbia to Augusta, Georgia, and on to Atlanta. Aiken and Edgefield counties are both tied economically to Augusta on the I-20 route.

MSA counties reflect the extensions of the original metropolitan concentrations along the interstate highways or the spillover from large cities in neighboring states. Some MSA counties—Pickens (93,894), Cherokee (44,506), Edgefield (18,375), and Dorchester (83,060)—have populations of less than 100,000 but have a metropolitan designation due to the rate at which their populations commute to work in core cities such as Greenville, Spartanburg, and Charleston and Charlotte, North Carolina, and Augusta, Georgia.

The Economic Challenge

A steadily available supply of cotton, cheap post–Civil War labor, falling water for electricity, and a friendly state government combined to support the textile industry as South Carolina's original industry. After earlier decades of development and growth, state policymakers, especially since the 1930s, have encouraged the textile industry to stay and expand. However, since World War II the state has also sought more diversified industry because of the relative decline of the textile sector. The result is a more mixed and resilient economic base than was possible with cotton-based agriculture and textiles.[23]

Textile mill workers and textile apparel workers have steadily dropped from more than 15 percent of the state's nonagricultural workforce in 1980 to less than 9 percent in 1990. During the 1980s, textiles and associated industries in the state lost almost 44,000 jobs.[24] Based on projections made in 1987, the fastest-growing economic sectors in the period up to the year 2000 are expected to be services (45.9% increase and 158,046 jobs); finance, insurance, and real estate (37.9% and 23,004 jobs); and wholesale and retail trade (37.3% and 114,778 jobs). Today, agriculture, forestry, and fishing employ less than 3 percent of South Carolina's workforce.[25]

The Social Challenge

The hunt for new business and industry coincided with a determination by local political and business leaders to establish a stable social environment in South Carolina. The status quo was especially important to the traditionalistic elite because of uncertainty about the economic and social impact of changing race relations. Under a policy of managed change, they attempted to create a "separate but equal" racial system by providing more funding for public schools for African Americans under the leadership of Governor James F. Byrnes (1951–55).

When the U.S. Supreme Court's 1954 *Brown* decision and federal civil rights legislation made Byrnes's strategy shortsighted, state leaders responded delicately but positively to the new federal policies.[26] They encouraged piecemeal changes in the status quo and moderate accommodations of federal requirements rather than wholesale resistance or sharply negative reaction. Leaders sought by all means to maintain a favorable view by outside investors of the state's business climate.

There was much apprehension about racial integration in higher education institutions. Developments focused first on Clemson University in 1963, but events did not generate the violence one might have expected from thinking simply of Clemson's origins in the political turmoil of the farmer's movement of the 1880s.[27] Instead, Governor Ernest Hollings announced to the General Assembly that the state had exhausted its routes of judicial appeal. He exhorted lawmakers, policymakers, and citizens to stick to the dignified pursuit of government by law and order and not to give in to the appeal of anger or emotion that could only result in racial conflict and scare away business investors.

Generally, formal racial segregation faded through quiet, determined, and persistent efforts throughout the state. State and local officials and African American and white leaders were all involved in this broad-based, cooperative effort.[28] Today, although a few scattered private clubs and country clubs have refused African American members, racial integration of economic, political, and public life is a generally established reality in South Carolina.

These broad physical, demographic, economic, and social changes suggest different lifestyles, contrasting political values, and a more varied political culture than before. The presence of more African American voters and an increasingly active and vocal group of business leaders not native to the state has had an effect on traditional attitudes and the old elites. In the next section, examination of selected county characteristics gives more definition to this growing diversity.

PATTERNS IN THE SOCIOCULTURAL-POLITICAL ENVIRONMENT

Ira Sharkansky notes that research using Elazar's concepts "may signal predispositions that affect the behavior of state citizens, and the programs of state or local governments."[29] Elazar's concepts continue to spark debate among political scientists though many experts apply his models.[30] Significant studies have illustrated the utility of Elazar's conceptual model in analyses of the American states and of specific states.[31]

Having had a deeply rooted traditionalistic political culture, South Carolina was generally able to absorb or "corrupt" moralistic immigrants, such as the French Huguenots and the Scotch-Irish. This is a useful beginning generalization from which to explore developing patterns in South Carolina's sociocultural-political environment.

Although not specifically related to measures of political culture, a wide variety of United States Census data is available to describe the characteristics of populations in individual counties. Data on county populations cover an assortment of social, economic, and governmental conditions that collectively depict varying circumstances within the state. Among these variables are age characteristics of county residents, the size and intensity of agriculture, education levels and crime rates, per capita rates of governmental expenditure and debt, and family housing and household characteristics, as well as measures of employment, business, and manufacturing activities.

Examination of these measures provides a way to identify patterns among county populations and to speculate about South Carolina's sociocultural and political environment. Factor analysis using principal components is one way to reduce these varied and numerous measures to a more manageable set of new variables, or factors. After each new factor is created, it may be named and associated with an underlying general pattern.[32]

The factor analysis highlights two general sociocultural-political patterns among population attributes measured by county. One pattern may be named "static" because it describes conditions that seem little changed from the traditionalistic past. The other pattern may be named "dynamic" because it groups conditions that appear to be developing or changing more rapidly as well as circumstances that can be more easily associated with challenges to the traditionalistic past.

The static pattern includes higher birthrates, more persons per household, and higher levels of economic involvement in agriculture. The variables composing this factor most closely resemble the social and economic situation underlying the general historical background of traditionalistic South Carolina. This is the customary pattern; there may be growth and pressure for change, but the potential for achievement is capped by a restrictive agricultural base and widespread poverty.

Another group of variables relates to conditions that often associate with social and economic development and political change. This factor includes higher education levels, increased levels of business sales, and political change such as more votes for Republican presidential candidates. It suggests a more dynamic environment marked by the addition of nonagricultural markets and the presence of mobile populations that typically represent the contemporary social and economic characteristics of the American mainstream.

Cluster analysis is a useful method for describing specific county populations as static or developing. Through cluster analysis, county populations that tend to be similar can be grouped statistically around selected examples, or "typical" counties in each category.[33] As shown in map 2, roughly the same number of counties "cluster" or fall into one group of counties that illustrate traditionalistic, static conditions (twenty-two counties) and another group of "dynamic" counties that demonstrate more change and development (twenty-four counties).

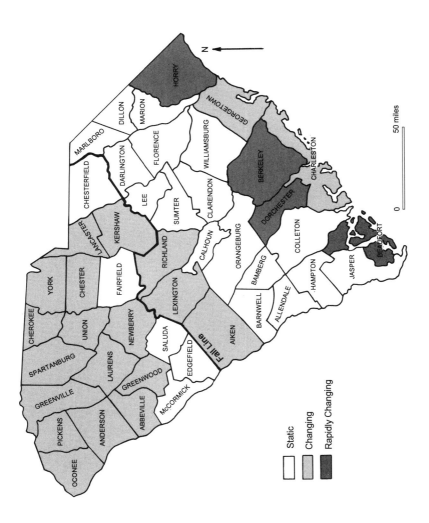

Map 2. Counties by General Sociocultural-Political Characteristics.

A small number of "dynamic" counties (four) are of immediate interest, since they stand out in their group. These counties are all fast-growing coastal plains counties.

Horry County gained the largest number of new residents (25,300) of any county in the state from 1980 to 1985. During the 1980s, its urban population increased 143.4 percent, far more than any other South Carolina county.[34] It is an area for many new retirees, but, more significantly, it is also the state's major tourist area. The Grand Strand, centered at Myrtle Beach, attracts many Canadian and midwestern tourists. Large concentrations of hotel and motel rooms and restaurants are located in this county. Horry's Myrtle Beach Air Force Base was closed in 1993 as a part of Department of Defense budget reductions. The base is extremely valuable because of its long concrete runways for commercial air operations and newly available land to help satisfy the area's intense needs for housing and commercial development. Horry citizens occasionally mark their independence by noting with pride that they live in the only county totally separated, despite modern highway bridges, from the rest of the state by major rivers and swamps. In 1993, about four hundred county residents assembled in a "Convention on Horry's Future" to contemplate countywide growth and development for the next two decades.[35]

Hilton Head Island, an extensive resort area, is located in Beaufort County. Many Hilton Head Island vacationers and residents come from outside South Carolina. It is noted nationally through network television coverage of the annual Heritage Golf Classic. Recent national media attention focused on Hilton Head Island in early 1993 due to President-elect Bill Clinton's participation in the "Renaissance Weekend" held on the island during year-end holidays since 1981.[36] Beaufort County also has a major Marine Corps facility and naval air station.

Berkeley and Dorchester counties are fast-growing suburban counties close to the major military installations north of Charleston. These counties are populated by many mobile non-natives, and extensive new markets and suburbs have developed to serve them. Both counties may have their fortunes reversed as current recommendations for closure of major Charleston-area naval facilities (including the shipyard and naval base) by federal administration officials become reality.

The developing counties in the "dynamic" pattern are almost exclusively Up-Country counties. The Up-Country counties have strong Scotch-Irish traditions that have been diluted to some extent by population and economic growth. They are no longer exclusively agricultural counties, but they still contain significant segments of relatively nonmobile, aging residents, especially where textile mills were located. The older population contrasts with suburban growth and development within the counties in this cluster.

Social and economic development in the more rapidly changing county populations reflect new conflicts as some residents respond to the impact of economic growth while others try to preserve their lifestyle by opposing significant changes.[37] Many of these counties have developed strong county councils that have increased zoning, building, and land-use regulations as well as law enforcement. The growing suburbs clamor for a voice in countywide taxation, spending, and policy decisions. These counties have to balance strong feelings of how they will respond to the larger political realities of growth, changing views of work and personal freedom, and new demands on public institutions along with the sizable groups of elderly citizens and social service beneficiaries.

The cluster of counties characterized as "static" on map 2 demonstrates customary socioeconomic conditions in South Carolina. Allendale, Jasper, Lee, and Marlboro are good examples. These counties are typically small and rural. They have relatively little industrial or manufacturing development, and they have high numbers of African American residents. They represent the part of South Carolina that may not have changed very much demographically or politically. One would expect to find in these counties a relatively closed political structure that does not warm to political or social change from outside and that may not be very tolerant of changes stemming from within. Exceptions in this group may be the MSA counties—Florence, Sumter, and Edgefield—because of growing economic activity. Florence County, for example, is the site of a major new plant built by a European-owned company.

CONCLUSION

This chapter has reviewed the geological, political, social, historical, and economic background of South Carolina and examined current patterns in these conditions through analysis of population characteristics measured by counties.

Historically, South Carolina had a traditionalistic political culture. The early diversity of colonial population and society was harmonized by the spread of agriculture and the slave economy along with the absence of major social divisions among the state's elite. Economic development after the end of British colonialism extended slave labor and the prosperity of cotton agriculture. At the same time, the state's political leaders rejected broader democratic principles for its governance.

Faced with economic competition and national policy shifts, South Carolinians withdrew into a no-party political system, and ultimately they rebelled against the nation. Aggravated by Reconstruction poverty, agricultural dependence, and white backlash to federal policies on race and civil rights, the state hardened into a static, white supremacist shell by the beginning of the twentieth century. Since World War II, greater economic diversification, population growth, and more moderate political leaders have been sources of social and political challenge to the stagnation from the past.

However, the patterns of change have been uneven. County-based population data demonstrate the variety of sociopolitical-economic environments in contemporary South Carolina. County populations are about evenly split between contrasting groups of static and dynamic counties.

One group of county populations emphasizes the long-standing dependence on agriculture—typically in small, rural Low Country counties. This group most nearly resembles the South Carolina of a past time in which the traditionalistic political culture dominated exclusively. Their economic challenges are great.

The other group includes county populations in the Up-Country as well as the modernizing urban centers. Four coastal counties with rapid suburbanization and extensive tourism seem to be the most dynamic. There is extensive economic development in all of the counties in this group, and they are experiencing sharp challenges to the traditionalistic past.

South Carolinians and their long-standing traditionalistic political culture will be challenged by the continuing economic and social changes sure to come in the future.

CHAPTER TWO

Traditionalistic Culture and Constitutional Responses

Constitutions in South Carolina have developed in parallel with the tensions and events discussed in chapter 1. The description of constitutional developments starts with the Fundamental Constitutions, a detailed set of concessions to the colonists presented by the colonial proprietors in 1669. Subsequently, the description moves to the major constitutions enacted since statehood—their features and the major changes and developments affecting them—and then to some features of today's state constitution.

South Carolina's traditionalistic political culture produced a long series of efforts to protect the state from change. As illustrated in table 1, the state's insularity was virtually continuous for two centuries, from its colonial beginnings through its Golden Age of the mid-1700s down through World War II.[1]

One native South Carolinian, John C. Calhoun, was an especially influential advocate of the need for stability within the state and of opposition to unwanted change from without. This is not to say that Calhoun had a static view, since he was very much in favor of national and statewide change as long as it was in such a way as to protect South Carolina's "peculiar institution" of slavery along with states' rights. Calhoun's "state-centered" view became the frame of reference through which subsequent leaders could explain state policy and blunt a substantial portion of the contrary forces confronting them.[2]

The rhetoric changed from decade to decade, but changes in South Carolina followed Calhoun's model. Whether in opposition to Jacksonian Democrats, to the evils of federal Reconstruction policies, or to the influences of "gangs" or "rings" of local political factions, South Carolina's leaders uniformly extolled the virtues of limited changes that led to uninterrupted internal regularity well into the twentieth century. South Carolina became a state

Table 1: South Carolina: A Thumbnail History

Before 1670	Unsuccessful attempts to colonize by English, French, and Spanish in several coastal sites.
1670–1719	Successful English colonization followed by a period of growth and development. The Lords Proprietors became bankrupt in 1719.
1719–1776	Emergence of a powerful Commons House of Assembly while the colony was run by the British government down to statehood in 1776. Charleston was the state's window on the world and its seat of political and social influence. The major problem was how to balance African American slavery and free populations. Slaves came with the first English settlers, and African Americans were a majority by 1708. Whites became a majority by 1750, but many continued to migrate west. Leadership gradually consolidated into the traditional, agricultural elite of Low Country rice planters and Charleston merchants during the state's "Golden Age" (1740–1800).
1776–1790	A period of war and adjustment to independence. Sectional differences were formally recognized and limited moves were made toward unification of Low Country and Up-Country sections. Many with economic or political troubles moved away.
1790–1820	State dominated by large-scale agriculture. Many South Carolinians were active and prominent in national affairs. The 1790 constitution gave the state its first organized statewide government. African Americans again became a majority of the population by 1820, and the continuation of slavery became a national question.
1820–1850	Closing off of the state and the dominance of John C. Calhoun's state-centered views. There were many episodes of tedious negotiation and compromise with national policies.
1850–1877	Gradual separation from the nation; rebellion, secession, Civil War; defeat and Reconstruction.
1877–1890	Restoration of conservative ruling aristocrats and gradual emergence of anticonservative politics.
1890–1960	Triumph of the politics of white supremacy in a "separate but equal" policy implemented by a Farmers' Revolt. One-crop (cotton) agriculture persisted in the face of grinding poverty. Industrialization consisted largely of cotton-based textiles. African Americans left the state in large numbers after 1900.
1960–today	Politics of racial moderation; state modernization through increased African American voter registration and changes in governmental form; increasing diversity of political views within the state.

based on one-crop agriculture (cotton), one-industry manufacturing (textile), and white social and political supremacy that would have met with Calhoun's approval. These economic and social interests achieved almost holy status against internal or external pressures for transformation, even if the pressures proved more imagined than real.

Contemporary political leaders, beginning particularly in the 1960s, have had to confront this solid bloc of common opinion and balance it against the risk of distrust by social critics or advocates for change. Still, chip by chip and degree by degree, pragmatic leaders have sculpted today's forms of South Carolina society and government from rock-hard traditions that reach deep into colonial life and experience.

The earliest attempt at colonial governance was the arrangements of the Fundamental Constitutions that provided for an appointed upper legislative body, or council, and an appointed governor along with an elected lower legislative body. The orders from royal governors soon found competition from the elected legislative body, or the Commons House of Assembly. The Commons House institutionalized the state's first traditionalistic political elite and provided the means to incorporate and unify new and different political interests as the population changed in number and composition.

Legislative rule in South Carolina is often traced to the colonial practices of direct legislative control of local affairs and legislative defiance of external authorities. In the century from colonization to the American Revolution (1670–1776), the Commons House gradually expanded into the dominating governing force. Especially after proprietary rule ended in 1719, the Commons House asserted more and more authority over the governor and council. It concentrated governing power over both state and local affairs in legislative hands. These practices were often subsequently made a part of the state's constitution and its approach to the practice of government.

Since the colonial period, the legislature has continually dominated and controlled other state officials and their decisions. Coupled with its control of spending power, the story of the South Carolina legislature is the story of South Carolina government throughout the state's history.[3] It is the extent and persistence of legislative dominion into contemporary times that has led observers to characterize South Carolina as the "legislative state."[4]

COLONIAL BACKGROUND

John and Sebastian Cabot, under the authority of England's King Henry VII, were among the first European visitors to the region of the present-day

American Southeast in 1497. The Spanish and French also initiated ventures in the region. The English first called the entire region *Virginia* but later applied the name *Carolina* to the lower part. For a long time the English did nothing to colonize the Carolina territory. Then, in 1629, Charles I of England granted all the territory south of Virginia as far west as the Mississippi River to his attorney general, Sir Robert Heath.[5] When the Heath charter failed, King Charles II restarted the colonial project by granting the land to some of his political supporters. The grant was made in a charter dated March 24, 1663, to eight "Lords Proprietors."

The Fundamental Constitutions

The Lords Proprietors were allowed by the charters to develop a code of laws for the colonies with the advice and consent of the inhabitants. John Locke, later a noted English political philosopher, was secretary and physician to one of the Lords Proprietors, Anthony, Lord Ashley. A popular story is that Locke collaborated in the initial design of an approach to social and governmental structures contained in a fundamental code of laws for the colony.

Set out as the "Fundamental Constitutions," five major versions were developed between 1669 and 1698.[6] The proposals never really worked in the colony because the formal power was in the hands of the Lords Proprietors, who lived in England. Nevertheless, the tone of the arrangements did much to set the political culture and perspectives of colonial residents and South Carolina politics.

The conscious attempts in the Fundamental Constitutions to create a nobility in the new colony gave South Carolina very "English" traditions. The Lords Proprietors' plan for a colonial nobility may have reflected their support for the restored English monarch, but the realistic effect was that "their plan to award large acreages with contingent responsibilities and prerogatives to selected individuals [became] a very practical promotional device."[7] These first colonists appear to have been as interested in making money and enhancing their business reputations as they were in establishing any grand scheme for organizing their society and their state.

The Fundamental Constitutions provided for a two-house parliament to make and revise laws. The upper house was to be composed of the seven deputies of the proprietors, seven of the oldest noblemen, and seven men chosen by the lower house. The lower house, the Commons House of Assembly, consisted of representatives of the different counties and towns. The proprietors were given power by the charter to create counties; to build towns, cities, and forts; to establish a judicial system; to train soldiers and to wage war when necessary; and to confer titles of honor.

The charter also required that settlers be allowed to worship in the church of their choice. The Fundamental Constitutions required belief in God and regular worship, and affirmed the duty of a citizen to swear to the truth if called upon. Although full freedom of religious exercise and belief was allowed by the Fundamental Constitutions, it is probably accurate to say that the Church of England was intended by the charter as an established church. The proprietors had the right to appoint ministers to all churches in the colony, but settlers could join churches other than the Anglican one if they wished.[8]

Whether due to the physical absence of the Lords Proprietors from the colony, the spirit of the New World, or irregular settlement patterns, the nobility envisioned in the Fundamental Constitutions never materialized. Three counties—Berkeley (including present-day Charleston), Craven, and Colleton—were formed, but Craven remained sparsely settled.

The proprietors ordered in 1683 that the twenty-member parliament be elected ten each from the two populated counties rather than all twenty at Charles Town (later Charleston). The people paid no attention, and the proprietors could do nothing about it. The proprietors strained relationships further by objecting to an act of the colonial parliament that protected colonists from prosecution for debt incurred outside the colony. In the original land grants, the proprietors had permitted annual rents to be paid in either money or merchandise. Now, they insisted on payments only in money. Because money was scarce in the colony, the settlers resisted through their parliament.

In 1685, a parliament of eight deputies and twenty elected representatives first met to consider the proprietors' decision to put into effect a new constitution, proposed by the proprietors in 1682. Twelve elected members of the parliament walked out, claiming support for the existing version of the Fundamental Constitution of 1669. The remaining members of the parliament, under the leadership of a newly appointed governor, proceeded to pass all the laws. By 1686 this leftover parliament was concentrating on an invasion of the Spanish territory to the south (contemporary south Georgia and north Florida) and ignored internal colonial affairs and protests even more.

The Fundamental Constitutions became obscured on many fronts by the continuing struggles between old settlers, new settlers, and the proprietors. For example, trade between the colonies and transportation of goods in vessels other than English ones were prohibited by English laws. The colonists thought their charter and the Fundamental Constitutions allowed them to trade as they wanted. When a Charles Town court overturned the English revenue collector as he tried to enforce the navigation laws, the English king turned on the proprietors. The colonists added to pressures by demanding more independence, which put the proprietors under more strain and the people in closer allegiance with the king.[9]

Colonial Government under the British Crown

In 1719, the colonial inhabitants declared themselves independent of the proprietors. The problems that plagued the proprietors as they attempted to implement the Fundamental Constitutions had finally caught up with them. The formalized social structure envisioned in the Fundamental Constitutions, however, laid the groundwork for establishing and carrying on a traditionalistic political culture. This groundwork reinforced a coastal, agricultural aristocracy with the belief that its prominence and status gave it power and jurisdiction over new arrivals as well as settlers in the Up-Country.

The new colonial government after 1719 was administered by the British government and modeled after it. Governing power lay in a governor, a council, and an assembly. The governor was the king's representative and was appointed by him. The council became like the English House of Lords. It was appointed by the king and functioned as an advisory board to the governor. The assembly, or Commons House, was like the English House of Commons and consisted of elected representatives. The governor could convene or dissolve the assembly and veto its acts. Once approved by the governor, laws had to be sent to England to be approved by the king before they could be enforced officially.

Generally, the colony prospered under these arrangements. Rice was a major source of wealth, along with indigo and silk. Settlement expanded. In 1747, the white population was twenty-five thousand and the slave population was thirty-nine thousand.

The prosperous conditions changed because of the change in the English king perhaps as much as for any other reason. Under George II, South Carolina was treated quite favorably and given extensive considerations. The sons of South Carolina planters were generally educated in England. There were frequent and affectionate references to England as the "mother country."

Under George III after 1760, the number of English officials moving into the colony increased steadily. The colonists disagreed with many of the decisions of the British Parliament—such as the Stamp Act of 1765, though it was repealed in 1766—and subsequent taxes on products such as glass, paper, and tea. The opposition was expressed by resolutions of the Commons House. The legislature led and consolidated public opinion against British governance of South Carolina.

The actions of the colonial Commons House of Assembly had, over time, become increasingly at odds with the intentions of the Fundamental Constitutions and with the orders of royal governors. After the mid-1700s, the Commons House literally took over from the royal governor and the royal council. It was just as reluctant to decentralize its authority within the state. It avoided creating significant units of local government by providing for limited local government by a legislative commission for each specific area or problem.

CONSTITUTIONS AFTER STATEHOOD

South Carolina adopted its first state constitution March 26, 1776. Since then, it has had six more (1778, 1790, 1861, 1865, 1868, and 1895). As highlighted in table 2, some of the constitutions (1790, 1868, 1895) have been more extensive and politically significant than others.

The major constitutions were adopted at critical turning points in the state's history: in 1790 at the time of federal statehood, in 1868 during Reconstruction and in 1895 after general economic distress. Although a totally new constitution has not been proposed specifically since then, significant revision and modernization of the 1895 constitution have been ongoing since 1968 in response to federal civil rights policies and practical state and local reform pressures.

Revolutionary Era Constitutions (1776, 1778)

With pending revolution, state affairs were assumed by a Provincial Congress. It formed a committee to draft a plan of government for the state. On March 26, 1776, more than three months before the Declaration of Independence, the committee's report was adopted by the Provincial Congress as the first constitution of South Carolina as a free and independent state.

The Provincial Congress dissolved into a General Assembly that dominated the new government. The General Assembly was formed into two houses. The lower house was elected popularly. The lower house then elected thirteen of its members as a legislative council or upper house. It also elected a president (who was chief executive, like a governor), a vice president, and a chief justice. The president had veto power over legislation but

Table 2: Significant Historical Questions and Constitutional Responses

Historical Questions	*Constitutional Responses*
1. How to form the colony as an attractive development?	The Fundamental Constitutions
2. How to deal with an expanding colony?	The ascendance of the Commons House of Assembly
3. How to coordinate the established Low Country aristocracy with the new Up-Country settlers?	1790 constitution —extend representation to the Up-Country based on population, but keep property as a voting qualification —strip the governor of veto and keep the office weak —maintain legislative rule
4. How to reconcile the state with the Union?	Constitution of 1868 —popularity ratified —separation of powers —stronger, popularly elected governor with veto power —provisions for counties, free schools, personal freedoms and liberties
5. How to assert white dominance over a racially divided state?	Constitution of 1895 —made by a convention with few minority representatives —suffrage clause to exclude African Americans —maintain legislative rule through decentralization
6. How to modernize the structure and provisions for state and local government?	Revised constitution of 1895 —remove obsolete provisions to eliminate racial separation —rewrite often-amended parts —allow county self-governance —rework finance and taxation
7. Lingering problems: —how to strengthen the executive? —more judicial accountability? —reduce power of legislature to govern directly by commissions? —more coordinated or enhanced local government powers?	

could not be reelected. Practically, political power stayed firmly in legislative hands, and legislative representation did not change significantly.

The new constitution tried to deal with potential political differences between the Up-Country and Low Country, but it did not go very far. The Up-Country area had a large, white population but was able to elect only 64 of the 202 members of the General Assembly, or a little more than 30 percent.[10]

In 1778 some modifications were made by the General Assembly in the state's second constitution. "Governor" replaced "president" as the name of the state's chief executive, but the legislature continued to elect the governor as well as the lieutenant governor. The representation imbalance in the legislature was adjusted so that the Up-Country share approached 40 percent.[11] The upper house was no longer a legislative council; it became a senate. The new senators also were elected popularly.

In the process of constitutional change, the Anglican Church lost its special role in the government. All of the organized Protestant congregations became part of the established church, but none of them, Anglican or non-Anglican, was to get any financial support from the state as the Anglican Church had in the past. Without finances and because of the separation of church and state after the Revolution, church officials could no longer maintain vital statistics, register voters, or perform other duties of state that now devolved onto the government.

Despite the appearance of formal arrangements for the structure of a government, the presence of a real government remained somewhat ephemeral. Charles Town (Charleston) was captured by the British in 1780, and the British controlled large chunks of territory all across the state. British military occupation had mobilized the Up-Country.

British military regulars dealt with native partisan sympathizers by burning down their houses and barns, killing their livestock, and destroying their possessions. The British generated additional enemies by not being content with just passive conduct by the occupants of their conquered territory. Instead, they demanded that inhabitants actively support their efforts.[12] Whether mobilized into a partisan militia or forced into reluctant participation in public life as apparent British subjects, the Scotch and Irish people of the backwoods found themselves more deeply involved in state affairs during and after the Revolution. They developed a hunger to get involved in state government. Among their interests were more equitable legislative representation and the redevelopment of legislative activity. Interrupted by war, the General Assembly did not meet until the last stages of the war (January

1782) at Jacksonborough, a settlement about thirty miles southwest of Charleston on the Edisto River.[13]

Members of the legislature came from a victorious but disordered army. General Nathanael Greene had his hands full keeping the peace among officers who had not been paid for two years. There are even tales that some of "South Carolina's finest" argued over rank and took public property (horses) for their own use, perhaps even selling them for private profit.[14]

However, the Jacksonborough legislature provided a new feeling of achievement and success for the state's elite. They had been physically challenged by organized outsiders and agitated by economic hardship, but they had won against heavy odds. Speeches at Jacksonborough heaped praised upon South Carolina's heroic Revolutionary War generals: Thomas Sumter, whose troops were as feisty as the "fighting chickens," or gamecocks used in local sport;[15] Francis Marion, leader of Low Country campaigns as the Swamp Fox; and Andrew Pickens, a significant Up-Country leader. Even the militia came in for congratulations. Continued physical and economic challenges in the nineteenth century evoked similar legislative admiration of militaristic actions.

After the close of the Revolutionary period, the General Assembly focused on such problems as confiscating the estates of British supporters. Emotions surrounding the treatment of British supporters were no small problem for the struggling legislators. Many South Carolinians, prematurely measuring the political winds, concluded that the British had won in 1780 when Charles Town fell, so they swore loyalty to Britain. After the comeback of the Patriots and the expulsion of the British, how were these "friends and neighbors" to be assessed? The answers ranged from exile to heavy fines, confiscation of property, and even lynching.[16]

Historian David Ramsay provides an understated description of the contrast in the years after the American Revolution. "The eight years of war in Carolina [1776–82] were followed by eight years of disorganization [1783–90], which produced such an amount of civil distress as diminished with some their respect for liberty and independence."[17] Nevertheless, helped by a need to focus on economic decisions formerly left to the British Board of Trade, South Carolinians soon forgot about punishing each other and generally set about dealing with a whole new set of issues.

Significant economic and social changes lay behind events that converged on the new constitutional arrangements devised in 1790. The mainspring for change was the continuing imbalance in legislative representation that gave the overwhelming advantage to the Low Country. Before 1790, even the political symbolism appeared tarnished—the legislature sat in Charleston, so it seemed foreordained that Charlestonians and their associates would have their way against everybody else.

The legislature relocated the capital from Charleston in 1786 and created a new one in Columbia, the geographic center of the state, to symbolize increased statewide unity. In 1787, the General Assembly banned the importation of new slaves. On May 23, 1788, South Carolina ratified the United States Constitution. In the 1790 legislative session, the first in Columbia, the General Assembly ratified another state constitution—its third, but this time a more significant constitution that remained in force until 1861. The 1790 constitution was framed by a convention of delegates specifically elected by the "People of the State of South Carolina."

The Constitution of 1790

In many ways, the 1790 constitution was a recognition of the need to conciliate the interests of two geographic sections, Low Country and Up-Country, and two distinct groups, aristocratic planter and backwoods farmer. At one pole was a century-old, established agricultural aristocracy that thought it had the power and responsibility to define the terms by which it conveyed its privileges to others. At the other pole was an emerging population mass that demanded democratic solutions based on perceptions of popular sovereignty and personal liberties validated by the Revolution. As part of the American constitutional base, the 1790 constitution may be one example of "the mediating force between the pressures of politics found universally in all political systems."[18]

The Up-Country (defined at the time as the "upper district"—the judicial districts of Cheraw, Camden, Ninety Six, and Orangeburg) led the charge to get the General Assembly to authorize a constitutional convention. The Low Country "district" made of the judicial circuits of Georgetown, Charleston, and Beaufort defended the status quo. Although the population differences were "upper" 111,534 white inhabitants versus "lower" 28,644 white inhabitants, representation at the convention was unequal.[19] Each election district sent a number of delegates equal to its number of representatives in both houses of the legislature. The Low Country aristocracy was in complete control.

The constitution of 1790 continued the colonial legislative traditions, but it also reflected the conflicts and accommodations of the ideals of the American Revolution between the wealthy planters and slave economy of the Low

Country and the white small farmers typical in the Up-Country. The triumph of the established Low Country interests is demonstrated by the 1790 provisions for representation according to wealth and population, a governor without veto power, and separate "upper district" and "lower district" court divisions. After primogeniture was abolished and religious equality recognized, the new constitution placed political power in the hands of a propertied, slaveholding aristocracy that exercised its power through the legislature.[20] Social division came quickly to be treated as a dangerous political threat in South Carolina's fragile post-Revolutionary political order.

The 1790 constitution firmly instilled aristocratic control and provided for its regular and authoritative exercise through government and politics. David D. Wallace characterizes it as "aristocratic stability."[21] The key to aristocratic dominance was the institutionalization of political control by white male owners of land and slaves. A House member had to own five hundred acres of land and ten slaves in his district. One could also qualify as a House member by owning debt-free real estate worth 150 pounds sterling or, if not a resident of the parish, 500 pounds sterling. Senators needed to have twice as much worth in each circumstance. Voter registration was limited to males; a man could vote in any district where he owned fifty acres of land or a lot in town or in his residential district if he paid tax there of three shillings sterling. Although primogeniture was abolished, the qualifications to vote or be elected to the legislature were more restrictive than in any other American state. Perhaps because of the type of person who could go to the General Assembly or because of the power centered in the legislature, South Carolina rapidly became one of the most influential states in the new American Union.

The power of the 1790 legislature was virtually supreme over all matters of government in South Carolina. The separation of church and state was complete. The legislature made all the laws and elected the candidates for all other major offices. A governor (with no veto power), presidential electors, United States senators, and even many local officials were elected by legislative, not popular, vote.

Wallace suggests that the system worked because the slaveholding class needed constant protection, not only from forces of change outside the state but from changes within as well. The established interests in the state needed loyal representatives in the legislature, so they selected themselves. The officers of the state needed to be controlled so they could not upset these interests, so the self-selected legislature elected them too. The resources of the landowners or persons of wealth serving as legislators allowed them enough personal time to attend to legislation and other public matters. Wallace concludes that "the mere business man was long made to know and keep his place by the landed aristocracy and the bar."[22]

Cotton planting spread across the state so that the Up-Country farmer became more and more like the slaveholding Low Country rice planter. In 1808, the state constitution was amended to split representation in the General Assembly equally between the upper and lower divisions.

The traditionalistic political culture enshrined by the 1790 constitution was challenged little until the 1860s. Events surrounding the lifestyles of prominent Charleston families of the time illustrate the values of aristocracy and patriotism underlying the establishment and continuation of traditionalistic South Carolina politics, economics, and society.[23]

Secession and the 1861 Constitution

The Secession Convention met in Columbia in December 1860 but adjourned to Charleston because of a case of smallpox just across the street from Columbia's First Baptist Church, where the convention met. South Carolina's Ordinance of Secession was adopted and signed in Charleston on December 20, 1860. The Secession Convention also made some changes in the wording of the 1790 constitution to accommodate withdrawal from the federal union. The constant and total military mobilization of the state during secession placed concerns for the operations of government in the hands of military officers as much as elected officials. Nevertheless, elections to the legislature were held and the legislature proceeded to elect the governor as always.

One might maintain that there was no new state constitution because the existing provisions for internal governance were not changed significantly. However, once South Carolina seceded from the Union in 1860, the existing state constitution did exist outside the United States Constitution and thus is usually counted separately.

South Carolina soon dispatched commissioners to other states to invite them to meet to organize a new Confederate nation based, in its view, on a proper interpretation of the United States Constitution. A southern convention was convened in Montgomery, Alabama, in February 1861 to frame the new Confederate constitution, elect a president, create a Congress, and put into effect the laws of the United States with which it agreed. The members of the Confederate cabinet could sit, but not vote, in the Confederate Congress. The Confederate president was limited to one six-year term and had an item veto on appropriations bills. To adopt appropriations not requested by its president, the Confederate constitution required a two-thirds vote of its Congress.

Many of South Carolina's ideas of a good national constitution were not enthusiastically received at the southern convention. South Carolina tried and lost in efforts, among others, to prevent appeals from a state Supreme Court to the Confederate Supreme Court, to count all slaves when defining the population to apportion representation (since South Carolina had a tremendous slave population), to require state legislatures to elect presidential electors (South Carolina was the last state to allow popular election of presidential electors), and to prohibit admission to the Confederacy of any non-slaveholding state.

Although the state legislature ratified the new Confederate national constitution, South Carolina did not act with the same enthusiasm as it did when seceding from the United States.[24] Robert Barnwell Rhett had been an active secessionist and was probably disappointed that he was not made Confederate president. As editor of the Charleston *Mercury,* he used the newspaper for a constant and blistering attack on the Confederacy and Jefferson Davis.[25] Other state leaders joined with Rhett, increasing South Carolina's sense of isolation in an ill-conceived conflict that would only lead to military and economic defeat and to an immediate necessity to recognize outside influence.

The Constitution of 1865

Once Confederate leaders, including General Robert E. Lee at Appomattox and General Joseph E. Johnston at Durham, surrendered their armies, South Carolinians began to return home. South Carolina faced major economic and social problems: (1) its major cities, Charleston and Columbia, were burned to the ground; (2) military courts governed the state; (3) agriculture was revolutionized from slave to free labor, but, without adequate money resources, roots were being laid for sharecropping and the crop-lien system;[26] (4) the Freedman's Bureau reallocated coastal lands and islands that had been occupied by federal troops in 1861, and federal tax policies provided other land for redistribution to freedmen;[27] and (5) some citizens emigrated to Mexico, to Brazil, and to the western United States.

The task of rebuilding or reconstructing the defeated Confederate states was first attempted by the president of the United States. A new state constitution was a requirement for readmission to the federal union. President Andrew Johnson appointed a provisional governor, Benjamin F. Perry, on June

30, 1865. Governor Perry's first task was to find and register eligible voters (those who had taken an oath of allegiance to the United States) in order to elect delegates to a state constitutional convention. He required that each parish and district (there were no counties) elect as many delegates as it had members in the lower house. Thus, the legislative powers of the local areas declined somewhat because there was no representation for senators. Through this arrangement, Governor Perry avoided too sharp a break with the representation tradition in South Carolina while simultaneously moving toward greater representation equity based on population in the constitution of 1865. It was ratified September 27, 1865.

The representation compromise by the 1865 constitutional convention created closer parity between the Up-Country and Low Country. First, the parishes were abolished as election districts. Then, local areas were more uniformly defined as districts. Each district was given one senator except Charleston, which was given two by the convention, perhaps because Charleston represented the concentration of ten old parishes. The House of Representatives was apportioned on the basis of white population and of wealth, measured by taxes paid. To promote balanced representation according to wealth, all property was assessed at its real, current value rather than arbitrarily arranged fixed values. The new constitutional arrangements were not voted on popularly but were implemented by the convention directly. A governor with veto power, a four-year term, and popular election was arranged, but the convention did not require popular election of presidential electors.[28]

The legislature under the new constitution dealt with many problems. The state had a large debt, and both the legislature and the military governor attempted to deal with it. Imprisonment for debt was abolished, and a homestead exemption for debt relief was defined, first by the federally appointed military governor, Major-General Dan Sickles, but later in a statute by the legislature as well.

The legislature and General Sickles fought bitterly over the Black Codes, an attempt by legislators in several southern states to restrict the civil liberties of newly emancipated African Americans. Sickles declared the Black Codes void in South Carolina, and the United States Congress passed the Civil Rights Acts of 1870, 1871, and 1875, in part to provide federal statutory relief for individuals punished by these codes in South Carolina and across the south. Amendments to the United States Constitution (the Thirteenth, Fourteenth, and Fifteenth, but especially the Fourteenth) abolished slavery, gave African Americans the right to vote, and placed state actions that denied equal protection or due process of law under the purview of the federal Constitution. Subsequent social developments largely reflected conflicts between attempts by outsiders to create more democratic institutions and attempts by insiders to return to the stability that excluded or restricted African Americans and uncooperative whites from meaningful participation in politics.

The new constitution in 1865 moved toward increased democracy in limited ways. It provided for the election of the governor and presidential electors by direct popular vote, rather than by indirect election by the legislature. It abolished property qualifications for holding office. It also abolished slavery, but it did not define the civil rights of the former slaves satisfactorily. Aggravated by South Carolina's insistence on electing former Confederate heroes to the Congress and its passage of the Black Codes to regulate former slaves, the U.S. Congress directed formation of a new state government in 1868.

The Constitution of 1868

Under authority of the congressional Reconstruction Acts, the head of the United States military government in South Carolina, Major-General E.R.S. Canby, ordered a state constitutional convention in Charleston on January 14, 1868. Under military supervision, African American men voted in South Carolina for the first time in the elections for the constitutional convention delegates. Seventy-six of the 124 convention delegates in 1868 were African American. For the second time after the Civil War, a constitutional convention was used to draft a new South Carolina constitution. Whites in the state did not vote in the ratification election for the proposed new constitution, despite the fact that it was, and still is, the only whole constitution to be submitted directly to the electorate for approval. It was ratified by the United States Congress April 16, 1868.

The 1868 constitution was equally revolutionary for the times for South Carolina, because it embodied many principles of democratic government.[29] Even though it was termed a radical Reconstruction constitution, possibly because of the number of non-natives who served as convention delegates, it was a reflection of the typical American state constitution of the time. In the eyes of many Americans, it had only the modest aims of bringing South Carolina up to the levels of American democracy already enjoyed elsewhere.

At least formally, South Carolina's government was given a more representative framework. For example, for the first time, the new constitution provided for population alone, rather than wealth or the combination of wealth and population, to be the basis for House representation. It also continued popular election of the governor rather than election by the General Assembly. The 1868 constitution abolished debtors' prison, provided for public education, abolished property ownership as a qualification for holding office, granted some rights to women that they had not had before, and created counties. The foundations of today's counties were laid in the change of name of local administration areas from "district" to "county."

A full set of state officers was also elected under the provisions of the new constitution. The governor was given a veto that required a two-thirds vote of the General Assembly to override it. A two-thirds legislative vote was also required to issue any bonded debt. The turmoil and accompanying fraud of the administrations elected in the period resulted, in 1873, in an additional requirement that a two-thirds majority of the voters confirm an increase in the general obligation debt of the state.

The 1868 constitution's Article X on education is one of its highlights. Offices for state superintendent of public instruction and for an education commissioner in each county were created. The article also provided for a uniform system of free public schools. Although not implemented, the constitution mandated that the schools should operate for at least six months each year. Further, all children had to attend school at least twenty-four months (four years) as soon as enough facilities were available. A reform school for juvenile offenders was also mandated, but it was not a reality until in the early 1900s. Proper provisions for the deaf and blind were also ordered. The schools were financed by a poll tax, and in 1878 an amendment added a tax of an additional two mills for the schools. Maintenance of the state university was made mandatory, and the creation of a normal school and an agricultural college were also required by the new constitution.

The status of the newly freed slaves was also confronted in the 1868 constitution. Race was abolished as a limit on male suffrage. Disfranchisement could be only for murder, robbery, and dueling. Some policymakers may have thought that African Americans would be more vulnerable to losing the vote through these additional requirements. The Black Codes that had flourished under the constitution of 1865 were essentially forbidden by the 1868 constitution. There was no provision against intermarriage of African Americans and whites, and all the public schools were open to all races.

The 1868 constitution represented advances in democratic government and was adopted by an overwhelming majority in the popular referendum that followed the convention.[30] Within thirty years, however, the democratic visions of the Reconstructionists were replaced by another constitution, one written at the direction of angry farmers.

The Constitution of 1895

Stirrings that led to the development of a new South Carolina constitution began in the 1880s with the work of the Reform party. The Reform party represented the efforts of agricultural and labor groups under the leadership of Benjamin R. Tillman to change the political order.[31] Tillman organized state politics along lines of economic, social, and racial differences and was elected governor in 1890. His agrarianism appealed to white farmers who did not govern the state, although they were the majority of the voting population.

The reason for framing a new constitution was the perceived danger for the numerical minority of whites from the potential African American vote. Alleged dangers were a return to the politics of Reconstruction or the manipulation of the large African American majority vote by an active, conservative white minority of planters, professional men, and business leaders.[32] Under Tillman's leadership, the state steered the narrow course of disfranchising South Carolina's African Americans without disfranchising poor, illiterate whites or stirring the national government to act on the provisions in the United States Constitution protecting African Americans.

Due to their social position and economic status, which were interdependent and not directly competitive with African Americans, the traditional leadership group, the conservatives, became the fall guys. An open appeal for the support of African American voters by the conservative candidate Colonel A. C. Haskell provided proof to Tillman and his followers of the need for an immediate change. The Democrats and small farmers rallied behind Tillman in an unbending, iron-hard effort to eliminate all but whites from South Carolina politics.

The white conservatives tried to appease the demands of the Tillmanite Democrats by promising, for example, that African Americans would receive no offices in a conservative government. The Tillmanites saw this as a deception or "conspiracy" of upper-class whites with African Americans to dominate the mass of poor white farmers and mill workers. It was an alleged conspiracy based on buying out the African American votes with money that would ultimately grant them offices in the future despite conservatives' promises. Once in office, African Americans would be dependent on and only an extension of upper-class interests against the poor, working white masses.

Social division again became a political threat, but this time the fear was that a split among whites would allow a patronizing aristocracy to manipulate the African American numerical majority to the special advantage of the traditional power structure. "Buying out the Negroes" was styled in Tillmanite rhetoric as a worse abomination than the carpetbag rule. The carpetbaggers had been encouraged or imposed from outside by federal authority, and they in turn had been driven from the state. Conservative appeasement of African Americans was worse to the Tillmanites than carpetbaggers, because it would result in an abomination imposed by neighbors.

The 1895 constitution was also adopted by a convention, but its specific aim was to exclude African Americans from politics. The Black Codes would reemerge under the 1895 constitution as "Jim Crow" laws in forms subtle enough to avoid immediate conflict with the Fifteenth Amendment to the United States Constitution. The political and social consequences stemming from the convention that produced the 1895 constitution were significant.

African Americans in 1900 made up 58 percent of the state's population. The means for their disfranchisement was through the suffrage clause in the 1895 constitution. The new provision gave the right to vote to all males who were paying taxes on property assessed at three hundred dollars or more and who were able to read and write the English language. Even if an African American male voter could qualify on the basis of property ownership, the constitutional literacy tests could be used by local, white voting registrars to disqualify him. Literacy tests could be used to exclude poor whites also. The poll tax was not abolished until 1951, and unsupervised local voter registration continued until passage of the federal Voting Rights Act in 1965.

The South Carolina tradition of legislative control of local government, as old as colonial times, was continued in the 1895 constitution through the failure to provide for locally elected county governing bodies. The legislative delegation from each county became the county governing board. A special "local government" session was reserved for the end of each legislative year to pass a budget, or supply bill, for each county.[33]

The 1895 constitution made specific use of the county as a base from which to organize politics and representation. The dispersion of political power to the county as an organizing jurisdiction led to dominance by the rural areas. Each county was allowed one senator regardless of population. Through a system of delegation governance, individual senators were able to influence the course of legislative and governmental affairs by their control of special legislation and with the supporting customs of senatorial courtesies. Special legislation applied only to one county and senators customarily did not interfere with the special laws or local appointments proposed by another senator.[34]

The long-standing political influence of the Low Country was partially diminished through the influence of single senators in the more numerous Up-Country counties. In turn, the growth of political influence from developing urban areas was precluded by the large number of small, rural counties across the state.

Nevertheless, some of the typical and therefore more reform-oriented features of the 1868 constitution were retained. Among them were the governor's veto, legal rights for women, and the provisions for public education. However, the practical side of the 1895 revisions was that the executive department was still split into many offices, including elected department heads. The formal powers of the governor were generally restrained, especially by limits to a two-year term with potential for only one reelection.

The 1895 constitution was not submitted to a popular referendum. The theory was that because the convention delegates were chosen by the people, the convention could put its provisions directly into operation.

CONTEMPORARY REVISION OF THE 1895 CONSTITUTION

As early as the 1920s, Professor David D. Wallace questioned whether the 1895 constitution needed replacement.[35] By the middle of the twentieth century, the inappropriateness of the 1895 constitution was evident on several fronts.

For one thing, it was cluttered by numerous amendments required for local government actions. Through the 1966 election, 330 constitutional amendments had been passed.[36] About three-fifths of these amendments dealt with bonded debt limits for local governments, especially school districts. It was not until 1968 that a constitutional amendment to change the bonded debt of a county could be voted on just within the county and not statewide. South Carolina along with Florida had the ninth longest constitution in the country in 1960 when measured by the number of words in the document.[37] The constitution was crowded with matters that could have easily been accomplished through statutes.

Many citizens and organized groups had recommended constitutional revision, but before the 1960s there were no practical results. A study committee was created by the General Assembly in 1966 to evaluate the need for revision. Based on its evaluations, the committee was additionally charged "to recommend provisions which may be included in a new constitution, to suggest methods to eliminate archaic provisions, and to propose methods to bring about changes."[38]

The Committee to Make a Study of the South Carolina Constitution of

1895 made its report to the General Assembly in July 1969. In the course of its work, the study committee focused on each section of the 1895 document, painstakingly reviewed it, and made a specific evaluation whether the section should be carried over or deleted. If carried over, needed revisions were recommended. Based on its general evaluation, the study committee also demonstrated the need for some new sections in the constitution and recommended them.[39]

The result was a proposal to the General Assembly of seventeen new articles that could be substituted on an article-by-article amendment process for the original seventeen articles in the 1895 constitution. The General Assembly also approved the study committee's proposal for the appointment of a legislative steering committee of five senators and five representatives. The steering committee was headed by Senator Marion Gressette (*D*-Calhoun County) and its purpose was to shepherd the individual articles through the legislature and on to the voter referendums.

Originally, it was thought that the article-by-article revision could be accomplished by submitting the proposed changes in all seventeen articles at the same time in the 1970 general election. However, the steering committee needed more time before proposing the changed articles. A critic might suspect that the legislature was dragging its heels to prevent deterioration in legislative preeminence.

Each proposed article had to be authorized by a two-thirds vote of each house and be approved or disapproved by a majority of the voters in the next general election. If approved by the voters, the changed article had to be ratified by the General Assembly before it was included in the constitution. All the approved amendments were ratified, but the ratification process was important because it set the effective date for the new amendment to take the force of the constitution.

Despite all the extensions, debates, approaches to article-by-article revision, and then questions about amending the revised articles, the legislature and the people marched steadily ahead with the revision process. The 1970 and 1972 elections produced several completely revised articles.

Five newly revised articles were ratified in 1971. Revised Article I deals with personal rights. The longtime formal constitutional guarantees for freedom and liberty were left intact. Many provisions similar to the 1868 constitution were not changed, such as provisions to vest the power in the people and to establish religious freedoms, freedom of speech, and the right of assembly and petition. Among other fundamental freedoms and liberties carried over were guarantees of privileges and immunities, due process and equal protection of the law, and prohibitions against bills of attainder, ex post facto laws, and titles of nobility. The complete list reads much like the Bill of Rights to the United States Constitution.

Revised Article II treats the right of voting. The revised article essentially establishes up-to-date requirements for voting. In a 1974 amendment, the voting age was set at eighteen years and the residency requirement at thirty days. The article also provides for the registration of voters.

The new Article IX arranges for corporations. The revisions updated this article and streamlined the constitutional procedures by which corporations are regulated. Common carriers, publicly owned utilities, and privately owned utilities are specifically mentioned.

Article XII distributes the functions of government. The revisions updated the older version of this article that was called "Charitable and Penal Institutions." The new article requires the General Assembly to provide appropriate agencies for "the health, welfare, and safety of the lives and property of the people of this State and the conservation of its natural resources." It provides for the building of prisons, the care and control of convicts, and the separate confinement of juvenile offenders.

New Article XV is the impeachment article. Very few changes were made in this article, which provides conditions for the removal of judges, the governor, and other officers that the General Assembly identifies by law.

In the 1972 election, voters approved seven more revised articles. One of these articles dealt with alcoholic beverages and was proposed directly by the General Assembly rather than by the study committee. After all these articles were ratified, the comprehensive result was one article essentially carried over into the new constitution (Article XV, Impeachment), ten articles revised, and one new article (Article VIII-A, Alcoholic Liquors and Beverages).

Article IV deals with the executive department. Executive powers are not increased, but rules regarding gubernatorial succession and who governs in the absence of the governor are clearly established. The most significant change came in 1981 when this revised article was amended again to allow the incumbent governor to run for reelection to a second four-year term.

Article V treats the judicial department. The revised article provides for a unified court system under the supervision of the state Supreme Court. It included old Article VI from the 1895 constitution, which dealt with jurisprudence. This article was overhauled again after a successful constitutional referendum in 1984 to add a Court of Appeals between the state Supreme Court and the sixteen Circuit Courts. A 1988 amendment established a statewide grand jury to give the state attorney general more flexibility in prosecuting cases, especially drug cases. Experts feel that handling evidence to win indictments is easier through the statewide grand jury than through a jury with authority limited to a single county.

Revised Article VI clarifies and increases the removal powers of the governor by allowing the governor to suspend any state or local official, except for legislators or judges, if they are indicted by a grand jury. This article also includes the "long ballot," whereby South Carolina elects a secretary of state, an attorney general, a treasurer, a superintendent of education, a comptroller general, a commissioner of agriculture, and an adjutant general to terms coterminous with the governor.

Article VIII, on local government, is a significant revision that allows local governing bodies for counties to replace the General Assembly's tradition of special legislation. The article also requires alternate forms of local government. It combined two articles from the 1895 constitution (VII, Counties, and VIII, Municipalities). The specific circumstances surrounding this amendment and the implications of its approval are discussed in more detail in chapter 11 in this book.

The article on alcoholic liquors and beverages (Article VIII-A) established the minibottle policy in South Carolina. The state had been plagued historically with different approaches to regulation of liquor ranging from prohibition to a cumbersome "brown-bag" arrangement. Consensus was difficult because of "wet versus dry" debates and preferences across the state. By letting the voters decide, the legislature could reach a decision on the problem, define a productive source of tax revenue for public education as well as for alcohol programs, and improve the image of the state for tourists and businesspeople.

Article XI, Public Education, requires a free public school system and permits indirect state aid to students. The article creates a State Board of Education made up of one member from each of the sixteen multicounty judicial circuits. Members are elected by the legislative delegation within each circuit, and the position rotates among the constituent counties. The governor appoints an additional member to the board.

CONTINUING TO OVERHAUL THE 1895 CONSTITUTION

Since the earliest flurry of legislative changes in the constitution, developments have gone more slowly. Among the developments in the remaining sections of the constitution have been some changes in Article III regarding the legislative branch. The article has not been revised, but an amendment in 1977 fixed the times and terms of the legislative session. In 1979, a general reserve fund requirement was ratified under this article.

Revised Article X on finance and taxation was ratified May 4, 1977. It is an extensive overhaul that identifies categories and formulas for the assessment of property and defines approaches that the General Assembly may take for classifying property and setting the assessment ratios for different categories of property.

The original 1895 Article X was the constitution's most amended section. The new article restricts the right of the state, its political subdivisions, and school districts to issue bonds and gives the General Assembly power to define limits and additional procedures for incurring general obligation debt. These restrictions guard against assaults on the constitution in the form of specific amendments as a means to incur debt that might actually be excessive or careless.

Provision for the militia (Article XIII) and eminent domain (Article XIV) have not been changed. The article on the militia has a section that requires pensions for Confederate veterans and their indigent widows. The last Confederate widow, Daisy Cave, who married an elderly Confederate veteran while a young woman, survived until the early 1990s, and her state pension check was regularly delivered in person by the elected comptroller general. The other articles deal with the amending and revising processes (Article XVI) and with Miscellaneous Matters (Article XVII). These articles were changed to the extent necessary to accommodate the revision process.

In 1992, legislation was introduced to call for a referendum to restructure state government by limiting the number of state agencies to fifteen and by authorizing the governor to appoint state agency heads. The legislature did not authorize the referendum, but in the 1993 session, it passed legislation that combined more than six dozen agencies into eleven agencies run directly by the governor and six agencies with some gubernatorial control in place of predominant governing commissions.

CONCLUSION

For the most part, today's South Carolina constitution is modern and up-to-date. The revisions eliminated the obsolete and troublesome provisions that conflicted with federal policy requirements. Formalized white supremacy, especially as reflected in the 1895 suffrage clause, is gone. There have been referendums for amendments in recent elections, but the voters have not been inundated, as before 1970, with thirty or forty proposed amendments, most of which dealt with specific borrowing issues of local jurisdictions across the state. The sections that dealt with financial borrowing limitations and that had to be amended so many times are now matters to be dealt with by action of the General Assembly.

Today's constitution is no different in function from the earlier constitutions. It establishes the foundation on which legislative and court decisions derive and on which the executive branch of government operates. Despite encouragement and pressures from historical circumstances, South Carolinians have taken only timid departures from past traditions and customs. Constitutional arrangements imposed from outside were emptied and refilled with negative views at the turn of the last century, and it has taken until the end of this century for these views to be revised and replaced.

The 1895 constitution is still the authority, but the contents of the constitution today are derived as much from amendments as from the old text. The amending process began in the mid-1960s to study the problems of conforming the state constitution with federal policies that demanded racial integration and a population-based representation. Economic pressures highlighted the awkwardness of lengthy and restrictive taxation and borrowing provisions in the constitution.

There will always be need for change as parts of the constitution fall out-of-date. For example, liquor store hours, permission to have a lottery, clarification of gambling or divorce regulations, or the election of officers named in the constitution may become topics for proposed constitutional amendments or even a constitutional convention. Hence, South Carolina is joining other states such as North Carolina that increasingly rely on their state constitutions for directing important public policy decisions.[40]

The revised state constitution voluntarily declares a more workable approach to the practical problems of governing internally while maintaining compatability with the United States Constitution. The following chapter explores selected aspects of South Carolina's experiences in dealing with the national government.

CHAPTER THREE

Intergovernmental Relations: Nation and State

This chapter treats South Carolina's experiences as a state in the context of the federal union. The opening discussion underscores traditionalistic political culture as the central theme in South Carolina's relationships in the federal system. The discussion then highlights recent interactions between South Carolina and the nation in such issue areas as voting rights and fiscal affairs. These highlights are a convenient way to look at the internal effects of current federal-state connections.

PERSISTENCE OF TRADITIONALISTIC POLITICAL CULTURE

Banner writes that "the political culture of South Carolina differed from that of every other state."[1] It did not have a two-party system because it failed to develop a diffused social and economic base that would promote party competition. By the time of the American Revolution, two ideas were well established in South Carolina's political culture. First, internal division was unnatural and dangerous, and second, political opposition was external and undesirable. Unwanted changes of any kind were easily interpreted by the established leadership as major challenges to the state constitutional order. External political opposition was not a force with which to negotiate, and internal division was just not tolerable. Banner calls such politics a "no-party" system.[2]

The lack of a political party or party competition was due to many factors. One important factor was race. The practical impact of African American slavery was to enlist poorer whites in an obligatory relationship with aristocratic white political leaders against the superior numbers of slaves. Although the "color line" was not a hard and fast one,[3] fear of African American rule or political power allowed all whites to see a common adversary. The result was a social pecking order that constantly put African Americans on the distant bottom.

Other important factors included the comparative homogeneity of the state. Although colonial South Carolina had considerable ethnic and religious diversity, the size of these "different" groups was small and they were geographically scattered. Perhaps due to their relative isolation, different ethnic and religious groups were typically absorbed into the prevailing local culture and quickly became "home folks."

Also, the local cultures across South Carolina were not very different. Charleston ideals were soon widespread. Charleston was not an urban center to which people moved; instead, Charlestonians, their family members, or their connections moved all over the state. After contagious diseases became more controlled, the state's scattered cities and towns became centers for regular commerce and expanded social activities.[4] The result was a continued decline in the sharpness of eighteenth-century sectional isolation and differences in local places. Low Country planters moved into the Up-Country. Important white citizens in the countryside and from all over the state became more alike and united rather than competitive.

The common result was a clublike feeling of ideological conformity, a solidarity of community and politics that persists even today among natives and those "properly socialized" to the South Carolina way of doing things. The underlying atmosphere of traditionalistic politics is still a visible force of social and political resistance to "pushy outsiders" who attempt to do things their new way without consultation, coordination, and "necessary seasoning."

The most visible manifestation of South Carolina's traditionalistic political culture, over time, has been in the structure and operations of its legislature. The political power of South Carolina's legislature is comprehensive and the power of selected legislators is legendary. As the most powerful state legislature in America, it elected the governor until 1865—longer than any other state legislature. South Carolina's John C. Calhoun warned that if the people elected the governor, high politics would be polluted by popular influence. The South Carolina legislature also chose presidential electors down through secession in 1860.

The legislature was the primary focus of power for state and local governments because it elected all state officers, court clerks, and many local officials. Through a variety of local commissions, the legislature essentially ran county and city governments. Not only did the legislature cut off the president, the governor, and many local officers from the popular vote, it shifted congressional districts so often that a party structure was impossible to sustain in these elections as well.

The absence of competing party structures to mediate extremism contributed greatly to the success of the secessionist movement. South Carolina had a state-centered view of its relationship with the nation. After John C. Calhoun's death, his guiding hand was no longer available to steer the delicate balance between the state and the national constitution, and there were no credible challenges to the increasingly radical views that carried the state out of the Union. In the mid–twentieth century, native journalist Ben Robertson articulated the bedrock view of white South Carolinians that, unchecked, makes their loyalty to the state vulnerable to exploitation by extremists: "We know why we were fearful of adopting the Federal Constitution—it took from us a part of our power. . . . We have been told to ask about everything: Will it leave us free?"[5] The lack of party politics allowed the scattered local gentry to develop and act on a political view emphasizing the state, not the nation, as the center of political power.

During Calhoun's time, South Carolina was a prime example of an approach to federal-state relations based on the concept of dual federalism. Although appearing to emphasize the state, leaders were really emphasizing the local community. Each went about local business separately until jeopardized by a common threat—at the time, usually a national policy that threatened some aspect of plantation society.

The national debate between advocates of federal preeminence and advocates of state preeminence was lively and continuous. Alexander Hamilton, John Marshall, and Daniel Webster were noted nationalist advocates; James Madison, Thomas Jefferson, and John C. Calhoun argued for the states.

It is important to separate Calhoun's genuine views from the later mythical role they assumed in South Carolina in support of secession.[6] Calhoun did not advocate complete sovereignty for the individual state. He was a Unionist and a nationalist who favored maintaining a state-centered federal union. He believed that the states were the true organic societies with original sovereignty. By comparison, the federal government was a compact among the states. In cases of conflict between state and federal sovereignties, state sovereignty should prevail, but not at the price of destroying the federal compact. In that respect, Calhoun was thoroughly different from the advocates of secession. They interpreted him out of context and distorted his views to make him the authority for their secessionist ideology.

Another controversial interpretation of Calhoun is Richard Hofstadter's now famous essay that touts Calhoun as the "Marx of the Master Class."[7] Hofstadter suggests that Calhoun foreshadowed many of the ideas later developed so extensively by the European political theorist Karl Marx. One of these common ideas is the class struggle in history that results from extensive exploitation of one social class by another. In his book, *Disquisition on Government,* Calhoun predicted that differences between the rich and the poor would become more significant and that the percentage of ignorant and economically dependent people would increase.[8]

Calhoun also wrote that financial capital would destroy and absorb the property of society, draw out all the profits from labor, and leave the laborer to shift alone and become destitute with old age or disease. According to Hofstadter, this view anticipates Marx's labor theory of value and of a surplus appropriated by the capitalists.

While Calhoun did examine conditions similar to the roots of some of Marx's ideas, his primary argument was for the perpetuation of an organic agrarian-based society. Only in such a society could everyone have a place and be well taken care of. Thus, Calhoun sharply differed from Marx's conclusions about the inevitability of revolution. Calhoun simply did not envision a political revolution. He proposed an alliance of planters and capitalists in which the South would act as a conservative, stabilizing force. Then, logically, conservative northern elements would join with southern views and limit the moralistic demands of the abolitionists in New England to end slavery. The northern conservatives would realize that freeing slaves in the South would only prepare the grounds for an equally unsettling social revolution in the North and thus would oppose the abolitionists.

The protective tariff advocated by Andrew Jackson for the nation was a major bone of contention in the South. Because of Jackson's birth in South Carolina, Calhoun may have expected him to sympathize with southern views. Instead, they argued. Calhoun and Jackson were politically and ideologically on opposite sides and they were competitors for office. South Carolina was entirely a cotton-growing state by the 1820s. Planters, working already worn-out land, could not compete with the fresh western land being farmed by new settlers and could not pay the tariff. In pre-Marxist fashion, Calhoun called southerners "serfs of the system" and seized on the idea of state nullification within the context of dual federalism.

Calhoun argued that a state should have the ultimate authority to interpret the Constitution of the United States. Constitutional interpretation was a three-stage process. The first stage was that a state could nullify, or make inoperative within its boundaries, any act of Congress that the state found to be in violation of the Constitution. Second, if the federal government insisted on enforcing its law, then approval of a state in its own convention or by constitutional amendment would be necessary to make the national law valid within a state's jurisdiction. Third, if three-fourths of the states ratified the national law in convention or as an amendment, then the disagreeing state would either go along with the law at its initiative or else assert its sovereignty within the federal compact to ignore the national law internally.[9]

Many South Carolinians and other southerners would argue later that Calhoun's state-centered constitutional theory did not end with Confederate surrender at Appomattox and Durham; only the feasibility of armed resistance to the federal union came to an end. As an idea of politics, state-centered federalism has endured and is still applied as a way to interpret federal policies—except that today's supporters do not usually misinterpret Calhoun to describe him as an advocate of secession. In the 1980s, South Carolinians warmed to President Ronald Reagan's revival of part of Calhoun's theory when he talked again about state sovereignty and not just states' rights.

The traditionalistic politics of South Carolina placed it on a collision course with the Union when extremists were able to win political support for secession. After the harsh lessons of war, the state persisted in rural isolation well into the twentieth century, and its agrarian heritage was relatively unaffected by widespread industrialization until after World War II. Along the way, state leaders built on political tactics such as restrictive legislation for emancipated slaves and on constitutional doctrines such as the "separate but equal" policy to obstruct the implementation of unwanted federal policies. Calhoun's fear of national political power, the devastation of the Confederacy, and late nineteenth-century agrarian reactions continued to perpetuate internal misgivings for productive associations with the federal union.

SOUTH CAROLINA IN THE MODERN FEDERAL SYSTEM

The New Deal and the world wars began to replace South Carolina's insular suspicion of national preeminence with guarded trust for Washington. Military expenditures for infantry training camps and the development of ports and New Deal programs gave a hint that the federal government could be a positive, friendly force for state economic growth and development and for individual well-being. However, before long this post-war idealism gave way to the familiar tensions of a "second Reconstruction" in which the state had to deal with federal policies that appeared once again to threaten its traditional way of life. This time the tensions surrounded federal civil rights policies.[10]

National civil rights policy gave South Carolina's predominately traditionalistic political culture a set of challenges to which it could have responded in the testy traditions of the nineteenth century. Although there were tensions, they were primarily challenges in federal courts that, when finally adjudicated, gave more open-minded legislators, governors, and civic leaders the basis on which to prevail politically. It is a story, happily, that reflects the triumph of state restraint and individual social responsibility as federal action belatedly brought equal voting rights and expanded civil rights for African Americans to South Carolina.

A deliberate effort was made by the highest levels of state government to change the public's view of the federal government from fear into the more positive image of partnership in a "cooperative federalism." Cooperative federalism emphasizes such principles of government and administration as national supremacy, broad national legislative and appropriations powers, noncentralized government, and maximum local control.[11] Local control and decentralization have been attractive approaches for solutions to policy problems that have long been on the South Carolina political agenda.

Emphasizing responsible efforts by individual localities, a network of post–World War II government and business leaders sought first to build the economic base to fund separate but equal facilities. Led especially by a number of active but nonideological governors who stressed the importance of legal compliance rather than violence or protest, the state developed to the point that Governor John West could proclaim the state "color blind" in his 1971 inaugural address. The consequences of the 1964 Civil Rights Act and the 1965 Voting Rights Act are essential elements that define social and political developments in South Carolina today.

Voting Rights

Voting rights are rooted in the Fifteenth Amendment (1870) to the United States Constitution. The amendment was forced on South Carolina by an activist Congress, at least from the perspective of a traditionalistic state. Under the Fifteenth Amendment, no state or local government can deny or restrict voting rights on the basis of race. As a practical matter, the amendment led to increased voting by African American citizens and the increased election of African American officials in the reconstructed southern states.

The election of 1876 spotlighted the controversies of Reconstruction and helped to restore a large measure of home rule to the southern states. Soon after, the issue of African American rights came to be deemed unimportant by the dominant whites across the nation, reflecting the impact of underlying racism in American society. Neither congressional nor presidential requirements for changes in conventional federal and state practices that depreciated the status and rights of African Americans were forthcoming. Essentially, national leaders held that racial questions required state political answers. Until the mid–twentieth century, federal judges did not recognize African American voting disputes as legal questions for federal courts to decide.

It was in reaction to the Fifteenth Amendment's impact on state politics that South Carolina's white political leaders began to develop a variety of ways to discourage African American voting and political participation. While the state's white conservatives trusted African American voters enough to attempt political alliances with them, most whites did not accept the prospect of a government based on the African American numerical majority. Indeed, they accused the conservatives, most of whom were former slaveholders and Confederate leaders, of conspiring with the freedmen to dominate the white minority through a "corrupt" government.

Among the measures used to thwart African American voting was a complicated tangle of laws that included poll taxes, literacy tests, white primaries, and racial gerrymandering of electoral districts. The laws often overshadowed manipulation of voter registration practices by county registrars, for example, denying a voting registration application because of a spelling or clerical error such as writing above or below the printed lines on the application form. It was possible to restrict qualified electors to a narrow band of white and African American voters considered trustworthy by the self-appointed managers of the system.

The formal system of laws went much further than restrictions on voting. African Americans became segregated from whites by law in public places from schools to cemeteries. Informal social contact reinforced the political and economic segregation of the races. For example, an African American was expected to refer to a white person by a title such as *Mr.* or *Mrs.*, while a white always used a first name or nickname for an African American. The result was a racial caste system, called generally the "Jim Crow" system.

For more than six decades the federal government ignored the segregated conditions in the southern states. Slowly, however, changes in national policies began to build. White primaries were declared illegal by the United States Supreme Court in 1944 and racially gerrymandered electoral districts were not permitted after the 1960s.[12] In 1964, ratification of the Twenty-Fourth Amendment to the United States Constitution outlawed the poll tax as a specified requirement for voting in federal elections.

Federal involvement in South Carolina's voting practices speeded up when the Congress passed the Voting Rights Act of 1965. Now, federal officials could become directly involved in registering voters in any state or state political subdivision where less than 50 percent of the eligible population either registered to vote or voted in November 1964 or where a literacy test had been used to register voters in the 1964 presidential election.

Largely because of its past use of obvious as well as shrewd tactics of racial discrimination, South Carolina was subject to the Voting Rights Act. South Carolina had argued that the Voting Rights Act of 1965 violated the state's right to design and administer its own election laws according to the state's constitution.[13] The state lost, and the United States Supreme Court upheld the act and the role of the United States attorney general in enforcing it. South Carolina and its cities, counties, and other substate units now had the burden of proof to show that they were not discriminating if any one of them was alleged deficient under the standards of the federal statute.

The 1965 act also included, in section 5, a preclearance or "prior approval" requirement for changes in voting laws, voter qualification requirements, or municipal boundaries for the political subdivisions where voting examiners had been appointed. Section 5 is critically important because "it prevents the deliberate alteration of election laws, boundaries, and systems of representation to negate the impact of black voters."[14]

The administrative fallout from compliance with the registration part of the act was relatively limited. The state created an election commission to report the compliance records of the various county election commissions across the state. African American voter registration increased from 23.5 percent of the state's registered voters in 1968 to a high of 28.3 percent in 1986.[15] Perhaps equally relevant is the percentage of those of voting age who are registered to vote: in January 1992, 46.1 percent of eligible African Americans were registered, compared to 51.4 percent of eligible whites.[16] African American leaders actively promote the registration of eligible voters in their communities (eighteen years old or older) in order to increase the percentage.

In 1895 the total "minority" population was about 60 percent of state residents. African American men could have been a voting majority then if they had all been allowed to vote. Today, a racial minority is a voting majority only in small, relatively isolated rural counties or in specific inner-city election districts.

The political fallout from federal policies leading to increased minority voter participation was ruinous for the state Democratic party. State Democrats were viewed by many independent white voters as being connected with the national Democratic party's support for civil rights changes. As a consequence, the white independents voted for a specific candidate who took the "right" position, not exclusively for Democratic party candidates as before.

Another area of extensive federal-state involvement is in intergovernmental transfers of funds through grants and federal spending. Federal funds have become an integral part of public programs in South Carolina. Selected aspects of these relations are explored in the following section.

Intergovernmental Fiscal Relations

The state's congressional delegation has touted its reputation for being able to "deliver the goods" when federal spending decisions are made. The ability of representatives from the southern states to be reelected allowed many South Carolina delegation members to become heads of committees because of their seniority. For example, Congressman William Jennings Bryan Dorn (D-SC; 1947–49, 1951–74) was instrumental as chair of the U.S. House of Representatives Public Works Committee in securing funding in the 1970s for a second medical school at Columbia's Veterans Administration Hospital as well as approval to extend highway I-77 from its original end at Charlotte, North Carolina, to a new terminus at Columbia. Congressman L. Mendel Rivers (D-SC, 1941–69) was chair of the House Armed Services Committee and supported extensive military spending in the Charleston area as well as across the state.

Senators Strom Thurmond (R-SC) and Ernest Hollings (D-SC) have worked actively to promote federal defense spending and to oppose reductions or closure of military facilities within the state. For example, the South Carolina Air National Guard is so well funded that it gets the most current fighter airplanes and in 1989 won the "Top Gun" award in competition on Nevada firing ranges. Both senators routinely announce a steady flow of other types of federal funds into the state, although with the federal government's budget deficit problems beginning in the late 1980s, neither senator appears to step forward to claim credit for federal spending as eagerly as before, when it was more politically popular.

South Carolina has about the same per capita share of federal dollars used to aid state and local governments ($531) as the nation as a whole ($533).[17] South Carolina's per capita share ($3,868) of total federal funds falls about 2.5 percent below the national per capita level of $3,939.[18]

There were 32,000 federal civilian employees in the state in 1989, a rate of about 9 federal employees per 1,000 state residents. What is extraordinary is the percentage of these federal civilians who work in defense-related areas. About 59 percent (19,100) of federal civilian employees in South Carolina work for the Department of Defense. This is almost twice the national rate (31.4%) and the rate of South Atlantic states (33.8%) and higher than any other single state except Hawaii (77.8%). From 1985 through 1990, Department of Defense contracts in South Carolina grew from $490 million to $985 million and the payroll increased from $1.6 billion to almost $2.622 billion.[19] The federal decision to close most of the naval operations in Charleston as part of national military reductions will have a significant impact on these trends as the cuts are phased in.

MANAGING FEDERAL FUNDS IN SOUTH CAROLINA

The administrative transformation of the state due to the impact of federal aid is important. When intergovernmental officials across the country ranked the significant trends affecting their tasks between 1960 and 1980, they found the increased flow of federal dollars to state and local governments as the most important development over the two decades.[20]

South Carolina's major concern was that operations of many of the federally funded programs were not being monitored by state government. The state's budget agency, the Budget and Control Board, simply catalogued the grant proposals and the grant funds as they flowed through the state auditor's office. There was no central accounting system. This haphazard approach to funds management and control led to many problems.

One problem was state government growth. A qualified person would first be hired with grant funds (or "soft" money), but then when the grant money ran out, the employee would be picked up on state appropriations (or "hard" money, called "hard" because once the position existed, funds were typically reappropriated year after year without any questions). Making these new spending decisions with little debate and without close evaluation led to some criticisms from legislators and taxpayers.

Other administrative practices clouded intergovernmental funds management. For example, the state was so eager to get the federal money that appropriations for matching funds were often considered only after the federal grant was awarded in many cases. Using the power of federal dollars, state agencies could operate relatively independent of the General Assembly, maybe even contrary to General Assembly preferences. Thus, federal funds moved some state agencies or local governments beyond their authorized mission in the eyes of many legislators. Frequently, no officials questioned whether a state agency should take on a federally funded mission or how to manage it organizationally.

In some instances, a federally funded program may not even have been within the general objectives of the state government, especially if the question had been asked, "Would we do this without the federal funds?" South Carolinians may have been too starved for economic opportunity and the venture capital represented by federal aid, and some may have been overly motivated by narrow, professional interests in an all-out approach to federal funding. The legislative branch soon reacted to strengthen its control of state agency budgets. For example, in the mid-1970s it created a Legislative Audit Council.

Early reports of the new Legislative Audit Council illustrate the continuous tug-of-war between the executive and legislative branches over budgetary issues. A 1977 report noted that the General Assembly's control over the growth and direction of state government was limited because of the existing state budgetary process. The report stated that legislative priorities were hindered and altered in many cases by the influence of programs funded from federal and other sources and noted that, in essence, the budgetary process was open ended.[21]

There were other moves to increase the role of the legislature in budgeting as well. An administrative procedure act was passed to regularize legislative oversight of agency rules and regulations, standing legislative committees were staffed with professional research personnel to counteract agency or executive branch expertise, and several powerful joint committees with specific statutory responsibilities were created and professionally staffed.[22]

Nonetheless, gubernatorial administration of federal funds continues to be extensive. In 1988, for example, between $150 million and $200 million was targeted for South Carolina through the governor's office. These targets included Community Development Block Grants, Highway Safety Funds, Juvenile Justice Funds, Equal Opportunity Funds, and Job Training Partnership Funds. The governor's office influenced how these funds were distributed geographically in the state as well as how the funds were utilized. For example, it was decided to use $800,000 of the Job Training Partnership

Funds to set up a workforce to target improvement of basic literacy in South Carolina.[23]

South Carolina's business advertising is another aspect of its broader image. The state tries hard to shed the national stereotype of an ineffective population that ranges from barefooted, rural silliness to snaggle-toothed meanness to overly polite, crafty, scheming gentleness. Instead, South Carolina advertised its "golden egg" image for business and its "Grand Strand" image for tourists.

Recently, the State Development Board promoted prime-time television commercials on CNN and a print campaign for national business publications with the theme "South Carolina is taking off in all directions." The messages emphasize a diversifying economy by describing the Tower Computer construction facility run by NCR corporation (National Cash Register, now a subsidiary of American Telephone and Telegraph, AT&T, Company), Wal-Mart corporation's distribution center, and the state's transportation system. The interstate highway network offers easy access to major national markets from South Carolina. Companies that have operations in the state— Michelin Tire Corporation, Union Camp, Porsche Cars of North America, Wal-Mart, and NCR—are featured by showing pictures of their trucks moving down an uncrowded highway at dawn. This image was accelerated by the 1992 decision of the German automaker BMW to build a major production facility in the state.

South Carolina today is also a full partner in the federal union and participates just as any other state in interstate compacts, legal battles with other states or with the federal government, and constant administrative actions.

Interstate Compacts

South Carolina lobbied the Congress to shift administrative responsibility for low-level nuclear waste away from exclusive federal authority. The federal Low-Level Radioactive Waste Policy Act of 1980 encourages and recognizes an interstate compact as a desirable way to deal with nuclear waste from such sources as nuclear power plants, hospitals, and pharmaceutical companies.

The result is a variety of compacts that group states into identifiable regions of the country.[24] South Carolina has a compact with six other southeastern states for storing low-level waste at the Barnwell site in the Savannah

River Facility near Aiken. Unfortunately, other regions have a compact but no suitable disposal site. South Carolina and two other states (Nevada and Washington) have had to accept everybody's nuclear waste so that nuclear power plants and hospitals could keep operating. The main problems are how to coordinate low-level nuclear waste disposal nationally and how to provide safe transportation of waste materials. Solutions have taken the form of ultimatums and deadlines, often announced by one state acting alone, that have been renegotiated because of the general reluctance of states to develop new sites.

Congress's 1980 statute required every state to have its own low-level nuclear waste site or to have an agreement with a neighboring state to use its facility by January 1, 1993. On that date, however, the Barnwell site was the only one open to the rest of the country. The site in Nevada closed December 31, 1992, and Washington will only accept waste from the Rocky Mountain states and the Northwest. The South Carolina legislature voted to keep Barnwell open to states other than the seven southeastern ones until mid-1994, but it raised charges $220 per cubic foot. This will reduce the amount of outside waste but continue to generate state revenue.

After December 1995, the southeastern states will no longer be permitted by the South Carolina legislature to dump at Barnwell. Then, under the compact, North Carolina is scheduled to provide a site. North Carolina is considering disposal site alternatives, one of which is within ten miles of the South Carolina border. If that site is chosen, South Carolina will close the Barnwell facility to North Carolina immediately and to the other southeastern states in mid-1994.

A Court Battle with the United States

South Carolina v. Baker is a U.S. Supreme Court case instigated by South Carolina's state treasurer, Grady Patterson.[25] The suit challenged section 310(b)(1) of the Tax Equity and Fiscal Responsibility Act (TEFRA) of 1982.[26] The contested section in TEFRA requires states and their political subdivisions (counties, cities, special districts, and authorities) to register their bonds in the name of the purchasers if the interest on the bonds is to continue to be exempt from federal personal income tax. This tax exemption makes the bonds more attractive to investors and helps reduce the interest rate that the state and local governments have to pay to the bond buyers.

The tradition of states, including South Carolina, was to issue bonds to "bearer." No records were kept on the names or identities of the actual owners. Given that no income taxes are levied on the interest payments,

South Carolina argued that registering the bonds in the names of the owners is an extra and unnecessary administrative expense. United States officials argued that the records are needed because the bonds are subject to federal estate and gift taxes. The United States Treasury also held that bearer bonds constituted a "currency" in illegal transactions because they are not registered to any one person. In the course of the debate, the states contended that the change was part of a long-standing effort by the federal government to tax the interest paid to investors on state and local debt instruments.

Also, South Carolina maintained, in the traditions of state sovereignty and "dual federalism," that TEFRA was an unconstitutional attack on state government that violated the Tenth Amendment to the U.S. Constitution. The argument was that, historically, the freedom of states to exercise their borrowing power for proper public purposes came before the federal Constitution both in time—the states existed before the Constitution of 1789—and authority—the states ratified the federal Constitution and at no point gave away their borrowing power. Therefore, states were "immune" from federal restrictions, such as TEFRA registration, and, furthermore, this immunity had been reaffirmed in challenges to the Sixteenth Amendment (1913) that created the income tax in the first place.[27]

Twenty-six other states joined South Carolina's argument. Even the *Wall Street Journal* editorialized on behalf of the states.[28] The U.S. Supreme Court voted 8–1 to hear the case as an original jurisdiction case, so that it did not have to go through lower federal courts in a long and expensive process. A special master, Chief Justice Samuel J. Roberts of the Pennsylvania Supreme Court, was appointed to study the facts, derive findings, and present them to the U.S. Supreme Court. The states did not prevail when the Court decision came down; hence, one more remnant of dual federalism fell.

The message in *South Carolina* is that the federal Constitution contains no specific textual protections for the states and their local governments from federal regulation. Instead of the federal Constitution, states must look to the national political process, mainly their representatives in the Congress, to protect their powers against federal encroachment. The most obvious lesson is also a general one: in matters of interstate commerce and taxation, "American federalism has been construed by the Court as a political and administrative relationship rather than a constitutional one."[29] Questions of federalism today call for the states' best political and legal talents to defend their interests.[30]

It has not been easy for the states to deal with the United States Supreme Court, but they have had to do so. Two South Carolinians started it in 1792 by suing the state of Georgia over a debt. Georgia would not participate, lost, and thereby the federal courts asserted jurisdiction over a suit between a state and citizens of another state.[31] The Eleventh Amendment to the U.S. Constitution was required to stop a rash of ordinary suits against states in federal courts by making it necessary for citizens to sue states in state courts, not federal courts.

Even so, rigid legal arguments are, at the present, mostly old-fashioned, as South Carolina learned once again. American federalism today is largely a political relationship among the federal, state, and local governments, and the courts play a big part. In the 1987–88 term of the United States Supreme Court, state and local governments were involved in three out of five cases decided. The states' record was not totally dismal; they won in forty-three of the seventy-five cases they brought.[32]

The Challenge of Hurricane Hugo

It does not take a creative legal problem to illustrate the complexities of relationships among governments; a major natural disaster tests the system as well. Of the more than one hundred hurricanes that struck the United States between 1900 and Hurricane Andrew in 1992, South Carolina's September 21–22, 1989, Hurricane Hugo was the tenth most intense. More than half of the storm's total destruction fell in South Carolina, where there were twenty-nine deaths and over $6 billion in damage.[33] It was an enormous storm that affected an extensive, predominately rural part of the state as well as Charleston and its suburbs. The response to such a widespread disaster involves governments at all levels.

The first level of response is local government. As its capacity and resources are exhausted, the response level moves up to the state. If the state government is unable to handle all of the demands occasioned by a major disaster, federal law authorizes the governor to request federal assistance.[34] The Federal Emergency Management Agency (FEMA) reviews the request from the state and makes a recommendation to the president of the United States. If the president agrees, a formal announcement is made and a federal coordinating officer (FCO) is appointed to represent the chief executive in the disaster area.

One view is that the intergovernmental administration of relief from Hugo's effects led to a "confusion" response in South Carolina. An effective response was hampered "because there was no clear-cut line of communication from counties and municipalities through the state to the national government."[35] Among the factors that contributed to the disappointing lack of coordination were the immensity of the storm, FEMA's policies and the limits of its resources, and the weak capacities of local agencies and state disaster-response units. FEMA turned out to be only a tiny coordinating agency with a primary mission to deal with nuclear attacks, not storms. Its focus was on the governor's office, and it was not prepared to deal with the countless requests from local governments.

One lesson that did sink in for South Carolina's governments was the importance of disaster preparedness planning and proficiency by local governments, so that self-help is the first line of defense against natural disaster.[36] The hurricane's damages may have also prompted more legislative interest in uniform, statewide building-code legislation. Counties have had an option to adopt and enforce building codes. Before 1989, seventeen of South Carolina's forty-six counties had a specific building code.[37] Even though the hurricane affected rural areas as well as metropolitan ones, uniform building requirements might have been helpful in reducing dangers from wind and flooding.

A Help for Intergovernmental Relations

In one of his first acts after taking office in 1979, Governor Richard W. Riley created a state advisory commission on intergovernmental relations (SCACIR). Governor Riley was appointed in 1977 by President Jimmy Carter to the United States Advisory Commission on Intergovernmental Relations and concluded, "While serving on the national ACIR, I realized that South Carolina could benefit greatly from a similar experience."[38]

The commission became permanent in 1984; it provides a forum for discussing and studying intergovernmental issues. One of these issues is how local governments in South Carolina interact with the federal government. The SCACIR's primary emphasis, however, is on the relationships between the agencies of state government and the counties, cities, and special districts. A more specific discussion of these problems follows in chapter 11.

CONCLUSION

The politics between states and the federal government result from constantly changing intergovernmental relations.[39] The federal-state connection today is best described generally as a stabilized federal role with most change coming from the revival of the states, including South Carolina. The federal halt in spending and policy making has also sent local governments that formerly found policy responses exclusively in Washington more and more to the state capital.

There are a variety of reasons for the "resurgence of the states" in American political life.[40] One reason has certainly been the widespread public dissatisfaction with the federal government. In 1980 President Ronald Reagan was elected on a campaign to "get the government off the people's back" and to "get the government out of Washington." This meant, among other things, substituting state government for the federal government in dealing with local governments and advancing state responsibility for block grants, for general regulatory authority, and for raising the revenues to offset decreased federal funding efforts. South Carolina has steadily supported the Reagan-Bush style of government, as the upcoming description of recent elections will illustrate. It has also tried new approaches to improving state policy decisions and management.

South Carolina has successfully initiated reform of its 1895 constitution and strengthened the formal capacities of its governors to perform with slightly more executive strength. Federally inspired legislative reapportionment has developed more politically diverse representation at state and local government levels in South Carolina and a more vigorous public policy debate in state and local deliberative bodies.

Daniel Elazar has maintained that each state has a political will of its own. The states are separately organized polities, not mere appendages of a central govenment. South Carolina's century of colonialism and its history of more than two hundred years in the federal governmental system demonstrate a variety of attitudes. Leaders in eighteenth-century South Carolina came to view a strong federal union as the best way to continue their political dominance of the state. Through the dramatic political, economic, and social upheavals before, during, and after secession, South Carolinians came to see the federal government as an enemy. The general economic Depression of the 1930s made federal relief programs more attractive, and many welcomed the development of national forests on old worn-out farmland, the generation of electricity by the Rural Electrification Administration, and the employment programs of the New Deal. Great Society civil rights legislation was a temporary setback of friendly relations for some, but negative voices were limited by less defiant views as moderate political leaders prevailed.

South Carolina is among the states that currently use their independence as a basis to revive their positive political capacity to deal with important policy problems in cooperation with the national government. South Carolinians today express their traditionalistic independence through protest when the federal government closes a military base. But unlike earlier generations, they do not withdraw in the face of adverse federal actions. Instead, they think about development alternatives and how the federal government could assist with them. Even as the Charleston naval facilities were listed for closing, rumors were circulating that the Mercedes-Benz company was surveying the area for a factory site. Similarly, cutbacks in the benefits from an entitlement program such as Medicaid would rally the state's leaders into a debate about how to deal with the lack of federal money. Today, the federal system is more an ally than a foe because the federal government has the power to relate in concert with the state to its major problems, such as trade restrictions on foreign textiles or the health and education of its people.

CHAPTER FOUR

Political Parties and the Electorate

In a 1949 book, V. O. Key Jr. entitled his chapter on South Carolina "The Politics of Color." Key observed that the state's preoccupation with race muffled debate about the really important issue—the poor condition of the state's economy.[1] Whites, in groups ranging from large-scale, plantation-style farmers to mill workers, wanted to keep African Americans in their place while ignoring and supressing important problems, such as jobs and education.

South Carolina, like many other states in the South at the time, was locked in the grip of a one-party system composed of politicians who empha-sized states' rights and racial segregation. All politics revolved around the Democratic party. Within that structure, the state had a loosely organized political system. Typically, a single faction dominated local politics. The state legislature was an assembly of those local factions. Successful legisla-tive proposals depended on majority combinations of local factions. State politics was defined by multifactional alliances among local interests. These alliances frequently reflected dominant legislative personalities.

Down to the 1960s, only the faces of the dominant players changed. The state remained trapped in the memories of Calhoun's fear of national politi-cal power, the ravages of war with the federal union, and the late nineteenth-century agrarian reactions. All of these forces underpinned continued re-strictions on the growth of competitive political parties in South Carolina. Statewide political outcomes were routinely limited by narrow, local, race-oriented choices.

South Carolina was locked into the traditionalistic culture dominant throughout the South. The economy was limited by the single crop, cotton. The resulting social and intellectual vacuum guaranteed South Carolina's continued isolation. Political change, whether from within or from without, was resisted by the state's agrarian leaders.

Two visible social categories were associated with the traditionalistic political culture. The first was a class of farm owners and the second was a class below them, which worked for little or no cash wages at the backbreaking labor of the crop-lien system of farming.[2] The lower class consisted of the farm tenants, laborers, and private household workers. The agrarian middle class of farm owners controlled politics and sought to maintain the status quo under the umbrella of the Democratic party, while the lower class was generally restricted from voting.

As in other southern states, South Carolina's Democratic party excluded African Americans from participating in its primary to nominate candidates for the general election. This prevented African Americans from having a meaningful voice in the electoral process. When there were no Republican opponents, victory in the Democratic primary was equivalent to election.

The Republicans seldom opposed the Democratic primary nominee in the general election. However, in 1944, the U.S. Supreme Court, in *Smith v. Allwright,* declared the white primary unconstitutional throughout the country.[3] After the Court's decision, South Carolina took steps to forestall an attack on its own white primary.

In April 1944, Governor Olin D. Johnston called the General Assembly into special session to recommend repeal of all laws regulating primaries so that the Democratic party could be defined as a private organization rather than a state-regulated public entity. Said Johnston, "White supremacy will be maintained in our primaries. Let the chips fall where they may. . . . We South Carolinians will use the necessary methods to retain white supremacy in our primaries."[4] Within one week, the General Assembly enacted 147 laws separating party primaries from state control. Johnston's action propelled him into the U.S. Senate. In July 1944, he defeated thirty-five-year Senate veteran Ellison D. "Cotton Ed" Smith in the Democratic primary by forty-five thousand votes.

Three years later, the Negro Citizens Committee in Richland County sued in federal court for the right to participate in the Democratic primary. The committee claimed that the primary, whether supported by state law or by party rule, controlled the choice of officeholders in South Carolina. Federal District Court judge J. Waties Waring decided in favor of the African American plaintiff, calling the repeal of the state primary laws a mere subterfuge. He added that he did not think the sky would fall if South Carolina were put in the same class as other states.[5]

After the decision was upheld on appeal, the state Democratic Committee tried to impose one last obstacle to African American participation. It was an oath that included the following phrase: "I believe in and will support the social and educational separation of the races."[6] This too was struck down by Judge Waring, and in July 1948, the Democratic party began enrolling African Americans. This was the same year that southern Democrats broke with the national party and planted the seeds for two-party development in the state and the region.

BEGINNINGS OF A TWO-PARTY SYSTEM

Southern dissatisfaction with the national Democratic party had begun to develop in the 1930s and 1940s over economic and social issues. This alienation led to an open revolt by southern Democrats in 1948 when the governor of South Carolina, J. Strom Thurmond, ran for United States president on the "Dixiecrat" or States' Rights Democratic party ticket. The revolt was triggered by the party's adoption of a pro–civil rights plank in its national platform.

The 1948 presidential election marked the turning point in southern support for the national Democratic party. Thurmond carried four southern states. In these states—Alabama, Louisiana, Mississippi, and South Carolina—Thurmond and his running mate, Governor Fielding Wright of Mississippi, were listed under the Democratic party's column on the ballot. In fact, in Alabama Harry Truman was excluded entirely from the ballot. Overall, in the South Truman received 50 percent of the vote, Republican Thomas Dewey 26.6 percent, and Governor Thurmond 22.6 percent. In South Carolina, Thurmond polled 102,607 votes to Harry Truman's 34,423 and Thomas Dewey's 5,385. Thurmond carried forty-four of the state's forty-six counties.

V. O. Key Jr. noted that South Carolinians would begin to talk about the virtues of a two-party system as they became more disenchanted with the national leadership of the Democratic party. He went on to say, however, that few South Carolinians realized: "what a genuine two-party system would mean in the way of raising issues and of activating the masses politically. By the same token, few of them realize[d] the capacities of a one-party system for muffling protest, postponing issues, and preserving the status quo." Key agreed with a local observer that "no person who makes more than $20,000 a year wants a two-party system in South Carolina. If there were two strong parties, each would compete for the lower-level vote. With the present

Democratic party structure, the $20,000-a-year men can keep control of the situation."[7]

Even while Key was writing, economic changes were occurring that would have significant political implications. These changes had begun with the New Deal programs of President Franklin D. Roosevelt. Under the New Deal, the federal government encouraged diversification in agriculture, and federal wage and hour laws began to push up personal income. During World War II, a flood of defense spending in the state began to foster diversification of the industrial sector.

These changes gradually led to a decline in the agrarian middle class and lower tenant class. They were replaced by the steady increase of two new classes located in cities and towns. One new class was a largely urban working class composed of individuals employed as craft workers and supervisors, operatives, transportation workers, service employees, and laborers. The other was a new middle class consisting of individuals with professional, technical, managerial, administrative, sales, and clerical skills.[8]

These class changes have had a significant impact on South Carolina's political landscape. For example, urban- and suburban-oriented political divisions are replacing the traditionalistic, rural units within the state. Today, about two-thirds of the population is concentrated in only about one-third of the forty-six counties. The rapidly growing population concentrations in the counties along the interstate highway system provide the foundation for the new partisan developments in the state.

There have also been changes in the number and distribution of African Americans. In 1880, 60.7 percent of the state's residents were African Americans. By 1920, this percentage had declined to 51.4 percent. It has continued to decline to a 1990 level of approximately 28.9 percent. Some African American suburbs have also developed along with a growing African American middle class. However, a large percentage of African Americans continue to reside in the rural, lesser-developed counties located away from the intersections of the interstate system.

Over the last twenty-five years, the rise of the Republican party has been one of the dominant themes of southern politics. Numerous studies have examined both the electoral strength and the composition of the Republican party in the South. Jack Bass and Walter DeVries describe these new Republicans as fitting into four major categories. They include migrants who moved into the region and brought their Republicanism with them, native middle- and upper-middle-class southerners who migrated from farms and small towns, a small group of reformers who were interested primarily in building a two-party system, and southerners who were conservative on racial and economic issues and who were attracted to Barry Goldwater's candidacy in 1964.[9] Clear examples of all of these groups except two-party reformers are found in South Carolina, as in other southern states.

The Goldwater Republicans were the first southern Republicans to gain recognition. The most visible figure nationally who fits this category is senior Republican U.S. senator J. Strom Thurmond. While accepting the nomination as the presidential candidate for the States' Rights Democratic party in 1948 in Birmingham, Alabama, Thurmond told his audience, "We believe that there are not enough troops in the army to force southern people to admit the Negroes into our theaters, swimming pools, and homes."[10]

Thurmond remained a Democrat until 1964, when he switched to what he referred to as the Goldwater Republican party. In a September 1964 televised speech to the people of South Carolina, Thurmond asserted that the Democratic party "of our fathers is dead" and that "those who took its name are engaged in another Reconstruction, this time not only of the South, but of the entire nation."[11] Claiming that the Democratic party had abandoned the people and was leading the United States to a socialistic dictatorship, Thurmond said that he realized the political risk involved and that because of this step, his chances for reelection might be jeopardized. Political columnist Lee Bandy, however, pointed out that Thurmond also realized that the Democratic primary would become a major obstacle to him once African Americans started to vote in large numbers.[12]

A second major political figure to become a Republican in this era was Second District congressman Albert Watson, a segregationist who openly supported Barry Goldwater. After congressional Democrats stripped him of his two years of seniority, he resigned from Congress and successfully ran for reelection as a Republican, receiving 70 percent of the vote.

Still another former Democrat, James F. Byrnes, the most significant political figure at the time in South Carolina, continued his support of Republican presidential candidates. Byrnes, who had supported Eisenhower and Nixon, was a critic of the U.S. Supreme Court's 1954 *Brown* decision. With support from such visible political figures in the state, other South Carolinians began to change parties, and the Republican party, under the leadership of J. Drake Edens Jr., began to grow in South Carolina.

Combining with the Goldwater Democrats was the new urban middle class. This class of southerners represented a new generation that found itself in positions requiring greater training and expertise than had been required of the southern worker in earlier times. In addition, these were higher-paying positions. This new middle class was replacing the shrinking agrarian middle class. Its ideology was conservative and its party loyalty was increasingly Republican. This group has provided much of the vote for Republican candidates in South Carolina over the last three decades.

The last group of southern Republicans consists of "Yankees who moved South" and brought their politics with them. These northern Republicans are to be found in the growing urban centers of the state and in the resort and retirement centers, such as Hilton Head. The result of all this change has been a gradual development of two-party competition in South Carolina following the Dixiecrat revolt of 1948.

THE ELECTORATE: DEALIGNMENT OR REALIGNMENT?

One way to understand voting patterns in the state is by comparing self-perceptions of partisan loyalty. In general, party identification in South Carolina seems to approximate the national pattern. The Democrats now find their greatest support in the state among African Americans as well as citizens with low incomes and low education levels. In 1986, for example, 55 percent of those with annual incomes under thirteen thousand dollars, 56 percent of those who were not high school graduates, and 63 percent of African Americans in South Carolina identified with the Democratic party. Republican party support was greatest among white college graduates with incomes over twenty-five thousand dollars a year. There is also movement away from party identification. By 1986 a plurality of South Carolinians (38%) called themselves independents.[13]

While this trend may seem to indicate a movement toward dealignment, a 1990 study indicated that the Republican party was still gaining momentum. This poll, undertaken by Mason-Dixon Opinion Research in October 1990, questioned probable voters about their party loyalty over the previous ten years. The results are shown in table 3. Based on this survey, Democratic party support declined from 52 percent to 41 percent over the ten-year-period while Republican party identification increased from 27 percent to 40 percent. Perhaps even more significant is that among whites, identification with the Democratic party declined from 40 percent in 1980 to only 27 percent in 1990. Identification with the Republican party showed an increase from 34 percent to 51 percent over the same period.[14]

There is a trend among younger voters in the state toward the Republican party. Table 4 reveals that Democratic voters are those who became eligible to vote between 1942 and 1961. They are products of the old, solidly Demo-

Table 3: Partisan Self-Perception, 1980, 1985, 1990

		Partisan Identification (in %)		
		Democrat	Republican	Neither
1990:				
In terms of South Carolina	All	41	40	19
state politics, do you	White	27	51	22
consider yourself a	African Amer.	78	10	12
Democrat or Republican?				
1985:				
Five years ago, did you	All	46	33	21
consider yourself a	White	34	42	24
Democrat or Republican?	African Amer.	80	10	10
1980:				
Ten years ago, did you	All	52	27	21
consider yourself a	White	40	34	26
Democrat or Republican?	African Amer.	84	7	9

Source: Mason-Dixon Opinion Research, Inc., Charleston News and Courier, October 30, 1990.

cratic South. In contrast, those reaching political maturity during the era of the changing South, during the 1970s, contain the most Republican identifiers. The strong support for Bush among the eighteen to twenty-nine-year-old voters in 1992 suggests that this trend may be accelerating.

The movement away from the Democratic party by whites in South Carolina has led some analysts to suggest that the Democratic party is in danger of becoming the party of African Americans. The 1990 Mason-Dixon Poll attempted to measure that sentiment by asking voters if they agreed with the statement "Blacks have too much influence in the South Carolina Democratic Party, that's why many whites are voting Republican." Among whites, 21 percent strongly agreed and 23 agreed with the statement, while 21 percent disagreed and 25 percent disagreed strongly. African Americans, however, did not agree with their white counterparts. Fifty-seven percent strongly disagreed with the statement and another 23 percent disagreed, while only 2 percent strongly agreed and 12 percent agreed.[15]

Race has affected party politics in South Carolina, however. In a 1989 study of party chairs in South Carolina, one Democratic chair noted that party efforts to attract minorities were "perhaps too successful" and that "many white moderates and conservatives believe the party is becoming the black party." An African American Democratic county chair noted that "white candidates want the Democratic vote, but will do nothing in return

Table 4: Distribution of Party Identification of South Carolinians by Age Cohort

Ages	18-24	25-34	35-44	45-54	55-64	65+
Party (in %)						
Democrat	36	36	35	40	46	37
Republican	26	34	23	27	24	19
Independent	38	30	41	33	30	44
N=508	(106)	(120)	(88)	(70)	(67)	(57)

Source: Michael Maggiotto, "South Carolinians' Political Attitudes," in Charlie B. Tyer and S. Jane Massey (eds.), Government in the Palmetto State: Perspectives and Issues (Columbia: University of South Carolina Bureau of Governmental Research and Service, 1988), p.143.

for it. White candidates run their own campaigns [and] do not want the party connection [because it is] too black for them."

The Republican party has moved cautiously in trying to recruit African Americans. One county chair stated, "[I]t is extremely important for our party and country to have racial minorities as members of both major parties. I know in my heart that there are many blacks that share my views but do not feel comfortable in my party." Another chair indicated that "although we're making some progress, it is extremely slow."[16] This sentiment is supported by election data. For example, in 1986, only 1.3 percent of the voters who participated in the statewide Republican primary were nonwhite.

The predominance of African Americans in the Democratic party does make race a potential issue in political campaigns where white Republican candidates face African American Democrats. Although overt racist tactics are seldom employed by Republican candidates, more subtle techniques have been used in some elections. One of the more commonly utilized techniques is to run campaign ads or flyers with pictures of the two candidates, the white Republican and the African American Democrat, side by side. Republicans deny that the tactic is racially motivated, but the message is obvious. The use of this technique is not limited to general election campaigns.

Within the Democratic party, the same technique may be utilized when both African American and white candidates are seeking the same office. The repercussions, however, make it less likely to be utilized by white Democrats.

Ideology is more important than race in explaining the decline in support for the Democratic party in South Carolina. In 1949, Key optimistically concluded that "southern liberalism is not to be underestimated" and that "fundamentally within southern politics there is a powerful strain of agrarian liberalism."[17]

However, the new southern white middle class and white working class have both opted for political conservatism. Approximately two-thirds of the South's white middle class express some affinity for the political Right, while 53 percent of southerners who think of themselves as working class express an affinity for political conservatism.[18] White South Carolinians fit this pattern.

The 1990 Mason-Dixon Poll asked the question "I feel the Democratic Party in South Carolina has grown increasingly liberal, and no longer represents my views." Among the white respondents, 35 percent strongly agreed and another 23 percent agreed.[19] A variety of polls on various political, social, and economic issues consistently reveal the conservatism of the state's white population.

A 1988 University of South Carolina poll shows that a majority (56.6%) of South Carolinians favor a limited ban on abortion, 84.3 percent either strongly or moderately support prayer in public schools, 68.2 percent support the death penalty, and almost three-fourths feel that the best way to handle the national debt is to cut spending. There were some differences between Democrats and Republicans. For example, Democrats were less supportive of the death penalty than Republicans (60.8% compared to 87.5%) and were less supportive of cutting spending in order to reduce the national debt (71.4% to 80.9%); however, in general, both groups can be classified as conservative on these issues.[20]

This fundamental conservatism also appears among party leaders, especially Republicans. In 1989, county chairpersons were asked to place themselves on a five-part ideological scale. Table 5 shows that the Republican chairpersons strongly identify as conservative, while the Democratic chairpersons reflect both the demographic and ideological diversity of the party. All but two (93.7%) of the Republican chairpersons consider themselves to be right of center. None is to the left of center. For the Democrats, 33.4 percent consider themselves to be right of center while 47.3 percent identify themselves as being either moderately liberal or liberal. These orientations are consistent with the chairpersons' positions on issues. Republican leaders are more conservative on a variety of social and political issues, ranging from favoring a balanced budget amendment to the United States Constitution to opposing abortion. Democratic chairpersons are less conservative and represent a wider range of ideological viewpoints.

White southerners frequently state that the national Democratic party has abandoned them and that the party of their ancestors is no more. In 1989, six Democratic party chairpersons in South Carolina noted that they split their

Table 5: South Carolina Party Chairs' Self-Perception of Ideology, 1989 (in %)

Characteristic	All Chairs	Democratic Chairs	Republican Chairs
Conservative	33.8	5.6	65.6
Moderately conservative	27.9	27.8	28.1
Middle of the road	13.2	19.4	6.3
Moderately liberal	16.2	30.6	0.0
Liberal	8.8	16.7	0.0
TOTAL	*99.9	*100.1	100.0
*rounding error			
n=	(68)	(36)	(32)

Source: William V. Moore, "Party Development in South Carolina: County Chairmen Revisited," a paper presented at the annual meeting of the South Carolina Political Science Association, Florence, S.C., April 1989.

ticket and voted Republican in national elections because they perceived the national party as having become too liberal.[21] These chairpersons, however, and many of their fellow citizens come back to the Democratic party in state and local elections.

In 1990, for example, 37 percent of white voters in South Carolina agreed with the statement "The Republicans have had stronger presidential candidates and several good state candidates like Strom Thurmond and Carroll Campbell, but I tend to vote for Democrats more often than not in state and local elections in South Carolina."[22] For the Democratic party to be successful in South Carolina today, it must field candidates who are moderate to moderately conservative at best. Liberal candidates, such as the national Democratic party's presidential candidates in 1980, 1984, and 1988 elections and the party's gubernatorial candidate in 1990, are unable to appeal to the conservative white voter in the state.

What has happened to the South Carolina voter, however, can best be described as dealignment as opposed to realignment. Most African Americans and many whites still perceive the Republican party as the party of the rich. In fact, 81 percent of African American respondents and 38 percent of white respondents agreed with a 1990 statement in the Mason-Dixon Poll that said, "I feel the Republican party in South Carolina is controlled by rich, country-clubbers, and the Democrats better represent the concerns of working people."[23] For realignment to occur, the Republican party has to overcome this image held by many South Carolinians.

For the Democrats to reassert their dominance, they will need to convince a skeptical majority of conservative whites of the fairness of their fiscal and social policies. If they are unable to do so, then the movement to the Republican party may accelerate, and the Democratic party in South Carolina may become the bastion of the more liberal African American voters and a small group of liberal whites.

POLITICAL PARTICIPATION AND PARTY ORGANIZATION

Despite the removal of various barriers to voting, the rate of voter participation in South Carolina is one of the lowest in the United States. For example, as illustrated in table 6, only 41.1 percent of the voting-age population in South Carolina participated in the presidential election of 1988. This was the lowest turnout in the country. In the 1990 primary elections, despite statewide races in both parties, the turnout was only 7.4 percent. This was the third lowest in the United States, behind Connecticut and New Jersey. Then, in the 1990 general election, an estimated 55 percent of the registered voters participated; however, this constituted approximately 27 percent of the potentially eligible voters.

In 1992, there was an increase in voter participation. Approximately 78 percent of persons registered actually voted in the presidential election. However, South Carolina's turnout rate, 46.9 percent of the voting-age population, was well below the national average 54 percent turnout, and the state ranked forty-ninth, just behind Georgia and ahead of Hawaii. One disturbing trend was a decrease in African American voter registration. It was down by about 3,000 while overall voter registration was up 90,000 to a record high of 1.5 million registered voters.

Voter registration continues to be an obstacle to participation. The voter registration procedure in South Carolina is comparable to most states. Any citizen who has resided within a county for thirty days prior to an election is entitled to register to vote. Mail-in registration is also permitted, provided it is accomplished forty-five days prior to elections. But despite the ease with which citizens can register, less than 60 percent of South Carolinians are registered to vote. In general, it is the poor, both African American and white, who do not register. As a result, elections in South Carolina continue to be determined by a minority of the voters. The difference between today and yesterday, however, is that alienation from the political process is now voluntary, rather than involuntary. Thus, despite the change in the political climate of the state, remnants of the traditionalistic political culture remain.

Political parties are still regulated by statute to some extent. The legal re-

Table 6: Voter Turnout for Presidential Elections (in Thousands)

Characteristic	1976	1980	Year 1984	1988	1992
Voting age population	1,993	2,213	2,386	2,534	2,567
Number registered	1,113	1,236	1,405	1,447	1,537
Percent registered	55.8	55.9	58.9	57.1	59.9
Number voting	803	922	1,018	1,041	1,203
Percent registered voters voting	72.1	74.6	72.5	71.9	78.3
Percent of voting age population voting	40.3	41.7	42.7	41.1	46.9

Source: Annual Report, South Carolina Election Commission, for indicated years.

quirements make party organizations resemble pyramids, but they are in fact more flexible, informal, and fragmented than a pyramid would suggest.[24]

The lowest level of party organization is the precinct organization or "club." Membership is loosely defined by participation in the party's primary election, although anyone who is a registered voter and who identifies with the party can normally participate in a party's precinct meetings.

One may also be a card-carrying member of a political party by paying party dues; however, the major benefit derived from this is to be placed on a mailing list for party newsletters. Club meetings must be publicized forty-eight hours in advance, and reorganization meetings must be held every two years. Those who attend these meetings may choose a president and other officers, including a district executive committee representative. The latter represents the club in the county organization.

The degree of actual organization varies tremendously among counties. In many instances, there are no precinct officers for one or both parties in particular counties. For example, the Republican party in Charleston County, one of the Republicans' most extensively organized counties, only has officers in 86 of 124 precincts.[25] While these elections are not normally highly competitive, some elections have been intense. For example, in the Republican presidential primary in 1988, Pat Robertson's supporters turned out in force in a number of precincts and captured control of some county party organizations. In 1993, members of the Christian Coalition did the same thing. As a result, a majority of the delegates to the state Republican convention in May were members or supporters of the Christian Coalition.

The county committee consists of one representative from each club or precinct and the state executive committee member. The duty of this body is to oversee party business between conventions. In theory, the county conventions of the parties are held on the first Monday in March of every statewide general election year (e.g., every two even-numbered years). Other dates in March may be selected, but two weeks' advance public notice is required. Delegates to the county convention are apportioned among various precincts based on the precincts' party votes in the previous general election.

The major function of the county convention is to select countywide officers (chairperson, vice chairperson, state executive committee representative, and so forth) as well as delegates to the state convention. Delegates to the state convention are allocated on the basis of the number of state House members from the county. Once again, the degree of county organization varies tremendously. The Republican party is organized in some but not all counties. Periodically over the last fifteen years, there have been several rural counties in the state without Republican county chairs.

The state committee and state convention are at the top of the party structure and are organized in a manner similar to the county organizations. The state committee is composed of one representative from each county, the state chairperson and vice chairperson elected by the state convention, and, as *ex officio* members, members of the national executive committee. Members of the state committee coordinate party activities statewide, nominate presidential electors, and fill any vacancies on the state ticket and the national committee of the party.[26]

Parties may also have municipal organizations that operate independently of the regular party structure. They function only within municipalities and are independent of the county party organization. For example, in Charleston County, the Republican party nominates candidates through primary elections; however, in the city of Charleston, the municipal party organization nominates party candidates by citywide convention.

Candidates seeking office as party nominees must file a statement of candidacy with their party's county executive committee between twelve noon on March 16 and twelve noon on March 30 on a form provided by the State Election Commission.[27] The parties may select candidates through party conventions or through primary elections. Conventions can be used to nominate candidates if three-fourths of the total membership of the convention decide the convention will be used for that purpose.

Until 1992, South Carolina's primary elections were managed by the parties, not the state. Numerous problems had occurred because of the party operation of primary elections. For example, some precincts failed to open, voting machines did not operate properly, and some voters ended up being deprived of their right to cast a ballot. In recent years, there were several proposals for the state to take over the conduct of primary elections; however, they failed to pass. The major stumbling block to a state takeover was not party opposition but cost. In lean budget years, politicians were reluctant to add the seven-figure cost of conducting primary elections to the state's budget. In 1991, such a proposal died in committee in the General Assembly. However, a bill authorizing state primaries was approved by 1992 by the General Assembly and signed into law by the governor. In August 1992, state-run primaries took place for the first time.

In presidential elections, South Carolina's Democratic and Republican parties have utilized different methods. The Democratic party has used the caucus system while the Republican party has used a presidential preference primary. The South Carolina Republican party scored a major national publicity coup in 1988 when it decided to hold its presidential preference primary on the Saturday before "Super Tuesday." Getting the jump on the Democrats is an accomplishment attributed by many to the influence of the late Lee Atwater, national Republican political activist from South Carolina. All eyes were focused on South Carolina to see if a front-runner might emerge from the state's primary to lead the other southern states.

In the ensuing primary vote, George Bush, with the support of Republican Governor Carroll A. Campbell Jr., won a landslide victory over his main Republican challengers. Bush received 42.5 percent of the vote in a seven-candidate field. His nearest challengers, Senator Robert Dole and evangelist Pat Robertson, received 22.9 percent and 21.1 percent of the vote respectively. Bush's victory propelled him into convincing victories on Super Tuesday, thus assuring him the Republican party's 1988 presidential nomination. Bush's success also vaulted Atwater into a political staff position in the White House and later to the position as chairperson of the Republican National Committee.

The state Democratic caucus results were much less politically indicative of eventual regional or national results. Native son Jesse Jackson easily outdistanced Albert Gore, Michael Dukakis, Richard Gephardt, Paul Simon, and Gary Hart as a result of his solid African American support. Prior to the caucus meetings, it was revealed that Democratic county chairpersons favored a change to a presidential primary. In a telephone survey, twenty-six of the county leaders said they preferred a change, twelve said they did not, and eight expressed no opinion.[28] In 1992, the South Carolina Democratic party moved to a presidential preference primary. Bill Clinton won easily with solid support from both whites and African Americans. On the Republican side, George Bush easily outdistanced Republican challengers Patrick Buchanan and David Duke.

CONCLUSION

The continuation of a traditionalistic political culture in South Carolina remains apparent. The Republican party has become the dominant party in national elections and a significant force in the state as well. The modern Republican party in South Carolina in the 1960s originated from racial issues. Today, it enjoys significant support from fiscal and social conservatives. For traditionalistic South Carolinians who feel that the Democratic party of the past has deserted them, about the only way to stay traditionalistic is to vote Republican.

The former executive director of the South Carolina Republican party, Mike Burton, attributes the more recent growth of the Republican party in South Carolina to Governor Campbell. Burton claims that Campbell has done more for the Republican party than any one individual in the state.[29] As governor, Campbell has been able to assist the party in building a structure and raising funds, and he has made it easier for the party to recruit candidates. The Republican party remains more concentrated in the suburban areas of the state where economic growth is concentrated. As a result, the party should continue to grow as the state moves toward the twenty-first century. Certainly, the first two elections of the 1990s reflect this trend.

Realignment or complete Republican dominance have not occurred, because the Democratic party remains in solid control of the legislature and most constitutionally elected state offices. In addition, Democratic control continues in most counties. But the message is clear: voters in the state today will split their tickets or switch their loyalty in specific elections depending on the issues and candidates. Because the Democrats have to rely heavily on African American votes, they take more "liberal" welfare-state positions that call for strong central national political leadership. This runs counter to the traditionalistic interests and ideologies of the past. Political dealignment has come to South Carolina.

CHAPTER FIVE

Recent Elections and Their Outcomes

Between 1920 and 1950, the Republican party was of no consequence in South Carolina. No Republican candidate for governor, the U.S. Senate, or the U.S. House of Representatives received as much as 5 percent of the popular vote.[1] In the 1944 presidential election, the Republican candidate, Governor Thomas E. Dewey of New York, received less than 5 percent of the popular vote (4,547 out of 95,148 votes for the two major parties). Perhaps the level of Republican futility in 1944 was best expressed by J. Bates Gerald, then chair of the South Carolina Republican party. Gerald, as quoted by Key, said, " 'There's no use fooling ourselves about' winning any seats in South Carolina in the congressional elections, . . . 'So we're offering no candidates in the general election, in order that every cent of money contributed in the state can be sent into doubtful states to finance campaigns there.' "[2] Gradually, however, Republican fortunes began to change.

VOTING FOR UNITED STATES PRESIDENT

In the 1952 presidential campaign, Democratic governor James F. Byrnes invited Republican presidential nominee Dwight D. Eisenhower to speak on the steps of the statehouse. Large crowds heard the speech and Byrnes publicly endorsed Eisenhower for president. In the election that followed, there were three slates of electors—Democrats, Democrats for Eisenhower, and Republicans. As shown in table 7, the Democratic candidate, Adlai Stevenson, received 50.7 percent of the vote, the Democrats for Eisenhower 46.4 percent, and the Republicans 2.9 percent. Eisenhower's strong showing was linked to Byrnes's endorsement plus continued opposition on the part of white southerners to the national Democratic party's support for civil rights.

Table 7: Presidential Voting Outcomes in South Carolina, 1948–1992

Year	Candidate (Party)	% of Vote	No. of Votes
1948	Truman (D)	24.1	34,423
	Dewey (R)	3.8	5,396
	Thurmond (State's Rights Dem.)	72.1	102,762
1952	Stevenson (D)	50.7	173,004
	Eisenhower (R)	2.9	9,775
	Independents for Ike	46.4	158,243
1956	Stevenson (D)	45.4	136,372
	Eisenhower (R)	25.2	75,700
	Byrd (Ind)	29.4	88,511
1960	Kennedy (D)	51.2	198,129
	Nixon (R)	48.8	188,588
1964	Johnson (D)	41.1	215,723
	Goldwater (R)	58.9	309,048
1968	Humphrey (D)	29.6	197,486
	Nixon (R)	38.1	254,062
	Wallace (AIP), Others	32.3	215,430
1972	McGovern (D)	27.7	186,824
	Nixon (R)	70.8	477,044
	Other	1.5	10,092
1976	Carter (D)	56.2	450,807
	Ford (R)	43.1	346,149
1980	Carter (D)	48.9	417,117
	Reagan (R)	49.4	421,117
	Anderson (Ind)	1.6	13,990
1984	Mondale (D)	36.0	316,746
	Reagan (R)	64.0	561,963
1988	Dukakis (D)	37.6	370,554
	Bush (R)	61.5	606,443
1992	Clinton (D)	39.9	479,514
	Bush (R)	48.0	577,507
	Perot (Ind)	11.5	138,872

Sources: Fowler, *Presidential Voting* (1966); various State Election Commission Reports 1968–92.

Backing for Eisenhower was strongest in the Low Country coastal region. In the counties in this region, African Americans were registered to vote in small numbers at the time. Eisenhower's support positively correlated with the percentage of the African American population in a county.[3] Since most voters were white, the positive correlation demonstrates white voter defection to Eisenhower, probably because of disagreement with the national Democratic party's stand for civil rights.

At the same time, there was an indication of the growing impact of the urban Republican vote in South Carolina. The two Eisenhower slates received 64.8 percent of the vote in Charleston County, 52.4 percent in Greenville County, and 61.7 percent in Richland County.[4] Overall, Neal Peirce characterized the Republican support in South Carolina as coming from traditional Democrats disaffected on the race issue, Republican businesspeople who had moved into the state bringing their party loyalties with them, and a small reform element upset with the generally unprogressive one-party Democratic rule.[5]

By 1956, many southerners had become disillusioned with Eisenhower. Many of them backed slates of independent electors who supported Virginia senator Harry F. Byrd. Although Democratic presidential candidate Adlai Stevenson won a plurality of the vote in South Carolina (45.4%), the Byrd electors won 29.4 percent, and the Eisenhower Republicans won 25.2 percent of the vote. Once again, upper-class urban whites and whites in rural counties with high percentages of African Americans provided the greatest support for the conservative Republican and/or independent candidates.

At the same time, Donald Fowler found that the greatest gains for Eisenhower between 1952 and 1956 came from the African American wards where Eisenhower's enforcement policies on racial issues apparently met with favor. Fowler described South Carolina in 1956 as a maverick state:

> [N]o other state gave as much support to an independent slate of electors; or metropolitan city gave as little support to Eisenhower and as much to an independent as did Charleston; and, as a whole the three metropolitan cities gave less support to the Republican candidate than did their counterparts in other southern states.[6]

The Democratic presidential candidate in 1960 was Massachusetts senator John F. Kennedy. Kennedy, however, balanced his ticket with native Texan Lyndon B. Johnson. In South Carolina, the Democrats allowed state party members to support any candidate without recrimination rather than fielding another independent slate of electors. The Kennedy-Johnson ticket received 51.2 percent of the vote in South Carolina. The Republicans got about one-third of their vote from the three metropolitan counties of Charleston, Greenville, and Richland. The Republican balance was added primarily from the states' rights, independent, rural, agricultural counties that had predominately voted for Byrd in 1956.[7] In fact, the gains made by the Republican party in the rural counties of South Carolina with high percentages of African Americans were unequaled in size or proportion in any other southern state.

In 1964, the candidacy of conservative Republican Barry Goldwater resulted in a Republican victory in South Carolina's presidential election for the first time in the twentieth century. Goldwater had established ties to South Carolina as early as 1959 when South Carolina Republican party chairman Greg D. Shorey took him to a meeting in Greenville and introduced him as a presidential candidate. In 1960, Goldwater addressed the Republican party's state convention.

In 1961, Goldwater spoke in Atlanta and stated, "We're not going to get the Negro vote as a bloc in 1964 and 1968, so we ought to go hunting where the ducks are."[8] In 1964, South Carolina's Republican delegates pledged their support to Goldwater. In addition, former Democrats Strom Thurmond and Albert Watson supported Goldwater for president.

In the 1964 presidential election, Goldwater carried the five Deep South states of Alabama, Georgia, Louisiana, Mississippi, and South Carolina in addition to his home state, Arizona. Goldwater's states' rights philosophy was especially appealing to white southerners. In South Carolina, his strongest support came from the white vote in the rural counties with the heaviest concentrations of African Americans, along with the urban areas of Charleston, Columbia, and Greenville. Donald Fowler drew two conclusions from the Goldwater voting patterns in South Carolina. First, in areas having a high percentage of African Americans, the racial factor dominated the voting behavior of whites. Second, in areas having relatively small percentages of African Americans, voting behavior was linked to income.[9] The whole pattern was propelled by low rates of African American voter registration.

Although race was an important factor in South Carolinians' voting Republican, a new group of Republicans was emerging in the 1960s. They were the urban and suburban middle- and upper-middle-class migrants from farms and small towns who developed negative attitudes toward social programs and hostility toward government spending and taxing.[10] They provided a core of strength in the 1960s for the modern Republican party in the New South.

The 1968 presidential election marked the emergence of the African American vote as an important force in southern politics. Following passage of the federal Voting Rights Act of 1965, African Americans began to register in increasing numbers. By 1968, African Americans constituted 23.5 percent of the registered voters in South Carolina and were becoming a force to be reckoned with in both national and state elections in South Carolina.

The 1968 presidential election was complicated by former Alabama governor George Wallace's candidacy on a third-party ticket, the American Independent Party. The Republican candidate, Richard M. Nixon, developed a southern strategy and had the endorsement of Republican U.S. senator Strom Thurmond. Prior to the Republican National Convention, Nixon and Thurmond met in Atlanta and agreed on a number of issues. In return for the support of southern Republican delegates at the party's convention, Nixon agreed to appoint "strict constructionists" to the United States Supreme Court, to oppose school busing, and to stem the growth of textile imports.[11]

Nixon's southern strategy appealed to a coalition of economic and racial conservatives once again. In the general election, Thurmond campaigned for Nixon, and, in a three-way race, Nixon carried South Carolina with 38.1 percent of the vote. George Wallace received 32.3 percent of the vote, and Democrat Hubert Humphrey finished a poor third with only 29.6 percent of the vote. Two major voting shifts were apparent in South Carolina in 1968. While working-class whites shifted to Wallace, rural counties where African Americans were now voting in significant numbers shifted to the Democratic party. Nixon's greatest support came from middle- and upper-class whites.

Thurmond's influence became evident when President Nixon appointed over twenty of Thurmond's associates to key federal positions. These included former Thurmond aide Harry Dent as political advisor to the president and J. Fred Buzhardt as general counsel to the Department of Defense. Another South Carolinian, Clement Haynsworth, was nominated by Nixon for the U.S. Supreme Court, but the Senate rejected him.[12]

Republican support in South Carolina reached its apex in 1972. The Nixon-Agnew ticket carried forty-nine states and handily defeated George McGovern. The McGovern brand of liberalism found few supporters in South Carolina. Nixon carried every county and received over 70 percent of the popular vote. Nixon's support came from virtually all of the voting groups that supported the Republicans or Wallace in 1968. McGovern ran well only among African American voters.[13]

In the 1976 presidential election, South Carolina returned to the Democratic column for the first time since 1960. The key to the Democratic party's electoral success was the candidacy of former Georgia governor Jimmy Carter. In the 1976 election, Carter carried ten of the eleven states of the old Confederacy. His electoral success was due to his image as a moderate, which resulted in interracial support from working-class whites and African Americans. Carter received 56.2 percent of the vote in South Carolina.

Carter's strongest support came from traditional white Democratic voters in the Up-Country and in the rural counties. The strongest Republican support came from the three largest urban areas, Charleston, Greenville, and Columbia, and the counties surrounding them.[14] Republican governor James Edwards considered the Carter candidacy to be a major reason for the stall in the development of the Republican party in South Carolina as well as in the South in general. Southerners typically felt that Carter was one of them. Coupled with the Wallace candidacy in 1968 and then the Watergate scandal in 1973, Carter's popularity momentarily slowed Republican gains in the region.[15]

The three presidential elections during the 1980s brought new energy to the Republican party for South Carolinians. In 1980, there was widespread discontent with Jimmy Carter's economic and foreign policies. In the March 1980 Republican primary in South Carolina, Ronald Reagan won a decisive victory over John Connally and George Bush. Reagan won every congressional district and received 54.7 percent of the vote compared to 29.6 percent for Connally and 14.8 percent for Bush.

Reagan's victory also marked a victory for new forces within the GOP in South Carolina. These forces moved away from the Republicans of the 1960s, such as James Edwards and Strom Thurmond, who had supported Connally. The leader of the new Republicans was Carroll A. Campbell Jr., the Fourth District congressional representative. In the November election, Reagan narrowly defeated Carter, receiving 49.4 percent of the vote to Carter's 48.9 percent. Reagan carried only fourteen of the state's forty-six counties. These counties, however, were the most urbanized areas of the state and reflected the "New South" in terms of economic development and growth.

The "Reagan Revolution" found its greatest support from sunbelt Republicans, as illustrated by the 1984 presidential election. Reagan's Democratic opponent, Walter Mondale, was identified with organized labor, African Americans, feminists, and a female running mate from New York—qualities having no appeal to traditionalistic, white southerners. South Carolinians responded with landslide support for Reagan. Reagan carried thirty-four of the state's counties. Once again, Reagan ran strongest in the urban counties. Mondale carried eight of the nine counties in the state that had a majority of African American voters. The only counties Mondale carried that did not have a majority of African American registered voters were Marlboro, Marion, and Edgefield.

George Bush's victory over Michael Dukakis in 1988 closely paralleled Reagan's 1984 victory. Bush's campaign manager in the South was Carroll

Table 8: South Carolina Republican Presidential Primary, 1988

Candidate	Percentage	Votes
Bush	42.5	74,738
Dole	22.9	40,265
Robertson	21.5	37,761
Kemp	12.8	22,431
Other	.3	597
TOTALS	100.0	175,792

Source: Neal Thigpen, South Carolina Election Commission.

A. Campbell Jr. The March 1988 Republican primary in South Carolina was held on the Saturday before "Super Tuesday." Bush won a solid victory over his six opponents, capturing 42.5 percent of the vote for delegates. His primary victory launched him to victory in the southern primaries that followed on Super Tuesday and effectively ended the campaigns of Republicans Robert Dole, Jack Kemp, and Pat Robertson.

In the November election, Bush's success followed that of Reagan in 1984. Bush carried thirty-four of the state's counties. Democratic candidate Michael Dukakis carried only three counties that did not have a majority of African American registered voters. They were Bamberg, Marion, and Marlboro. Overall, South Carolina gave Bush his biggest win in the South, with 61.5 percent of the vote.

What was true for South Carolina was also true for the rest of the South. In its study of the 1988 presidential vote, the Institute for Southern Studies noted that the counties with the largest voter turnout were generally the ones that favored George Bush. They were also generally richer, whiter, and growing nearly twice as fast as the counties carried by Dukakis.

In 1992, South Carolina reinforced its image as a Republican presidential stronghold when George Bush received 48 percent of the vote to only 40 percent for the Democrat, Bill Clinton. For Bush, this was the second highest percentage of the vote he received in the fifty states. Only in Mississippi, where he received 50 percent of the vote, did Bush top his South Carolina percentage. Bush carried twenty-four of the forty-six counties and received about 60 percent of the white vote. In addition, he ran exceptionally well among young voters. For example, it is generally estimated that he carried more than 50 percent of Palmetto State voters between the ages of eighteen and twenty-nine, compared to 34 percent in the rest of the United States. Clinton's greatest support came from the less-populated rural counties and

Table 9: Contested Senatorial Elections in South Carolina

Year	Candidate (Party)	% of Vote	No. of Votes
1962	Olin Johnston (D)	57.2	178,712
	W. D. Workman Jr. (R)	42.8	133,930
1966	Bradley Morrah (D)	37.8	164,955
	Strom Thurmond (R)	62.3	271,295
1966	Ernest Hollings (D)	51.3	223,790
	Marshall Parker (R)	48.7	212,032
1968	Ernest Hollings (D)	61.9	404,060
	Marshall Parker (R)	38.1	248,780
1972	Eugene Zeigler (D)	36.7	241,056
	Strom Thurmond (R)	63.3	415,806
1974	Ernest Hollings (D)	69.5	356,126
	Gwen Bush (R)	28.6	146,645
1978	Charles Ravenel (D)	44.4	281,119
	Strom Thurmond (R)	55.6	351,733
1980	Ernest Hollings (D)	70.4	512,554
	Marshall Mays (R)	29.6	257,946
1984	Melvin Purvis (D)	33.0	288,199
	Strom Thurmond (R)	67.0	585,130
1986	Ernest Hollings (D)	63.1	465,511
	Henry McMaster (R)	35.6	262,976
1990	Robert Cunningham (D)	33.5	243,465
	Strom Thurmond (R)	66.5	484,429
1992	Ernest Hollings (D)	49.8	570,070
	Tommy Hartnett (R)	47.4	550,854

Sources: For years 1962–66 various newspaper accounts; for years 1968–92 various State Election Commission Reports.

African Americans. General estimates are that Clinton received 90 percent of the African American votes.

VOTING FOR SENATORS AND MEMBERS OF CONGRESS

Incumbency, not party, has been the most important factor in determining electoral outcomes for U.S. Senate and U.S. House of Representatives elections since the Republican party began contesting them.

U.S. Senate elections have included Republican candidates since 1956. In that year, the Republican party fought for a seat when the mayor of Clemson, Leon Crawford, opposed Democrat Olin D. Johnston. Although Crawford only received 17.8 percent of the vote, it was more than any GOP candidate had received in South Carolina since Reconstruction.

Johnston faced Republican opposition again in 1962. This time it was Columbia newspaper editor William D. Workman Jr. Workman tried to link Johnston to the policies of the national Democratic party, a common Republican approach in the 1960s. Although Workman was defeated, he did receive 42.8 percent of the vote, the highest total for a Republican since 1877. Workman's support base paralleled that of the Republican presidential candidates. He carried the urban counties of Charleston and Greenville and ran well in rural counties with smaller African American populations.

In 1966, both Senate seats were contested in South Carolina. Strom Thurmond, who had not been challenged in 1960, faced competition from Democratic state senator Bradley Morrah of Greenville. Thurmond easily won reelection with 62.2 percent of the vote. African American voters supported Morrah, but Thurmond carried forty-five of the state's forty-six counties.

A special election was also held in 1966 to complete the unexpired term of Olin Johnston, who had died in 1965. Former Democratic governor Ernest F. Hollings of Charleston was challenged by Marshall Parker, a former Democratic state senator who had switched parties. Parker, who had the support of Thurmond, tried to link Hollings to the national Democratic party. In an unusually close election, Hollings received 51.3 percent of the vote. The election was significant inasmuch as the African American votes emerged as the key to Hollings's victory. Hollings carried only 40 percent of the white vote, but he received overwhelming African American support. Republican voting patterns also were illustrated by this election. Parker carried thirteen counties, including the urban/suburban counties of Greenville, Lexington, and Aiken.

Both Thurmond and Hollings have been reelected since 1966. In fact, the only election in which a challenger to Thurmond got over 40 percent of the vote occurred in 1978 when Charles "Pug" Ravenel challenged Strom Thurmond. Ravenel, a native Charlestonian, had graduated from Harvard University and had been an investment banker on Wall Street for seventeen years before returning to South Carolina. In 1974 he had won the Democratic primary for governor; however, he was declared ineligible by the state Supreme Court for not meeting the state's five-year residency requirement. In his second try for statewide office, Ravenel concentrated on Thurmond's opposition to traditional Democratic programs. Thurmond focused on his long record as incumbent senator and won the election, but by his narrowest margin (55.6%). Although Ravenel did make inroads among white voters, his support closely resembled the vote for George McGovern in 1972.[16] Other senatorial elections have been landslide victories for Thurmond. In fact, in the 1984 race, Thurmond carried forty-five counties, losing only Fairfield County by 21 votes out of 7,059 votes cast.

The 1990 senatorial election once again revealed Thurmond's electoral popularity. The eighty-seven-year-old Thurmond faced token opposition from Robert Cunningham. In 1984, Cunningham had opposed Thurmond in the Republican primary. Despite his change in party, Cunningham polled only 33.5 percent of the vote in the November 1990 election.

Hollings has also experienced easy election campaigns. In 1974 and 1980, his opponents failed to receive 30 percent of the vote. In 1986, Hollings's victory margin decreased when Henry McMaster received 35.6 percent of the vote. However, Hollings still carried forty-five counties. The only one he failed to carry was Lexington County, where he lost by 949 votes out of 39,673 votes cast.

However, in 1992, Ernest Hollings barely survived a challenge by former Republican congressman Tommy Hartnett. Hartnett, who had not run for elected office since having been defeated in the lieutenant-governor's race in 1986, mounted a surprisingly strong campaign. Although Hartnett was outspent by about a three-to-one margin, he benefited tremendously from the anti-incumbent sentiment. This, coupled with a political climate in the state that is more religious, more conservative, and more patriotic than the country as a whole, almost ended the veteran Hollings's career. Although Hollings won by about 28,000 votes, it was his closest race since his 11,000 vote win that put him in office in 1966.

Nonetheless, Hollings and Thurmond now have more years of service in the U.S. Senate than the two senators from any other state. In fact, in 1993 their combined service in the Senate totaled sixty-six years!

Elections for the U.S. House of Representatives are somewhat similar to their Senate counterparts. Generally, real party competition did not occur until the 1960s, both in terms of contested seats and vote totals. In addition, with the exception of the Sixth Congressional District, an incumbent had never been defeated in a House race until 1992.

The first really competitive House race occurred in 1962 in the Second Congressional District, which stretched at the time across the state's midlands from Columbia to Aiken and Orangeburg. Republican Floyd Spence garnered 47.2 percent of the vote in an unsuccessful bid to oust Democratic incumbent Albert Watson. Watson, who then supported Barry Goldwater in 1964, was stripped of his seniority by House Democrats in 1965. He subsequently resigned from office in protest on January 31, 1965. He ran as a Republican in a special election and was reelected to Congress. Watson thus became the first Republican congressman from South Carolina since Reconstruction. Watson served in Congress until he ran unsuccessfully for governor in 1970.

Watson's political campaigns were racially charged. For example, one of his campaign leaflets called for South Carolinians to support a man "who will represent the people in Washington" and who will oppose "further pro-Communist and pro-Negro rulings of the Supreme Court." This racial emphasis, which characterized Watson's congressional campaigns in the 1960s, was a visible factor in Republican politics in the state. This harsh Republicanism was as out-and-out racist as the traditionalistic political culture reestablished by turn-of-the-century Democrats in South Carolina under the leadership of Ben Tillman.[17]

Prior to 1970, Watson was the only Republican member of Congress from South Carolina. During the 1970s, as shown in table 10, Republicans became a more viable force in congressional elections. In 1970, Floyd Spence became the second Republican elected to Congress when he replaced Watson, who chose to run for governor. Spence has been reelected continuously since that time from a predominately suburban, New South–type district.

The next gain for the Republican party occurred in 1972 in the Sixth Congressional District, located in the eastern Pee Dee region. In that year, Florence dairyman Ed Young defeated Democratic nominee John Jenrette Jr. Young's victory, however, was related to a split in the Democratic party. In the party's primary, Jenrette, with significant African American support, defeated longtime House veteran John McMillan in a bitter campaign. In the general election, many McMillan supporters backed Young. That, coupled with the Nixon coattails in South Carolina in 1972, gave Young a victory. Two years later, with memories of 1972 fading and no presidential coattails, Jenrette defeated Young in a rematch.

The Republican party regained a second congressional seat in 1978 when Democrat James Mann retired from his Fourth District seat. In the November election, Carroll A. Campbell Jr. defeated Greenville mayor Max Heller in an angrily and unpleasantly fought campaign. This was a seat that Campbell would hold until he ran successfully for governor in 1986.

In 1980, the Republican party made history when it captured two additional congressional seats. In the First Congressional District, Mendel Davis chose not to seek reelection. In the November election, Republican state senator Thomas Hartnett narrowly defeated Charles "Pug" Ravenel. Hart-

Table 10: South Carolina Congressional Elections, 1948–1992

Year	Contested Districts	Election Results	
		Democrats	Republicans
1948	2	6	–
1950	0	6	–
1952	2	6	–
1954	0	6	–
1956	2	6	–
1958	0	6	–
1960	0	6	–
1962	2	6	–
1964	2	6	–
1966	3	5	1
1968	5	5	1
1970	4	5	1
1972	5[a]	4	2
1974	6	5	1
1976	5	5	1
1978	4	4	2
1980	5[b]	2	4
1982	6	3	3
1984	6	3	3
1986	6	4	2
1988	6	4	2
1990	5[c]	4	2
1992	6	3	3

Sources: Compiled from various newspaper accounts and State Election Commission Reports.

[a] In 1972 Floyd Spence, the Republican candidate from the Second Congressional District, was unopposed.

[b] In 1980 Carroll Campbell, the Republican candidate from the Fourth Congressional District, was unopposed.

[c] In 1990 John Spratt, the Democratic candidate from the Fifth Congressional District, was unopposed.

nett's victory, like Campbell's victory in the Fourth District, revealed the growing urbanization of this congressional district. In particular, the Republican party's strength was centered in Charleston County, suburban Dorchester County, suburban Berkeley County, and the retirement area of Hilton Head in Beaufort County.

In the Sixth Congressional District, Republican newcomer John Napier, a lawyer from Bennettsville, defeated incumbent John Jenrette, who had been convicted in the ABSCAM scandal and whose wife, Rita Jenrette, had been featured in *Playboy* magazine photographs.[18] With the addition of these two seats, Republicans held a majority of the congressional seats in the state. This control, however, was short lived. Two years later, the Democrats regained control of the Sixth Congressional District when Democrat Robin Tallon, a businessman from Florence, defeated Napier.

The stability of the congressional districts was evident in 1984. All six incumbents were reelected by margins ranging from 60 percent in the Sixth District to 91 percent in the Fifth District.

The South Carolina congressional delegation remained evenly divided until 1986. In that year, Carroll Campbell relinquished his seat in the Fourth Congressional District. In the November election, Democrat Liz Patterson narrowly defeated William D. Workman III 67,012 votes to 61,648. Patterson, the daughter of former U.S. Senator Olin Johnston, lost Greenville County but was able to carry her home county of Spartanburg and the rural county of Union. This congressional election was one of the most competitive and expensive elections in the country. Patterson spent $594,026, and Workman reportedly spent $639,859. Republicans targeted the district in 1988; however, Patterson retained her seat by a scant 7,441 votes over Republican Knox White, a Greenville city council member and lawyer. In 1990, all incumbents were reelected easily, including Patterson.

In 1992, however, Liz Patterson was upset by a thirty-two-year-old lawyer, Robert Inglis, in the Fourth Congressional District. Inglis used a door-to-door campaign and had the support of the Christian Coalition. Inglis won by almost 6,000 votes out of about 200,000 cast. Patterson, who favored abortion, blamed the Coalition for her defeat. Since the Republican party began contesting congressional seats in the 1960s, this is the only other congressional election in which a Democratic incumbent has been defeated.

The two districts that have remained safe Democratic seats are the Third District and the Fifth District. In the Third District, Butler Derrick was first elected to the House in 1968 and has served continuously since then. In the Fifth District, John Spratt Jr. was elected in 1982 and has been reelected easily three times. Spratt replaced Democrat Kenneth Holland, who declined to seek reelection.

In 1992, a new majority African American district was created mostly out of the Sixth Congressional District. Approximately 60 percent of the voters in this new district were African American. As a result, Robin Tallon decided not to run for reelection. State Human Affairs Commissioner James Clyburn easily won the Democratic party's nomination in a field of five African American candidates. In the November elections, he became the first African American congressman from South Carolina since the turn of the twentieth century. Clyburn received approximately 65 percent of the vote against John Chase, a white Republican who had defeated two African Americans in the Republican primary.

An analysis of congressional elections in South Carolina reveals once again the importance of incumbency. Changes in party control of House seats has normally occurred only when an incumbent has not sought reelection. Prior to 1992, the only exception to this rule had been the Sixth Congressional District. The successful challenges to an incumbent in that district have been linked to divisiveness within Democratic ranks. Jenrette's victory over McMillan in the Democratic primary in 1972 best explains the Republican victory in November of that year. Jenrette's ABSCAM conviction led to his 1980 defeat, but since the Democratic party regained the seat in 1982, it has been secure. In fact, in 1986 Democrat Robin Tallon defeated Republican Robert Cunningham 92,398 to 29,922. With Liz Patterson's defeat in 1992, the Democrats have now experienced the defeat of a second incumbent. For the rest of the decade, one would expect the congressional seats to stabilize at three for each party. Here, the Republican party has achieved parity in South Carolina.

VOTING FOR GOVERNOR

The Republican party did not contest gubernatorial elections until 1966. In that year Joseph Rogers, a native of Mullins, ran against Democrat Robert McNair. Rogers was characteristic of the South Carolina Republican candidates of the 1960s. He was a Democrat who became a Republican in 1966. Well known for his segregationist position, Rogers carried the counties of Aiken, Lexington, and Barnwell in the general election, while capturing only 41.8 percent of the vote. McNair easily won election and counted among his support a large percentage of African American voters.

The gubernatorial campaign of 1970 marked the end of an era of racial politics in South Carolina. The Republican party ran Albert Watson for governor, while the Democrats chose Lieutenant Governor John West, a racial moderate. Strom Thurmond nominated Watson at the party's convention and, for the first time, put the full weight of his office and prestige behind another state office seeker.[19] National Republicans, including Vice President Spiro Agnew and Julie Nixon, also made appearances in South Carolina on behalf of Watson.

Watson's campaign has been described by Jack Bass and Walter DeVries as blatantly racist. During the campaign, Watson made a speech in Lamar, South Carolina, at a freedom-of-choice rally protesting a court-ordered school desegregation plan. Watson told the audience: "*Every section* of this

Table II: Contested Gubernatorial Elections in South Carolina, 1966–1990

Year	Candidate (Party)	% of Vote	No. of Votes
1966	Robert McNair (D)	58.2	255,854
	Joseph Rogers Jr. (R)	41.8	184,088
1970	John West (D)	51.7	250,551
	Albert Watson (R)	45.6	221,233
1974	Bryan Dorn (D)	47.6	248,938
	James Edwards (R)	50.9	266,109
1978	Richard Riley (D)	61.9	384,898
	Edward Young (R)	37.8	236,946
1982	Richard Riley (D)	70.0	466,347
	William Workmam (R)	30.0	201,002
1986	Mike Daniel (D)	48.4	361,328
	Carroll Campbell (R)	51.6	384,565
1990	Theo Mitchell (D)	28.7	211,200
	Carroll Campbell (R)	71.3	524,166

Sources: Compiled from various newspaper accounts and State Election Commission Reports, 1970–90.

state is in for it unless you stand up and use *every* means at your disposal to defend (against) what I consider an illegal order of the Circuit Court of the United States." Nine days later, a white mob attacked an empty school bus at Lamar. Then two of Watson's aides were linked to an attempt to stage a racial confrontation at a high school in Columbia.[20] The racial issue reduced Watson's support from more moderate Republicans. For example, Watson ran better in lower-income white precincts than in upper-income white areas.[21]

Overall, Watson carried eleven counties and received slightly more than 45 percent of the vote. This was the strongest showing for the Republican party in a statehouse election since Reconstruction. Watson's defeat, however, marked the end of an era in which Republicans campaigned on the basis of race. Since then, election issues have focused on other concerns, and the Republican party has attempted to recruit African American members and supporters while maintaining a conservative stance.

In 1974, South Carolina became the first Deep South state to elect a Republican governor. It also marked the first time the Republican party held a primary election to select its candidate. In the primary, Charleston dental surgeon James Edwards faced retired army general William Westmoreland. Only 34,949 persons voted in the primary. Westmoreland carried thirty-five of the state's forty-six counties; however, Edwards received 58 percent of the vote. The key to Edwards's victory was Charleston County, where he received 8,152 votes to 688 for Westmoreland. In seventeen counties, fewer than one thousand persons voted in the Republican primary, including only ten in McCormick County. Two-thirds of the Republican vote was cast in only five counties—Charleston, Lexington, Richland, Greenville, and Spartanburg. Almost ten times as many voters, 319,100, participated in the Democratic primary as in the Republican primary.

In the Democratic primary, newcomer Charles "Pug" Ravenel of Charleston defeated longtime congressman William Jennings Bryan Dorn of Greenwood. Ravenel was seen as a new force in South Carolina politics and campaigned as a progressive reformer. For example, he openly supported the right to collective bargaining by public employees in a state that ranked forty-ninth in percentage of workers belonging to unions. When Ravenel was declared ineligible to run because he had not been a state resident for five years, the state Democratic convention selected Dorn as Ravenel's replacement. Ravenel refused to endorse Dorn. Rather, he said he would write Dorn's name in on the ballot in the November election.

The controversy over this selection process opened the door for the Republican party. Polls had shown Ravenel with a sizable lead over Edwards, but the chain of events resulted in Edwards's election. Edwards carried only fourteen of the state's forty-six counties; however, he carried the urban counties of Charleston (by 65%), Greenville (by 67%), and Lexington (by 67%). While Edwards's victory was a result of disunity in the Democratic party, his candidacy furthered the Republican shift away from the politics of race. As Edwards himself states, "I was a hard-nose conservative when I ran for governor, but on the race issue, I reckon I was as liberal as anybody in the state. . . . I appointed more minorities to boards and commissions than all the rest of the Democratic governors put together."[22]

That Edwards's victory was a political irregularity was confirmed in 1978. The winner of the Democratic primary was Richard W. Riley of Greenville. Riley was the ideal candidate for the Democratic party. He had the support of the business establishment, he was seen as a reformer, and he had ties to the African American community. This coalition was unbeatable. Riley's opponent in the general election was former congressman Ed Young. In the 1978 general election, Riley won with 61.9 percent of the vote while carrying forty-five of the state's forty-six counties.

Carroll A. Campbell Jr., then a member of Congress, explained Riley's appeal in an interview with Alex Lamis: "Riley is a moderate, not a conservative, but not a wild man. Dick was able to pick up some of your moderate conservative voters, pick up his black (supporters), and pick up virtually all of the liberal votes. You know that was a good coalition; it's good politics."[23]

During Riley's term in office, a constitutional amendment was enacted that allowed the governor to compete for a second consecutive term. Because of his personal popularity and the tendency of South Carolina's voters to reelect incumbents, Riley's reelection as governor was virtually assured. In fact, the Republican party had difficulty recruiting someone to challenge Riley.

Eventually, William Workman Jr., the retired editor of the *State* newspaper, agreed to run. At best, Workman, who had first run for office in 1962 as a Republican candidate for United States Senate, was a token candidate. In a lackluster campaign, Workman failed to carry a single county, while Riley received 70 percent of the vote. State Republican party chairman George Graham observed after the election that about 40 percent of the vote in South Carolina consisted of people who voted loyal, one-party politics and that a substantial percentage of these people were African American voters.[24]

The 1982 gubernatorial election marked the low point for South Carolina Republicans. The rebuilding of its electoral strength began in 1984 with presidential and state legislative gains. Then in 1986 the Republican party offered what it called its "dream ticket." Two young, popular Republican members of Congress representing the Up-Country and Low Country sections of South Carolina teamed together in a formidable ticket. Carroll A. Campbell Jr., the Fourth District representative, and Thomas Hartnett, the First District representative, were the candidates for governor and lieutenant governor respectively.

The Republican ticket was a result of skillful negotiation because each candidate had originally announced his intention to seek the governor's office. Hartnett eventually agreed to run for lieutenant governor, thus avoiding a costly and potentially bloody primary election. The alliance was fragile, but it held together and led to the election of Campbell as governor over Gaffney lawyer Mike Daniel.

An analysis of the election results shows the importance of the Campbell/ Hartnett ticket as well as sectionalism in the state. While receiving 51.6 percent of the vote, Campbell carried only seventeen of the state's forty-six counties, but ran exceptionally well in the urban counties throughout the state. Hartnett, however, received 24,145 votes fewer than Campbell. This resulted in the election of Democrat Nick Theodore of Greenville as lieutenant governor due to a significant amount of split-ticket voting in the Up-

Table 12: Selected Counties in the Statewide Gubernatorial Election, 1986

County	Up-Country Counties Candidate Vote Totals	
	Campbell	Hartnett
Anderson	15,339	13,547
Greenville	44,688	36,072
Oconee	6,047	5,186
Pickens	9,778	8,480
Spartanburg	26,107	23,722
TOTALS	101,959	87,007
Hartnett's Lag		(14,952)

County	Low Country Counties Candidate Vote Totals	
	Campbell	Hartnett
Berkeley	9,251	9,729
Beaufort	8,616	9,081
Charleston	30,978	32,154
Dorchester	8,480	8,725
TOTALS	57,325	59,689
Campbell's Lag	(2,364)	

Source: State Election Commission Report.

Country section of the state. Many voters in that region voted for the two Greenville candidates, Republican Campbell and Democrat Theodore. In fact, some people put bumper stickers on their cars advocating Campbell and Theodore.

In contrast, Hartnett was the only candidate on either ticket from the Low Country, and voters in that region were much less likely to split their ticket. In essence, Hartnett was instrumental in Campbell's success, but Campbell was unable to add enough votes to his running mate for a victory. In Greenville and neighboring Anderson County, a majority of the electorate voted for Republican Campbell and Democrat Theodore.

As shown in table 12, in five Up-Country counties won by Campbell, Hartnett lagged 14,952 votes behind. In the four counties of the First Congressional District, Campbell lagged only 2,364 votes behind running mate Hartnett.

Campbell's election did represent a milestone in Republican party development in South Carolina. For the first time, a Republican governor had been elected in an election where both parties were united. During his first term in office, Campbell consolidated his power base, and the Democrats struggled to find a viable candidate to oppose Campbell in 1990.

The 1990 gubernatorial election provides the best illustration of the changing nature of party politics in the state as South Carolina continues to modernize its traditionalistic political culture. The first example of this occurred in the June 1990 primaries where Democrats nominated an African American state senator, Theo Mitchell of Greenville, as their candidate for governor. Mitchell faced only token opposition from first-term state senator Ernie Passailaigue of Charleston. Mitchell received overwhelming support from African Americans and received 25 to 30 percent of the white vote to carry thirty-seven counties. Of note, however, is the fact that only about 193,000 people voted in the Democratic primary. This was only 60 percent of the 1986 figure. Analysts attributed the low turnout to the strength of the incumbent Republican governor, Carroll Campbell.

In comparison, the hotly contested statewide Republican primary for nomination of a candidate for lieutenant governor drew approximately 96,000 voters. In evaluating this turnout, Republican party officials noted that the rates of Democratic to Republican primary voters had declined from sixteen to one in 1978 to two to one in 1990. In fact, in 1990 Republican voters outnumbered Democratic voters in the primary elections in ten of the state's forty-six counties. Most of the counties were urban or suburban areas, once again illustrating the emerging individualistic culture in these areas.

In the general election, Campbell easily defeated Mitchell. Campbell won over 70 percent of the vote and carried forty-three counties. Campbell also carried seven of the state's ten majority African American counties and won an estimated 14 percent of the African American vote. His reelection, however, was seen more as a personal victory than a realignment of the state's voters. For example, in the lieutenant governor's race, Democratic incumbent Nick Theodore easily defeated Republican challenger Henry McMaster by carrying forty-three counties and receiving 58 percent of the vote.

Although Republicans did win three other statewide constitutional offices (secretary of state, superintendent of education, and commissioner of agriculture), these successes were linked to factors other than party. Both the secretary of state and the superintendent of education were defeated because of political tumult involving their departments. The incumbent secretary of state was scalded by his successful opponent for "taking a beach vacation" courtesy of lobbyists while laws regulating lobbyists were not being enforced. The education superintendent was forced into a negative campaign defending management practices. The agriculture commissioner was an incumbent Democrat who switched his party affiliation to Republican prior to the election.

VOTING FOR STATE LEGISLATORS

The continuing weakness of the Republican party at the grass roots is readily apparent in the legislature. In 1961, the Republicans captured their first legislative seat since early in the twentieth century. In 1970, Republicans held 8.9 percent (eleven) of the state House positions and 16 percent (eight) of the Senate seats. By 1980, Republican representation had increased to 14.5 percent (eighteen) in the House while decreasing to 10.9 percent (five) in the Senate. The Senate decrease was linked in part to a reduction in the size of the Senate from fifty members to forty-six and to the reapportionment that took place after the 1970 census.

The 1980s witnessed the greatest growth in Republican state legislative representation. Following the 1988 election, Republicans constituted 29.8 percent (thirty-seven) of the House and 23.9 percent (eleven) of the Senate. In addition, following the 1988 election, four Democratic House members and one Democratic senator switched party affiliation. The Republican party picked up one additional Senate seat in a special election. By the 1990 elections, there were forty-two Republicans in the state House. This increased to forty-four prior to the 1992 elections.

Redistricting, coupled with the growth in support of the Republican party by the state's voting population, resulted in additional gains for the GOP in 1992. After the dust had settled, the Republican party could claim fifty House seats to seventy-three for the Democrats and one independent. Republicans won three open seats and defeated three incumbent Democrats for their other new positions. In the state Senate, the Republican party gained three more seats, giving them sixteen seats. This means that the Republican party now has a veto-proof minority in both houses of the General Assembly.

A closer examination of the legislators illustrates the metropolitan base of legislative representation. Republicans in the House primarily come from the rapidly growing suburban areas in such counties as Charleston, Berkeley, Richland, Lexington, Greenville, Spartanburg, Aiken, and Horry. A similar pattern exists in the Senate, where the Republican senators represent the three major urban centers in the state—Charleston, Columbia, and Greenville-Spartanburg. In 1992, the Republican party did gain some seats from more rural areas; however, it is too early to tell if these gains will become more permanent.

These patterns suggest that the Republican party has historically been concentrated in the state's urban counties. Republican senator Strom Thurmond explains the still-entrenched nature of the Democratic party as follows. When South Carolinians vote Republican for president, "They feel that's way out yonder and if they vote Republican there won't be any stigma. But in state elections, especially among the less enlightened people, there's still that stigma against Republicans that goes back to the military rule of 1866 to 1876."[25]

Democratic senator Ernest Hollings, however, insists that the Democrats have maintained their power because they "have been habitually good public servants" and because they are more conservative than they are liberal.

CONCLUSION

Elections in South Carolina show varying patterns of Democratic party dominance. South Carolinians have not supported a Democratic candidate for president since 1960, except for Jimmy Carter in 1976. Democrats have not fared as badly in governors' races, but Democratic candidates today cannot depend on a consistent majority stronghold. Given the strong showing of Republican gubernatorial candidates in metropolitan areas, neither party had a clear advantage going into the 1994 election.

Today, candidates for governor or for the legislature from either party will be closely inspected by voters to determine their positions on taxing and spending issues. The perceived fairness of fiscal policies and the integrity of the administration in Columbia are key to the voters' sentiments.

CHAPTER SIX

Lobbyists and Interest Groups

Interest group activity in post–World War II South Carolina as portrayed by V. O. Key Jr. illustrates traditionalistic political culture and the struggle by reformers to redesign the state's excessive reliance on narrowly organized political interests. Key described South Carolina as being commanded by a strong banker/planter/lawyer, "Bourbon" ring in the Low Country, while manufacturing interests dominated the Up-Country.[1] Key showed how Up-Country manufacturing counties and Low Country Charleston often joined in a natural alliance of urban and manufacturing communities. For example, in 1947 legislators from York County and Charleston County joined forces to oppose anti-check-off and anti–closed shop bills.[2]

On most legislative actions, however, the textile industry dominated more than the urban-manufacturing alliance. Longtime legislative leader state senator Edgar Brown (*D*-Barnwell, 1929–72) once said that he steered South Carolina's state finances in such a way as to ensure that "the big fellows like Dupont, Stevens, Deering-Milliken, Fiberglass, Textron, Chemstrand, Lowenstein, Burlington, Bowaters, and others . . . have confidence in our stability."[3] On most other issues, the textile giants from the Up-Country would often clash with Low Country interests. They argued about patronage, state construction projects, which section of the state the governor would come from, and "virtuous" issues such as liquor referendums.

The practical emphasis of this conservative "Bourbon"/textile elite, whether in alliance or conflict, was to maintain the status quo. New government activities were limited, and the role played by government in the expansion of social service programs was given low priority. Reflecting on his service as House Speaker, Solomon Blatt (*D*-Barnwell, 1933–45, 1951–73) described his perception of the role of government as follows: "We believed in good government, good stable government, and a balanced budget. . . . we fit in the key to accomplish that [statewide] purpose of government, which is to serve its people at the least dollar that could be spent."[4]

Maintaining the state's AAA credit rating was seen by Blatt and other state leaders as more important than providing services to a population that ranked among the poorest in the country. Higher estimated state revenues and the clamor for increased spending have recently expanded state government rapidly—perhaps too rapidly. In 1993 the state's honored bond rating slipped a notch from the highest level of Standard and Poor's rating service.

INTEREST GROUPS: THE CONTEMPORARY PROFILE

Although interest groups are still a major political force, changes in South Carolina's economic base since the late 1940s have altered the character of individual interest group influence. From the 1950s through the 1970s, the state's economy was dramatically transformed. The textile elite remained important, but the agricultural sector became smaller and more diversified. For example, from 1950 to 1976 the number of farmers declined from 140,000 to only 47,000. The farm population declined by 38 percent during the 1950s and another 66 percent during the 1960s. Timber, tobacco, soybeans, corn, peaches, cattle, and poultry replaced cotton as the significant cash crops during the same era.

Despite the dominance of textiles in manufacturing, new industry began to appear. In 1973, textile employment totaled 156,000 workers, or more than 40 percent of the manufacturing workforce. The value of textiles produced totaled $4 billion. The allied garment industry employed 44,000 workers.[5] These interests were so powerful in the 1970s that they were able to discourage the location of a Philip Morris plant in the state because it was a unionized company, which "might drag the union here and raise wage rates."[6]

During the 1960s, nearly $4 billion was invested in new industry, not only in textiles but also in such fields as tool and die works, electronics design and assembly, chemical technology, and precision metalworking. Then from 1972 through 1977, new investments in South Carolina plants ranged from $500 million to $1.3 billion per year. International investment in South Carolina, which totaled $665 million prior to 1970, amounted to $1.4 billion between 1970 and 1977.[7]

By the end of the 1980s, textiles still represented one-third of all manufacturing employment. No other industry group could claim more than 10 percent of the industrial workforce. Other sectors of the economy, however, are growing much more rapidly today. Between 1972 and 1984, manufacturing employment grew a modest 7 percent (0.6% annually) while employment in the wholesale/retail trades combined and service industries increased by 64 percent (5.3% annually) and 92 percent (7.7% annually) respectively.[8] Between 1985 and 1989, the same pattern continued. Manufacturing jobs grew by 5.1 percent (18,638 employees; 1% annually), wholesale/retail trades by 23 percent (59,877 employees; 4.6% annually), and service industries by 38.3 percent (75,589 employees; 7.8% annually).[9]

These changes in the employment picture are now reflected in interest group activity in South Carolina. A survey of recent lobbying expenditures illustrates the pluralistic nature of interest groups. For example, banking and utilities have become increasingly important business interests in the state. In fact, the second highest reported spending among lobbyists in South Carolina in 1989 was by the representative of the League of Savings and Loans, who reported expenditures of $54,499. The only lobbyist reporting higher expenditures represented thirteen different clients.

The major utilities in South Carolina are Carolina Power and Light, Duke Power, South Carolina Electric and Gas, and Santee-Cooper. Formally named the Public Service Authority, Santee-Cooper is a state agency that resembles the federal Tennessee Valley Authority (TVA).[10] It provides electric power to the seventeen electric distribution co-ops in the state.[11] Collectively, utilities spent $186,318 on lobbying in 1989. Utility expenditures were unusually high in 1989 because of a statehouse battle between electric co-ops and the SCANA Corporation, the parent company of South Carolina Electric and Gas Company, over proposed legislation that would have made it easier to dissolve co-ops. The bill that eventually passed the legislature actually made it more difficult to dissolve co-ops.

Some interests, such as the Trial Lawyers Association, periodically become important. In 1989, for example, there was a proposal to put caps on insurance claims arising from automobile accidents. Both trial lawyers and insurance company representatives camped out at the statehouse, almost becoming permanent fixtures in the House and Senate balconies during the debate. One state representative said the trial lawyers, coupled with insurance company lobbyists, spent money into six figures fighting different sections of the one bill. He said,

> It bordered on a circus for those familiar with the process. . . . If money is power, the insurance industry and the trial lawyers have power because they

both have inexhaustible supplies of money. . . . Their lobbying wasn't effective, but they had so much money, it was effective.[12]

The measure died on the floor of the House. After the defeat, trial lawyer lobbyists were seen hugging each other in the House gallery.

In 1989–90, waste management became an important issue as legislators struggled with the state's reputation as a dumping ground for other states' refuse—including nuclear waste deposited at the Savannah River Facility's Barnwell site, medical waste burned at the Hampton County incinerator operated by Southland Exchange Joint Venture, or chemical waste stored at the Pinewood Dump. In 1989, the waste industry first reported lobbying expenditures of $67,448. However, after the state attorney general threatened to sue lobbyists who failed to report their lobbying-related income, nine lobbyists for GSX Chemical Services, Inc., filed reports that indicated that GSX paid them nearly $100,000 in combined "salaries"—that is, fees—in 1989.[13] Southland Exchange Joint Venture, which operates the medical waste incinerator in Hampton County, paid its lobbyists $90,000 in fees in 1989.[14]

GSX corporation, which operates the Pinewood Dump, was described by one state senator as the best-financed lobby in the state. GSX opposes reductions in the permitted amounts of waste that may be deposited at the Pinewood facility, higher dumping fees, and legislation requiring them to buy insurance for spillage and leakage. The Pinewood facility, which is near Lake Marion, is seen by some observers as a potential billion-dollar environmental disaster if it develops a leak. Lake Marion connects with Lake Moultrie and, through the Santee-Cooper hydroelectric plant at Pinopolis, Lake Moultrie empties into the Cooper River, which flows to Charleston. Also, the Santee River flows from the lakes through rich agricultural country before emptying into the Atlantic Ocean above McClellanville.

Government groups are also perceived to be relatively important. A variety of government agencies, both state and local, battle annually over funding. In addition to state agencies, legislators must contend with the South Carolina Municipal Association, the South Carolina Association of Counties, and the South Carolina School Boards Association. These groups are just as involved in taxing, spending, and regulating as is the state legislature. For some voters, local officials seem more significant than state legislators.

In the field of higher education, the state universities, colleges, and technical schools both cooperate and compete for state funding. Before the new ethics law, state universities, such as Clemson and the University of South Carolina, often courted legislators with free football and basketball tickets.

A lobbyist for Clemson University spent $28,000 in 1990 while entertaining legislators, most of it at football games. Another well-known advocate for a state agency, former University of South Carolina president James Holderman, reportedly gave expensive gifts to win key lawmakers' support for state-financed campus projects. A council of university presidents from the major state institutions is emerging as a significant lobbying effort intent on influencing the regulatory guidelines of the State Commission on Higher Education. The council of presidents also clashes with the legislature's apparent preference for spending to upgrade the state's technical colleges at the expense of the research universities.

Universities are just one example of the involvement of state agencies in lobbying the legislature. In 1990, state agencies reported lobbying expenditures of $747,000. Most of the money ($613,000) covered employees' salaries. House members often voice resentment of state employee lobbyists watching them from the gallery. The largest amount went to about forty state employees who spent more than 10 percent of their time lobbying.[15] That amount, however, is artificially low since state agency heads do not have to report how much time they spend personally trying to influence lawmakers.

One lobbyist noted that state agency lobbyists are in a stronger position than private lobbyists to get what they want because they have the favors of their agencies at their disposal to help them get additional appropriations. For example, a lobbyist for the Department of Health and Environmental Control noted that in 1991 he spent about half of his time fielding requests from legislators whose constituents needed a copy of a birth certificate or an answer about why an incinerator had been given a permit to operate in their neighborhood. A lobbyist for the State Highway Commission sat with the House subcommittee dealing with highways while it met and transacted business.[16]

The effectiveness of state agencies in lobbying is perhaps best illustrated by the fact that South Carolina has more employees per capita than all but seven other states in the country. Government in South Carolina is big business. In fact, the biggest single employer in South Carolina is the South Carolina government itself.[17]

In recent years, health-care interests have become increasingly important as government has become more involved in financing and regulating them—as, for example, the Medicaid program. These interests include doctors, insurance groups, and hospitals. They were cited as being important by 5 percent of legislators in the early 1980s. In 1989 lobbyists for health-care interests spent $153,532.

The changing nature of South Carolina's economy can best be illustrated by the fact that in a 1982 study of interest groups in the state, only 3 percent of the legislators cited farm interests as being powerful. Also notable by its absence is organized labor. Only about 5 percent of the state's private labor force is organized. In the public sector, only 16 percent of state and local workers are unionized.

Neither do national public interest groups seem very effective in the state. State chapters of organizations such as the League of Women Voters, the American Civil Liberties Union, and Common Cause, as well as civil rights groups such as the National Association for the Advancement of Colored People, are not typically credited by lawmakers as having much impact on legislation. However, state Common Cause members were active in promoting recently adopted state ethics legislation, and the other groups continue to provide important education, information, and commentary for broader public discussion of issues.

INTEREST GROUPS' METHODS

The technique most frequently identified with interest groups is lobbying. Today, lobbying is becoming a more important and visible part of the legislative process in South Carolina. In fact, in the twelve years from 1974 to 1986, the number of registered lobbyists nearly tripled, while their reported expenditures increased more than tenfold. The number of registered lobbyists in 1989 had increased by another 61 percent while their reported expenditures increased by over five hundred thousand dollars.[18]

One South Carolina lobbyist, Dwight Drake, attributes the increase in the number of lobbyists to the Reagan era of decentralized government. Drake, a former aide to two-term governor Richard Riley, represented nineteen different clients in 1989. Said Drake, "I know many of the clients that I represent now didn't have representation at all before 1980. That's because so many of the decisions have moved to the state level. There's been a real increase in lobbying activity."[19]

Among other things, lobbyists vie to entertain members of the General Assembly. In 1990, the Charleston *News and Courier* described the annual ritual by which lobbyists entertain legislators:

> When legislators come to Columbia each January, so do hundreds of lobbyists
> who crowd the House and Senate chambers seeking to influence members of
> the General Assembly on issues important to them. In the evening, the compe-

tition for a legislator's time turns to local restaurants, private clubs, and hotel rooms.[20]

On some past occasions, legislators did not even have to leave the capitol building to be wined and dined. During the 1984 legislative session, the state's electric cooperatives had lunch sandwiches and barbecue dinners sent to members on the floor of the legislature in hopes that they would consider a bill to protect their customers living in areas annexed by municipalities. When questioned about this attempt to influence members, a co-op spokesperson responded that the co-ops were not "attempting to bribe legislators with a $3.95 barbecue plate. The legislature has the sole option of deciding to adjourn or stay. We felt they were going to stay, so we offered to assist them."[21]

If lobbyists were not directly feeding legislators at work, the lobbyists were operating elsewhere throughout the statehouse during the legislative session. Senator Glenn McConnell (R-Charleston) noted that legislators could always tell what the body was discussing because the faces changed in the balcony. He added that lobbyists were "like a hungry herd" waiting to grab legislators when they got out of the elevator.[22]

Interest groups also hold social events for legislators. One of the larger events attended by members of the General Assembly is the annual meeting of the South Carolina Textile Manufacturers Association. At the fourteenth annual meeting of the association in March 1990, at least 64 of the 170 members of the General Assembly left a debate on ethics to travel to Hilton Head for a weekend as guests of the association. Jerry Beasley, the association's executive vice president, said that the purpose of inviting the legislators was to

> bring them in touch with the plant managers in this industry who are responsible for employing 90,000 people in South Carolina. . . . We try to make sure these people get to know their legislators well and have some casual time with them, as well as some business time.[23]

Legislators were split on the propriety of attending these functions. Representative Woodrow McKay (D-Florence) stated that he did not attend conferences or events like that

> because the perception that the public has is that we are indebted to them. It's not worth trying to overcome that. I just refrain from going to these things that are sponsored by lobbyists.

Senator Theo Mitchell (D-Greenville), who was running for governor at the time, reflected,

I just feel that a weekend of pleasure, all expenses paid, now that ethics are being raised—I shall endeavor to be as Caesar's wife: above suspicion and reproach.

In contrast, Senator John Land (*D*-Lee, Clarendon, Sumter, Florence), who did not attend, stated,

I don't think it's anything wrong with the South Carolina textile people putting us up and inviting us down. I think that's a legitimate way to curry favor, which is what lobbyists basically do. They try to make friends and cause you to be more inclined to support their positions, and of course that's what the process is all about.

Representative Tim Wilkes (*D*-Fairfield, Chester) noted,

I've got three textile mills in my district so I have an interest in what the industry's doing. We're losing a lot of jobs in that industry.

However, the executive director of South Carolina's Common Cause, John Crangle, saw it differently:

What's really going on is an effort to obtain influence and access by giving members of the General Assembly favors—free food, free liquor, free trips.

Legislators are required to report gifts of more than one hundred dollars received from lobbyists, but only eight of approximately one hundred who had attended the event the previous year had even acknowledged attending the event. House Speaker Robert J. Sheheen (*D*-Kershaw) in 1990 cited the Textile Association and other manufacturing associations as the most powerful lobbies in the state because they were active in monitoring legislation and talking to members of the legislature.

Interest groups also try to influence policy by contributing to the campaigns of candidates running for public office. Campaigns have become more expensive for those seeking to retain or win legislative seats. For example, in 1988 one Democratic Senate incumbent, James Waddell of Beaufort, spent $163,502 for his general election campaign. Two other Democratic incumbent senators, J. M. Long (Horry) and Nikki Setzler (Lexington, Aiken, and Barnwell), reported expenditures of $114,349 and $106,194 respectively. Neither were Republicans exempt from such levels of expenditures. State senator John Courson (*R*-Richland County) spent $104,556 on his successful reelection campaign. Altogether, Senate primary candidates filing disclosure forms reported receipts totaling $903,134 and general election receipts of $1,896,465 for the forty-six seats.[24]

State House candidates have also discovered the high cost of campaigns. The biggest spender for a House seat was Kenneth S. Corbett (*R*-Horry). Corbett reported 1988 expenditures of $49,121. Three other members of the House reported expenditures ranging from $33,252 to $36,903. Collectively, the 124 House members spent $2.2 million to contest the primary and general elections.[25]

Sources of contributions to campaigners vary in both bodies. Contributions from private individuals are the primary source of funds for candidates. For House candidates in 1988, two-thirds of the receipts for the general election and 54 percent of the receipts for the primary came from private contributions. Senate figures were somewhat lower. Forty percent of the general election receipts and 43 percent of the primary election receipts were from private sources.[26]

Political Action Committees (PACs) and business contributions together constituted 30 percent of the receipts for House members in the general election and 46 percent in the primary. In the Senate, approximately one-fourth of the receipts were from businesses or PACs. Of particular note is the insignificant financial role played by the political parties. Parties contributed only 1 percent of the receipts for state Senate races and only 5 percent for state House races.

INTEREST GROUP REGULATION

According to South Carolina law, a lobbyist is a "legislative agent . . . who is employed, appointed or retained, with or without compensation, by another person. . . . to influence in any manner the act or vote of any member of the General Assembly."[27] However, South Carolina laws governing lobbying have been known for their ineffectiveness.

Prior to 1990 all lobbyists had to register with the secretary of state and pay a ten-dollar filing fee. A 1990 bill proposed a registration fee of one hundred dollars. The reasoning behind the increase was that it would help raise the professional standards. As one lobbyist said, "[A]nybody could pay $10.00 and get a lobbying card. There are a lot of people on the list who call themselves lobbyists."[28] Today the fee is $50.

The law also required lobbyists to report how much they spent on entertainment, lodging, and travel; however, it did not require them to say on whom the money was spent or what specific legislation they sought to influence. In addition, the state law said lobbyists had to file expense and income reports with the secretary of state within thirty days after the legislature adjourned. These reports had to list "only that income or expense directly related to lobbying."

Enforcement of the law was given to the state attorney general. The maximum penalty for not filing lobbying income and expense reports was a fine of a hundred dollars and/or thirty days in jail. Many lobbyists, however, insisted that because of the way the law read, they were not required to report their salaries. For example, in 1989 approximately 390 lobbyists filed reports with the secretary of state's office. In their reports, about 110 left blank the space for salary.[29]

One lobbyist, Stephen H. Smith, president of the South Carolina League of Savings and Loans, called the law "vague and ambiguous." Spending had to be reported only on things "directly related to lobbying." Said Smith,

> Let's say I take two senators out for lunch or dinner and we never discuss any legislation, we're just buddies. Some lobbyists take the position that is not directly related to lobbying because you did not talk about a bill. . . . Right now the lobbyist disclosure is a total farce because some are filing, some aren't. It just depends on what position you take, and neither one of these positions is right or wrong because the law doesn't say which.[30]

The potential for special interests to influence legislative elections in South Carolina was also enormous, since businesses could legally contribute to campaigns and there were no legal limitations on the amount of money that any specific entity could contribute to a campaign. In addition, there were virtually no limits on the way campaign contributions could be spent. For example, candidates could buy a new car with campaign donations and even give money to other candidates.[31] In addition, the money could be carried over from one election to another.

Common Cause pointed out the weakness in the state's disclosure system for financial contributions. Candidates must file Campaign Disclosure forms with the House or Senate Ethics Committee and report all campaign contributions of more than one hundred dollars; however, there was not a uniform system of identifying contributors. For example, the disclosure forms for the candidates did not require them to categorize donation sources in sufficient detail to distinguish them from each other. In addition, no adequate system existed of monitoring or auditing candidates' filing to assure completeness and accuracy. The two legislative committees charged with the responsibility of receiving the forms lacked sufficient staff to monitor and assure compliance. At the beginning of the 1990s, as with the United

States Congress, the regulation of interest groups in South Carolina was weak and ambiguous.

Ambiguity and Scandal

Within the context of loosely regarded legislator–interest group interconnections, a major stumbling block appeared for the uninformed and unaware. The stumble began in July 1990, when the FBI launched a sting operation labeled Operation Lost Trust that investigated violations of the federal Hobbs Act and other federal laws.[32] At the center of the sting was a former lobbyist, Ron Cobb. As part of a plea bargain on other charges, Cobb worked for the FBI offering cash to state legislators in return for their votes on a pari-mutuel betting bill. The FBI set up a dummy corporation called the Alpha Group to push the pari-mutuel legislation, and an undercover FBI agent worked with Cobb.

The severity of the fall became clear when eventually twenty-eight individuals—legislators, lobbyists, and state officials—were indicted on a variety of charges ranging from bribery to possession of drugs. All but one of them either pleaded guilty or were found guilty in a federal court trial. Seventeen legislators were involved; sixteen were actively serving at the time, and one former legislator had been appointed as state circuit judge.

Most of the legislators had been charged with accepting bribes; one was charged with racketeering and one with cocaine possession. Six lobbyists, the Circuit Court judge, and a top Republican campaigner who had been chair of the state development board pleaded guilty to cocaine or marijuana possession. A former highway commissioner pleaded guilty to one count of extortion. The former director of legislative affairs for Governor Campbell pleaded guilty to obstruction of justice. A former employee of Clemson University pleaded guilty to cocaine possession. One legislator was tried and found innocent.

Two of the early arrests in the sting were a white Republican and an African American Democrat. They were then used by the FBI to continue the investigation, and they brought other legislators into the sting. Of the seventeen legislators who eventually became involved, eight were African Americans, including the Circuit Court judge, who was a former legislator. This led some African American leaders to claim that African American legislators had been targeted in the investigation. Senator Frank Gilbert (D-Florence, Marion, Horry) stated in September 1990 that "it certainly is no question that a disproportionate number of black legislators have been implicated

in the sting. . . . . [The fact that an] even higher percentage of blacks are being indicted than there are whites . . . speaks for itself."[33]

Minority leaders questioned whether the FBI had a *Fruhmenschen* policy
that singled out African Americans on the theory that they were inferior and
prone to crime. *Fruhmenschen* is a German word that means "primitive
man." In response to this charge, United States Attorney E. Bart Daniel
said,

> [S]ince this investigation became public several months ago, there has been
> some discussion that it might be politically or racially motivated. Neither is
> true. The indictments speak for themselves and will continue to do so over the
> next several months. They demonstrate that this investigation crosses all polit-
> ical, social and regional lines.[34]

For other critics, the legal problems inherent in an FBI sting outweighed the
worth of catching a few legislators taking a gift they interpreted as a campaign contribution.

For supporters of the sitting legislature, the turbulent times and apparent
general loss of trust in state government imposed by the FBI sting seemed ex-
traordinarily costly and disruptive. The *State,* the newspaper in Columbia,
suggested that since most of the legislators had either pleaded guilty or had
been found guilty, the better term for the sting was "juggernaut"—a formidable force that overwhelms everything in its path.[35]

Impact on Lobbyists and Legislators

Nevertheless, the FBI sting seemed to prompt several major changes in the
General Assembly in 1991, some of which may have impeded necessary legislative work. First, legislators became more cautious in their relations with
lobbyists because of a clear feeling among some legislators that they were
being watched. For example, freshman senator Glenn Reese (*D*-Spartan-
burg) was convinced that the phones in his Senate office were bugged. Representative John Rama (*R*-Charleston), president of a security systems firm,
told of some colleagues who believed they had seen fellow legislators wear-
ing hidden microphones.[36]

In addition, interaction between legislators and lobbyists declined significantly in 1991. Their relationship had to be redefined. Representative Ron
Fulmer (*R*-Charleston) described lobbying in the 1991 session as being
"dead on arrival." He noted that when legislators walked outside the chambers, lobbyists were nowhere to be seen. Instead, it was only representative

talking to representative. Fulmer stated that the most visible lobbyists were state agencies and the South Carolina Education Association. Business lobbyists were very quiet because they didn't want to jeopardize their lives and careers.[37]

L. Fred Carter, then senior advisor to Governor Campbell for finance and planning, supported Fulmer's assessment. Said Carter, "Lobbying has been substantially subdued this year. Most professional lobbyists have been very circumspect about approaching legislators."[38]

The social interaction between legislators and lobbyists also changed. First, there was less interaction. The *State* observed that when the House broke for a midday meal, a group of lobbyists and legislators headed to a sandwich shop as opposed to a private dinner club where lobbyists used to take lawmakers. At the sandwich shop, the legislators sat at one table, the lobbyists at another. An unidentified lobbyist observed that drink buying hardly existed. There were no private drinking parties. The bars were deserted at night and there were no dinner parties at the dinner clubs.[39]

Representative Fulmer stated that when legislators and lobbyists went out together, the legislator paid his or her own way. He recalled that when twelve to fourteen individuals had dinner one night with Jay Hicks, the lobbyist for Citizens & Southern National Bank (now NationsBank), Hicks said to the waitress, "[S]eparate checks please. It is the law."[40]

Representative Robert Barber (*D*-Charleston) felt that there were fewer lobbyists and fewer fund-raisers in 1991 than in the past. Barber described the legislator/lobbyist relationship in the past as being "arm-in-arm," but in 1991 it was "at arm's length."[41] Representative Barber assessed these changes positively. He noted that legislators were less distracted by lobbyists than in the past. For example, in 1991 when legislators broke for lunch, they were more likely to dine with fellow legislators where discussions centered around public issues and the General Assembly as opposed to dining with a lobbyist and focusing on specific issues of concern only to the lobbyist.

In addition, the number of bills on the House calendar dropped dramatically. Barber suspected that this was related in part to fewer special-interest bills being considered by the House.[42] House Speaker Bob Sheheen summarized these changes when he observed that there was an apprehension in two ways: the appearance of what legislators do with the outside community and of legislators' relationships with lobbyists.[43]

Reports filed by lobbyists at the end of the 1991 legislative session reinforce the image of the changed relationship between lobbyists and legislators. Money spent by lobbyists to wine and dine lawmakers dropped from $452,087.94 the previous year to just over half that amount, $227,191.65.[44]

In addition to a change in the customary legislator/lobbyist relationships, the General Assembly also moved toward enacting ethics legislation. In August 1990, House Speaker Bob Sheheen proposed several reforms to be considered by the General Assembly including the following:

1. Require full disclosure of all campaign contributions, regardless of amount.

2. Eliminate all cash contributions of more than fifty dollars.

3. Bar a candidate's family members from making donations that circumvent the rules.

4. Require full disclosure of all "in-kind" donations such as free travel and vacations.

Sheheen conceded, however, that laws regulating lawmakers and lobbyists would never be foolproof. "Nothing we do is going to keep bad lobbyists from offering money to legislators nor bad legislators from taking money," he said.[45]

While strong ethics legislation was being considered in 1991, there was evidence that support for reform was limited, especially among lawyer-legislators. For example, the original ethics bill passed by the state Senate in March 1991 banned lawyer-legislators from representing clients before state boards and commissions. This proposal was deleted from the final bill, which was approved by a two-vote margin in early April. The final bill allowed lawyer-legislators to continue representing clients before boards and agencies; however, it required them to disclose more about whom they represented before state boards and how much they were paid.

Several lawyer-legislators had a very tangible vested interest in this legislation. For example, fifteen lawyer-legislators in the 1990 General Assembly received $489,694 for work in cases before the Workers' Compensation Commission. Altogether, twenty-eight legislators either had active cases before the commission or got attorney's fees in 1990. Senator John Land topped the list with $145,731, while Senator Isadore Lourie of Columbia earned $139,771 in fees.[46]

Many had opposed the ban of legislators as attorneys before a state board or commission. For example, Senator Theo Mitchell stated that "an absolute prohibition . . . is absolutely ludicrous as well as vindictive and certainly has a tint of jealousy. . . . It's a vendetta." Another lawyer, Senator James E. Bryan Jr. (*D*-Laurens, Greenville) stated, "If that's what y'all want, to get lawyers who practice law out of the General Assembly, you're headed that way."[47] When the amended bill was approved, some legislators noted that the pressure tactics used were unusally strong. Senator Ernest L. Passailaigue Jr. (*D*-Charleston) said that "some people were threatened with reapportionment issues, intimidated in terms of other issues."[48]

State Ethics Legislation

The proposed ethics bill was finally passed during a special legislative session on September 23, 1991. It passed in the House by a vote of 108–0 after less than six hours' consideration with sixteen absences or abstentions. The Senate bill had five opponents, one of whom complained of major loopholes, such as one allowing lobbyists to buy meals for a legislator as long as the meal was for a group. Some observers characterized the new law as uneven but among the best ten or fifteen state ethics laws in the country nonetheless. Representative David Wilkins (*R*-Greenville) rated it as "9 or 9.5 on a scale of 10" with ten as the most rigorous.[49]

Among the major features of the bill, which went into effect January 1, 1992, are the following: (1) lobbyists cannot contribute to a legislator's campaign, nor can a lobbyist spend money on a legislator—for example, through entertainment; (2) legislators have to report business with lobbyists; (3) campaign contributions can be used only for running campaigns; (4) campaign contributions are limited to $25 in cash; (5) campaign contributions by a single contributor are limited to $3,500 per stage ($10,500 overall) for statewide candidates and $1,000 per stage ($3,000 overall) for other candidates; (6) campaign contributions by a political party are capped at $50,000 for a statewide race and $5,000 for a local one; (7) lawyer-legislators must report in writing when they represent a client before a state agency, and they cannot vote on legislation affecting that agency; and (8) legislators must provide for enforcement of the bill's various provisions.[50]

Before Operation Lost Trust, the line between a campaign contribution by a lobbyist (or anyone else) and a bribe was not clear. Many of the legislative defendants in trials testified that they thought they were getting a campaign contribution. The bill appears to be a specific reaction to these features of the sting, and it goes further than before in limiting potential influence by political contributors.

Before the bill, citizens could get information about political campaign contributions only after the election. Now, citizens may learn who contributes to any campaign before the vote. Critics of the campaign-finance provisions contend that the limits were set too high. A single source, such as a large corporation or major law firm, may give $10,500 overall to a single statewide candidate in an election cycle. For a local race, the overall single-source limit is $3,000. However, contributions are limited to $3,500 for each statewide stage and $1,000 for each stage of local elections—the primary if there is opposition, the runoff if one is required, and the general election. All three electoral stages have to happen if the single-source maximum is to be reached. Critics worry about influence not only because of the limits but also because twenty other states prohibit corporate contributions altogether.

The bill did not limit overall spending in a campaign, but it did limit the amount of personal money that a candidate may use to $200,000. Of course, the gamble for a candidate is to use personal money as "seed money" and hope that enough money is raised so that the candidate can get all personal money back. If it is not repaid, the most that a candidate can reclaim is $25,000 in a statewide race and $10,000 in a local race. One fear is that only the wealthy will run for public office, because only wealthy candidates would have that much private money to start and have the ability to withstand a "fine" of $175,000 or $190,000 for not being able to raise money on the campaign trail.

Another purpose of the bill was to reduce the impact of lobbyists, especially in races for the state legislature. The prohibition of political campaign contributions by lobbyists was intended by reform supporters to widen public participation in elections in order to change fundamentally the types of political campaigns run in South Carolina. Campaign financing will require more grassroots participation and reduce the significant public impact of lobbyists on elections.

A problem that some see in the new bill is weak enforcement. Enforcement lies with state trial court solicitors, the state law enforcement division, and the State Ethics Commission. Lobbyists must register with the State Ethics Commission, but Complaints are not disclosed. The reason frequently given in the legislative debate for keeping complaints confidential was to reduce frivolous charges. House rules require the State Ethics Commission to adjudicate a complaint, but the Senate will decide whether it or the State Ethics Commission will hear the complaint. Critics fear a "star chamber" atmosphere that will skew results.

Former state representative Robert Kohn (R-Charleston), who sold his vote for cash and recruited colleagues to take bribes before pleading guilty to one count of extortion, said that "the General Assembly has exempted them-

selves from the real thrust of the bill because they continue to police themselves. You will continue to have the fox guarding the chicken house."[51]

Among loopholes in the new law is a provision that allows lobbyists and
their employers to give promotional items worth less than $10 or plaques and
trophies worth less than $150 to public officials. To some, a $150 trophy is
expensive. Lobbyists' employers may also spend up to $25 per day or $200
per year on lawmakers if a lobbyist's employer invites the General Assembly, the House or the Senate, a legislative committee, a delegation, or a
caucus to a function. It is unlikely that many lobbyists will ask the whole legislature out eight times to a $25 meal. The problem is that the number of
small groups may grow larger so that legislators can get invited the maximum eight times by a single lobbyist. Also, there is still nothing wrong about
creating a "spontaneous small group" by asking a committee out in the evening a few hours before supper when most members have gone home. Neither is there anything wrong about legislators buying or bringing their own
food or drink to as many meals as they want. Activities will still abound because the number of lobbyists' employers has grown at almost the same rate
as the number of lobbyists.

The new law prohibits future legislators from becoming lobbyists until at
least one year after they finish public service. However, the law does not
prohibit current legislators from immediately becoming lobbyists if they
choose.[52] "That just stinks," Senator Glen McConnell said. "If it's good for
all of the folks in the future, it's just as good for those of us at the present
time. It's just basic fundamental fairness."[53]

THE SPECIAL ROLE OF MASS MEDIA

The almost daily parade of Operation Lost Trust revelations became fixed in
the state's print and broadcast media. Public officials bristled or cringed as
the next stories developed. Some compared the pictures on television or in
newspapers as equivalent to a modern-day "tarring and feathering" or to the
lineup of shady characters in the "most wanted" posters at the local post office. The major papers and television stations reported and editorialized
about the sorry state of affairs in South Carolina.

Columbia's *State* newspaper, under new ownership after its purchase by
the Knight-Ridder corporation from family ownership, launched an in-depth
inquiry into state government. Spurred on by its new "outside" editor, Gil
Thelen, the paper titled its series "Power Failure." The series, a Sunday feature for almost a year, exhaustively analyzed and described the state and its

government and explored reforms. One reform, a reorganized state government structure, is discussed in chapter 9. In the 1960s, another *State* editor, William D. Workman Jr., was instrumental in reforming the constitution of 1895.

In 1992, ten newsprint companies, eighteen radio and television organizations, and four news photography services were actively engaged in reporting activities of the General Assembly,[54] as well as of the governor's office and other state agencies. Researchers do not have very useful measurements of the direct influence of the mass media on the behavior of legislators, governors, lobbyists, or other public officials. Nevertheless, mass media remain as the major source by which a citizen learns about actions and events in government. This gives great weight to the potential for positive or negative public reaction to disclosures in the press and on television about government in general or about an individual official.

The media presence in Columbia is quite visible. Major media functions—such as media representatives for public officials, major news reporting services, and the major newspapers and television stations—all have offices in the capitol complex or nearby office buildings, including news conference rooms with television facilities. Offices for newspaper reporters and the Associated Press are in the capitol building in order for them to receive and send wire service bulletins.

Television cameras are not permitted on the floor of the legislative bodies. Instead, a special location is designated at the back of each chamber. Each chamber is lighted for television and still photography, and microphone networks ensure good audio recordings for broadcasts.

The major television coverage is by the state Educational Television Commission (ETV), which has a weekly summary of legislative actions. Other television coverage usually consists of spot interviews outside legislative chambers. The image and content of media broadcasts is uneven, at least from the perspective of many representatives. They believe that what the people think about them at home may depend on a chance encounter with a reporter. Comprehensive coverage depends on the ETV program and news analysis by the major newspapers. What is clear is that the mass media make a major impression on legislative minds by influencing what the public thinks of them.

CONCLUSION

The types of interest groups operating in South Carolina have undergone significant changes, which reflect the changing economy of the state. However, while interest groups became more diversified, the state did not respond very quickly to regulate such groups and/or to enforce regulations. In a recent classification of the impact of interest groups in state politics, South Carolina is one of nine states in which interest groups are rated as a dominant political force.[55]

Journalists, political scientists, other observers, and some legislators assert that a history of undefined ethical standards, weak lobbyist control laws, reluctant enforcement of the laws, and a divided governmental structure all made South Carolina government a scandal waiting to happen.

Common Cause's president for South Carolina, university law school professor Eldon Wedlock, considered that a laissez-faire approach to following strict rules was a long-standing part of the state's political culture. Said Wedlock, "There's a greater respect in South Carolina for the way things are done than for the way the law says they should be done." House Speaker Bob Sheheen claimed that the state's diffused governmental system made ethics harder to police. Sheheen noted that "different rules aren't going to change bad people wanting to do bad things," but the current system "makes it harder to discover and to know all the relationships that develop— much harder."[56]

Although the formal relationships between lobbyists and legislators have been redesigned, some members of the General Assembly were unwilling to remove all vestiges of the old lobbying system. Lawyer-legislators continue to be able to represent clients before boards and commissions that set policy for state agencies.

A June 1991 Mason-Dixon Poll revealed that South Carolinians continued to lack confidence in the honesty of their legislators. Only 13 percent of the state's voters felt that the legislators who represented them were very honest, and 56 percent perceived their representatives as somewhat honest. Twenty-eight percent said they felt their representatives were somewhat or very dishonest. Although 65 percent of the voters felt Operation Lost Trust would improve the overall operation of state government, 41 percent felt that the sting had not been effective in removing all of the state legislature's dishonest members.[57]

CHAPTER SEVEN

The South Carolina Legislature

The breezes of change blowing across South Carolina's traditionalistic political culture also stir within the General Assembly. Although its practices and attitudes change slowly, new patterns of partisan representation, greater diversity in the membership, greater professionalism in the legislative process, and new leadership have led to a legislative body that at least looks different from the mid-century description by V. O. Key Jr.

KEY'S VIEW OF SOUTH CAROLINA

"Legislative Government" was the term Key used to describe South Carolina's government in 1949. At that time, members of the General Assembly occupied two of the three positions on the State Budget Commission; they appointed all fourteen members of the State Highway Commission; they appointed the seven members of the Public Service Commission, the state's utility regulatory agency; and they elected all the judges in the state.

In addition to the control of state government, legislators constituted the real governing bodies for their respective counties. Key pointed out that the local legislative delegations held the power to appropriate county funds, to fix the local tax levy, and to appoint most county officials.[1] The result was an institutional structure that cast the governor into the political role of trying to challenge the legislature and its leadership domination. The General Assembly remained the defender of the policy status quo.[2] As the voice of "reason," the legislature could stand off an energetic or reform governor until the end of the governor's single four-year term.

Within this context of legislative government, observers found the real governing powers concentrated in the hands of a few traditionalistic, rural legislators. During the time of Key's studies and for a period afterwards, leaders came from only one rural county, Barnwell. In the Senate was Edgar A. Brown, a Barnwell lawyer, banker, and businessman. Dubbed the "Bishop from Barnwell" because he ran the state in the imposing manner with which a bishop might run a diocese, Brown was first elected to the Senate in 1929 after serving in the state House of Representatives (1921–26) and as its Speaker (1925–26).[3] Brown eventually became President Pro Tempore of the Senate in 1942 and chair of the all-important Senate Finance Committee. He held these positions for thirty years until his retirement in 1972 at the age of eighty-three.

Brown's counterpart in the House was Solomon Blatt, also from Barnwell County. Blatt, who was first elected to the House in 1933, was Speaker of the House from 1935 to 1945 and again from 1951 through 1973. Blatt kept political power concentrated in his hands by sharing it shrewdly with all the other small rural counties. For example, he would appoint no more than one member from any single county to the Ways and Means Committee. Since the county was the basis of representation at the time, this meant that not only would the twenty-four members represent more than half the counties in the state, it also ensured that the eight counties with half the state's population could never have more than one-third of the vote on the committee.[4] Thus, large, more urbanized counties had to deal with the small counties to fund anything, especially state-financed capital projects in large counties.

In addition to Brown and Blatt, for a time in the 1940s the chair of the House Ways and Means Committee and chair of the state Democratic party was Winchester Smith from Williston, another small town in Barnwell County. After Governor Burnet R. Maybank resigned to become a United States senator, the new governor also came from Barnwell. For a short time, from November 1941 until his death in February 1942, Lieutenant Governor J. E. Harley of Barnwell served as governor. Key and others referred to the Barnwell legislators and their concentration of power in one place as the "Barnwell Ring."

These Barnwell County legislators, along with like-minded conservative legislators, were elected primarily from the small, less-populated rural counties. They combined into transient but consistently aligned groups or rings that dominated the legislature—especially the Senate, where seniority determined committee assignments. To the supporters of change and urban advocates the Barnwell Ring, or subsequent political circles involving legislators from rural counties like Barnwell, must have seemed like a chokehold on state decision making.

Both Blatt and Brown, however, denied that such a "ring" existed. Sol Blatt deftly avoided discussing the true implications of rural dominance of an urbanizing state by noting that while he and Edgar Brown got along socially, they never discussed statewide legislation. Said Blatt,

> I used to ride up from Barnwell with him and we talked about the weather and other things. Very seldom did we mention legislation. He and I were a little bit different on the way the county should be operated, and he was never a political friend or ally of mine. . . . But, locally we differed, and Senator Brown and Mr. Winchester Smith stuck together. I was the third man in the party.[5]

News editor William D. Workman Jr. recorded Brown's version as recognizing that the key personalities in state government were located in Barnwell County, but that "there was no 'ring' and we didn't work together. There was no unanimity of action, even back in those times. We often split off on state issues, on state personalities."[6]

Even if it were attempted today, a dominant group of rural legislators probably could not be recreated due to the general relocation of the population from the countryside into suburbs. Additionally, federal policy has replaced county-based representation with single-member districts. The result is a more independent legislator who has to deal with more localized pressures and who works with more diverse colleagues compared to a generation ago.

THE LEGISLATORS

Demographic Characteristics of Members

The basic formal requirements for being a member of the General Assembly are to be a duly qualified elector and to be twenty-one years of age to serve in the House or twenty-five years of age to serve in the Senate. The 124 House members are elected from single-member districts, each with a population equal to about 28,111 per district. State senators are elected from one of forty-six numbered single-member districts. Each Senate district contained a population of approximately 75,800 in 1992. Candidates for House and Senate seats must be legal residents of the district from which they seek election.

Demographically, the major changes in the state House over the last twenty years have been increases in the numbers of female, African American, and Republican legislators. As suggested by table 13, these increases may, in part, result from the change to a single-member district system in 1974. Since 1971, women members have increased from two to nineteen, Af-

Table 13: Characteristics of Members, South Carolina House of Representatives, 1971–1993

Characteristic	1971	1981	1990	1993
Age				
Mean	45	45	49	50
Range	22–78	24–85	26–80	27–82
Sex				
Male	122	112	111	105
Female	2	12	13	19
Race				
White	121	110	107	106
African American	3	14	17	18
Party				
Democrat	113	107	82	73
Republican	11	17	42	50
Independent	0	0	0	1
Occupation				
Attorney	45*	32	34	27
Business	52	57	49	47
Farmer	15	9	11	9
Other	12	26	30	41
Education				
Law degree	48	34	34	27
College graduate	25	50	60	70
Less than college graduate	51	40	28	27

Source: South Carolina Legislative Manual.

* This number represents law school graduates, not practicing attorneys.

rican Americans from three to eighteen, and Republicans from only eleven to fifty. Ten of the women in the House are Democrats, three are Republicans, and three are African Americans. The African American members generally represent districts in which African Americans are the majority. The Republican legislators, with few exceptions, represent urban districts. Included among the forty-two Republicans in 1990 were five members who changed their party affiliation after being elected as Democrats in 1988. With their defections, the Republican party achieved a veto-proof minority in the House for the first time if all the Republicans voted as a bloc. Being able at least to obstruct legislation with the help of the governor became more certain with the increase in Republican membership to fifty in 1993.

As described by occupation, fewer South Carolina House members are

Table 14: Characteristics of Members, South Carolina Senate, 1971–1993

Characteristic	1971	1981	1990	1993
Age				
Mean	52	50	48	51
Range	35–78	31–79	37–78	27–81
Sex				
Male	46	44	44	43
Female	0	2	2	3
Race				
White	46	46	41	39
African American	0	0	5	7
Party				
Democrat	46	41	34	30
Republican	0	5	12	16
Occupation				
Attorney	25	25	23	18
Business	12	17	12	19
Farmer	8	2	2	2
Other	1	2	9	7
Education				
Law degree	23	28	24	18
College graduate	10	13	17	22
Less than college				
graduate	12	5	5	6

Source: South Carolina *Legislative Manual.*

practicing attorneys. The percentage was 39 percent in 1971 (forty-eight members), which decreased to 27 percent (thirty-four members) in 1990. Following the 1992 elections, the figure was only 22 percent (twenty-seven members), compared to 20 percent of state legislators nationally.

During the 1980s, House members also become better educated. Members with less than a college education decreased from 41 percent (fifty-one members) to 23 percent (twenty-eight members). Other changes in the last decade included an increase in the number of retirees as members (from two to twelve) and an increase in the number of legislators who were born outside of South Carolina (from thirteen to twenty-two). The average House member in 1993 was fifty years old and had served 5.2 years in the legislature.

The Senate has also changed demographically. Twenty years ago, the Senate was all white, all male, and all Democratic. As illustrated in table 14, three women (two Democrats and one Republican), seven African Americans (all Democrats), and sixteen Republicans were members of the 1993 Senate. In 1992 a forty-four-year-old Florence, South Carolina, educator,

Maggie Glover, became the first African American woman ever elected to serve in the state Senate. In general, the Republican members represent urban centers—Charleston, Columbia, or Greenville/Spartanburg. One represents the Beaufort–Hilton Head area, while two others represent mixed urban/rural districts. African American members represent majority African American districts.

In 1993, the average age of senators was fifty-one. There were only two farmers as members and the number of members with less than a college degree was six. Attorneys still represented the largest percentage of the membership. In 1971 there were twenty-five attorneys (54%); in 1993, there are only eighteen (39%). In 1980, seven members reported their birthplace as outside South Carolina; in 1993, eight members were born out-of-state. Four of the eight were born in the neighboring southern states of Georgia and North Carolina. One was born in Louisiana, two in Wisconsin, and one in Illinois.

Although these demographic characteristics appear as only small increments, they measure the important fact that the General Assembly is no longer exclusively a rural, white, male-dominated institution. However, African Americans and women are still underrepresented relative to their proportion in the population.

The most striking change has been the emerging Republican presence in the legislative process. These "New South" urban Republicans typically reflect the individualistic political culture of the state's urban areas. With the veto-proof Republican bloc in the House and Senate, Republicans have the potential for exercising real, though still negative, power in South Carolina politics. Despite this Republican growth, however, party identification has not proven to be a consistent source of voting divisions in the House, even though the Republican House members are less factionalized than the Democrats. This has generally been the case under both Democratic and Republican governors.[7]

Career Patterns in the General Assembly

Studies of state legislative membership across the nation show a substantial decline in turnover in the last fifty years, from approximately 50–60 percent in the early 1930s to 30–35 percent in the 1980s. Table 15 suggests that South Carolina legislators generally have lower turnover as well.

The South Carolina legislature is an institution where more and more people are building careers. During the 1980s, between 99 and 103 House members were reelected each year (80–83%). For the Senate, only 30 members

Table 15: Legislative Turnover Service Record of Legislators

| | House of Representatives | | | State Senate | | |
Year	Number Reelected	Prior Service	No Prior Service	Number Reelected	Prior Service	No Prior Service
1968	83	6	35	32	8	6
1970	89	10	25	—	—	—
1972	75	8	41	32	9	5
1974	73	9	42	—	—	—
1976	92	2	30	32	9	5
1978	100	3	21	—	—	—
1980	100	2	21	35	6	5
1982	99	3	22	—	—	—
1984	100	2	22	30	9	7
1986	103	1	18	—	—	—
1988	102	2	19	38	2	6
1990	96	2	26	—	—	—
1992	95	1	28	32	3	11

Source: South Carolina Legislative Manual, 1969, 1971, 1973, 1975, 1977, 1979, 1981, 1983, 1985, 1987, 1989, 1991, 1993.

were reelected in 1984 (65%). The 1984 election was exceptional because it was the first after the Senate changed to single-member districts from its previous system of sixteen multimember districts. Four years later, 38 senators were reelected (83%). After redistricting in 1992, 32 senators (70%) were reelected.

In June 1993, the U.S. Supreme Court rejected the redistricting plan approved by a three-person federal district court. The lower court was ordered to redraw legislative districts in order to increase majority African American districts. New House districts were drawn in 1994.

New members entering the legislature were not always new to the legislative process. A number of House members (ranging from ten in 1970 to one in 1986) had previously served in the legislature and were returning after an absence. In terms of the Senate, a number of members had previously served in the House. A description of these terms of service is in table 16. From 1968 to 1988, the largest number of senators with no previous legislative experience was seven (15%) in 1984.

Operation Lost Trust, the FBI undercover probe, claimed seven members of the 1991 class; another five became state judges. Overall, between the sting and reapportionment, the House had twenty-nine new members and the Senate fourteen new members following the 1992 elections.

Table 16: Seniority in the General Assembly

Seniority	House			Senate		
	1971	1981	1990	1971	1981	1990
Mean years of service	4.3	5.1	5.0	7.5	8.2	7.0
No. of members in 1st term	35	24	24	16	11	11
No. of members in 2nd term	30	26	16	15	13	15
No. of members in 3rd term	24	26	26	5	8	7
No. of members in 4th term	35	49	53	10	14	13

Not only are members being reelected, they also are remaining in the legislature for extended periods. While the mean, or average, years of service is about five years for the House, the number of members who had served at least four terms increased from thirty-five to fifty-three from 1971 to 1991. This was 43 percent of the membership of the House. However, following the 1992 elections, there were only thirty-two members (26%) who had served four or more terms. Marion Carnell (D-Greenwood, Abbeville, and Laurens) had served the most years in the House—since 1961 with the exception of one term from 1964 to 1966. Patrick Harris (D-Anderson) had served for the longest continuous time. He was first elected to the House in 1969.

Among senators, average service time was only 5.2 years in 1993, down from 8.2 years in 1981. The death of Marion Gressette (D-Calhoun, first elected in 1936) and the retirement of Rembert Dennis (D-Berkeley, first elected in 1943) from the Senate in the 1980s help to explain the decrease in average years of service. Some incumbents quit because of redistricting. The number of senators who have served at least four terms is still high (thirteen senators, or 28%). In 1992, nine Democrats and two Republicans did not seek reelection. In 1993, the senator with the longest service was Marshall Williams (D-Orangeburg, Barnwell) who had served continuously in the upper house since 1953, a period of forty years.

The decrease in competition may be related to the move to single-member districts by both houses of the General Assembly during the previous two decades. Before the switch to single-member districts in 1974, House district lines coincided with county lines, and representatives were allocated to counties based on population. Each county was guaranteed at least one representative. All elections were for at-large seats, though the seats were numbered for the first time in 1972. In addition to increasing the number of African Americans, women, and Republicans in the state House, the single-member district system led to fewer contested races. In 1972, 91 House races were contested; however, in 1990 only 60 seats were contested. In 1992, twenty representatives—twelve Democrats and eight Republicans—did not seek reelection. In fact, a total of ninety-two candidates for the House and Senate, including eighty-five incumbents, had no opposition in the general election. Only 32 races out of 170 had new faces.[8]

Lieutenant Governor Nick Theodore attributed the decrease in competitive races to the condensed nature of single-member districts. Said Theodore, "Obviously they are more accessible and the individuals certainly are in a position to develop a network of support that would normally repel opposition." House minority leader Terry Haskins (R-Greenville) agreed that "if the public felt like they were alienated and didn't have a voice in the government, there'd be a whole lot of candidates running to get in and try to correct that problem. I think it's a sign of general satisfaction." Political scientist Earl Black observes that South Carolina "now has a larger number of seats that are safe for one party or another. There is a greater representation of South Carolina's population. The price of that may be . . . less competition for those seats."[9]

Complicating the problem is the increased cost of contested elections. Incumbents raise money more easily than their opponents. In 1988, for example, winning incumbents collectively raised $666,560 for their primary elections while their opponents collectively raised only $235, 905.[10]

Incumbents also received a larger percentage of contributions from PACs and businesses. In 1988, incumbent Democratic winners received 31 percent of their receipts from PACs and 10 percent from businesses; incumbent Republicans received 37 percent from PACs and 9 percent from businesses. Losing non-incumbent Democrats received 6 percent of their contributions from PACs and 2 percent from businesses; losing non-incumbent Republicans received 13 percent and 3 percent respectively.

Although new varieties of legislators make the body more diverse, the method of election and the increased costs of campaigns may actually lead to the entrenchment of a new generation of traditionalistic legislators.

THE GENERAL ASSEMBLY: INTERNAL PROCESS AND STRUCTURE

The General Assembly holds annual sessions beginning on the second Tuesday in January. In 1993, members of each House were paid an annual salary of $10,400. Since 1990, legislators have received annual salary increases equal to the percentage received by other state employees. In addition, they are paid $79 per day for living expenses when the legislature is in session and 25.5¢ per mile for weekly round trips to the capital during the legislative session. Members also receive $35 per day compensation for committee or official business conducted when the legislature is not in session, $500 per session for postage, and $1,000 per month for in-district expenses. The President Pro Tempore of the Senate receives an additional $7,500 per year. The Speaker of the House gets an annual salary supplement of $11,000 and the House Speaker Pro Tempore receives $3,600 plus regular salary each year.

Before 1979, there was no limitation on the length of session. The General Assembly then acted to require adjournment at 5 P.M. on the first Thursday of June, unless two-thirds of each chamber votes to extend the session to override any gubernatorial vetoes, pass acts, or work on contested legislation that has been passed in different versions by both chambers. In only two years, in 1980 and again in 1990, has the General Assembly passed a resolution to extend beyond the June deadline for completing business.[11] Many times, however, the governor has convened special sessions to deal with major issues or business left over after the deadline.

The South Carolina legislative process is similar to that in other legislatures. As in the United States Congress, bills for raising revenue must originate in the House of Representatives. All other bills may originate in either house. The state Senate has a filibuster (unlimited debate), which can be ended only by a two-thirds vote. In the House, debate on bills can be ended by a majority vote. Gubernatorial vetoes require a two-thirds vote in each house to override.

The South Carolina General Assembly utilizes standing committees to evaluate bills introduced by members, debate policy issues, and perform legislative oversight. The number of standing committees in the Senate was fifteen in 1990, a reduction of three from the 1987 figure. The House of Representatives has eleven committees.

Senate Rule 19 defines the Senate's standing committees and their size and composition. The size of the Ethics Committee is set at six and the Invitations Committee at 10. The remaining Senate committees are allowed to vary in size from five to eighteen members.

Members of the Senate with seniority are limited to service on no more than five standing committees. Those with no seniority are limited to no more than four standing committees. However, the Ethics Committee and the Invitations Committee are not included in counting the number of committee assignments. Because these committees have little power, they are not highly sought-after assignments. Since passage of the Education Improvement Act in 1984, the Education Committee has become a more important committee.

Selection of committees occurs at the start of each session following the election of senators or at a special session called to select committees. The clerk of the Senate prepares a roll of the Senate listing the members in order of seniority. When two or more members have equal continuous service, they are listed in alphabetical order. Each member, when his or her name is called by the clerk, selects four unfilled standing committees on which he or she wishes to serve. The roll call is then repeated, with each member selecting one additional unfilled standing committee. Membership on one of the two most important committees, Finance or Judiciary, excludes a senator from serving on the other.

The chairs of the standing committees are elected by majority voice vote of the entire Senate. No member can chair more than one standing committee.

In the House, the Speaker and the Speaker Pro Tempore are elected by the members of the House. All House committees are appointed by the Speaker. The size of each committee is defined by House Rule 4. Each House member can serve on only one of the following six committees: (1) Ways and Means, (2) Judiciary, (3) Agriculture and Natural Resources, (4) Education and Public Works, (5) Medical, Military, Public and Municipal Affairs, and (6) Labor, Commerce and Industry. Members may hold a second membership on one of the remaining five committees, although the norm for members is one committee assignment. Members cannot serve as chair of more than one standing committee. The chair is elected by the committee.

The House and Senate committees, as well as joint committees, follow uniform rules of procedure. Committee meetings are open to the public, and one day's advance notice is required for a committee meeting.

Steven Haeberle has noted that the committee system in South Carolina is relatively weak because the extensive reliance on special and study committees undermines the effectiveness of the regular legislative committees. The variety of other committees includes special committees set up to study specific issues; study or joint committees drawn from both houses to examine specific issues; the conference committees, which work out the differences in legislation passed by both houses; and interim committees that meet between sessions to study specific issues.[12]

LEGISLATIVE RESOURCE DEVELOPMENTS

One of the most dramatic changes in state legislatures, including South Carolina, is an increase in office facilities and staff assistance since the 1960s. In the 1970s, all legislators were assigned offices in the Sol Blatt Building

(House members) or the Marion Gressette Building (Senate members). This ended the longtime practice of using the Wade Hampton Hotel across the street from the state capitol building as the unofficial office for most members of the General Assembly.

Second, research work was generally undertaken by legislative councils consisting of legislators meeting between sessions. Now, the Senate has both a clerk and a director of Senate research, an assistant clerk and director, and an office of Senate research, which consists of three staff counsels and three research analysts. Ten Senate standing committees have research personnel. The two most important committees, Finance and Judiciary, have five and two assistants respectively. In addition, all committees except the five-member Interstate Cooperation Committee have administrative assistance. Every two senators are assigned a secretary.

The House has an executive director for research. All House committees except for the Rules Committee have a staff. Staff size varies according to the importance of the committee. For example, the Interstate Cooperation Committee has only an executive secretary, while the Ways and Means Committee has a director of research, nine assistants, an administrative assistant, an executive secretary, and a secretary.

The General Assembly also has a Legislative Council. Created in 1949, it operates the research, reference, and bill-drafting facilities. The council consists of the President of the Senate, the Speaker of the House, the secretary of state, the chair of the Senate Judiciary Committee, and the chair of the House Judiciary Committee. They oversee a staff of approximately thirty-five individuals, including the director, the assistant director, three research assistants, and five attorneys.

Another body created in 1974 is the Legislative Information System. It is charged with providing services for administrative, legislative, and research-oriented data processing services to all offices of the General Assembly. The President of the Senate, the Speaker of the House, the chairs of the Senate Finance and Judiciary committees, and the chairs of the House Ways and Means and Judiciary committees make up a supervisory council for the fifteen employees of the system.

Oversight Capacity

Finally, the General Assembly made a greater commitment to legislative oversight through its creation of a Legislative Audit Council in 1974. The council is empowered to conduct investigations and audits of the operation

Table 17: Record of Bills, Acts, and Length of Session

	Days in Legislative Session		Total Bills Introduced			Total Acts Ratified
Year	House	Senate	House	Senate	Total	
1971	132	135	1,147	530	1,677	962
1976	109	109	769	319	1,088	466
1981	123	130	818	482	1,300	275
1986	91	94	588	459	1,047	328
1990	90	92	1,039	784	1,823	441
1992	65	65	882	556	1,438	387

Source: 1993 South Carolina *Legislative Manual,* p.518.

of state departments, agencies, or institutions and to submit reports of studies of problems as requested by the General Assembly, its members, or committees. All state agencies are required to submit quarterly financial statements to the council. This allows the General Assembly to review how funds, once appropriated, are spent.[13] The council's authority has been expanded to ensure that an appropriate amount is budgeted for audit purposes in all federal programs administered by state agencies. Also, the council is required to conduct sample audits to assess compliance with the provisions of the Education Finance Act of 1977 and to ascertain whether certain state agencies should continue to exist as stated in the 1978 "sunset" act.

Legislative Activity

Although the legislature's support staff, expenditures, and overall capacity have increased, the number of bills passed by the legislature has actually decreased. As shown in table 17, the legislature passed 962 acts in 1971. The number decreased by over 50 percent to only 466 in 1976. By 1981 it was only 275. The number has subsequently increased, while still not reaching one-half the 1971 figure. The number of bills introduced also decreased from 1,677 in 1971 to 1,438 in 1992.

One explanation for the decrease in bills passed is that before the 1970s, legislative delegations had typically governed local governments through special legislation. However, in 1973 limited home rule for local governments was established by amendment to the state constitution. The amendment prohibited special legislation for a city or county; only general laws that applied to all local governments were permitted. As a result of the amendment, bills that applied to a single city or county could no longer be a part of the legislative agenda. Limited local self-government reflects once again the movement of the state away from domination by small-town rural interests toward greater self-determination by different areas of the state.

THE GENERAL ASSEMBLY TODAY

New systems of election, new legislators, greater diversity in both houses of the General Assembly, and greater staff professionalism all reflect legislative changes in South Carolina. These developments have also led to changes in internal leadership as power in the legislature has passed from the hands of a few traditionalistic legislators representing the rural areas to individuals who may reflect, just as traditionalistically, new political energies and ideals from suburban parts of the state.

In the Senate, the change began with the retirement of Edgar Brown in 1972. First, senatorial power passed into the hands of two more rural legislators, Marion Gressette and Rembert Dennis. Gressette, first elected to the Senate in 1937, became President Pro Tempore of the Senate and chair of the Judiciary Committee. Dennis became chair of the Senate Finance Committee. These individuals continued their rural predecessors' policy of fiscal conservatism and dominated the Senate on most important issues.

Gressette, who often referred to the governor as "the man downstairs," was the last leader of the Senate who thoroughly understood the importance of the Senate rules and used them effectively. Senator Glenn McConnell (*R*-Charleston) referred to Gressette as the "Keeper of the Lodge." Under Gressette's leadership, senators were referred to as "the senator from Charleston" or "the senator from Calhoun" as opposed to their surnames, and a senator never took off his suit coat in the chamber.[14] Rules were sacred to Gressette. He might work around a rule, but he would not violate it.

In 1975, a reform attempt was mounted in the Senate by the "Young Turks" group from urban areas. The number of Senate committees was reduced from twenty-six to fifteen, and members were not allowed to chair more than one committee. The reform, however, was more of a paper change than a real redistribution of power. For example, in the first year of the reform effort, the big four committees still controlled 77 percent of all bills in the Senate, with 38.8 percent of the bills going to Gressette's Judiciary Committee and 18.4 percent going to Dennis's Finance Committee.[15]

Gressette was also able to control policy making through his domination of House-Senate conference committees. Senate tradition required the lieutenant governor, the presiding officer of the Senate, to appoint only the President Pro Tempore and other senior members to conference committees. In contrast, House conferees were by tradition appointed to represent the various sides of the issue. As a result, House members were much more likely to be outmaneuvered by the senior senators' leadership on vital issues.

Significant change in the Senate began to occur during the 1980s. First, the Senate was reapportioned following the 1980 census into single-member districts. This system replaced an apportioned system of sixteen Senate districts for the forty-six Senate seats. Under the apportioned system used in the 1970s, there were one to five members per district, depending on population. Both racial and political minorities found their voting strength diluted through this arrangement. The result throughout the 1970s was a continuation of the rural white power structure's domination of the Senate.

In 1980, the Senate had only five Republican members and no women or African Americans. The 1984 Senate election resulted in the election of sixteen new faces, including seven Republicans and three African Americans. When the Senate reconvened in 1984, ten Republicans, two women, and four African Americans were seated.

When Senator Gressette died in 1984, Rembert Dennis became President Pro Tempore. The sixty-nine-year-old Dennis had served in the House from 1939 to 1942 and had been a member of the state Senate since 1943. However, Dennis, in poor health as a result of two automobile accidents, was unable to continue the personal and dominant leadership of his predecessors. Dennis retired in 1988 after a legislative career spanning almost fifty years. By 1993 his successor, eighty-one-year-old Marshall Williams, a forty-year Senate veteran, was considered even less influential than Dennis by most observers and legislators. Republican senator Glenn McConnell described Williams in the following manner:

> What you've got is you have a president pro tempore who is a very good-natured person who doesn't try to impose his will on other people. . . . I don't think you're going to find that a lot of us are going to put up with somebody getting up there and thinking they're going to whip us into line.[16]

A newspaper reports Senator James Bryan's (*D*-Laurens, Greenville) description of the change in the Senate:

> "I think there is a different philosophy" about government today. "Used to be, the senior leadership frankly didn't care what the public thought. Most of the time they were doing what was right, but they just got up and said, 'This is

the way it's going to be,' " and the junior senators voted with them. "Now the junior senators are saying, 'you're going to have to explain to me why that's right.' "[17]

The power vacuum in the Senate has been filled by new personalities. First, Lieutenant Governor Mike Daniel (*D*-Cherokee) began in 1985 to appoint individuals other than senior members to conference committees. The result has been a greater diffusion of power in House-Senate conference committees. It has also, according to House Speaker Bob Sheheen, created "more and more difficult House-Senate conference committees."[18]

In addition to the leadership changes, caucuses formed in the Senate. Republicans, numbering twelve members in 1990, formed a relatively cohesive group that challenged the Senate leadership on a variety of procedural and substantive issues. Although the Republicans did not organize a formal caucus, they were referred to as "that group" by their colleagues.

In addition to the Republicans, a Democratic caucus and a minority caucus in the Senate developed about the same time. The Democratic caucus, led by Senators Isadore Lourie of Columbia and Tom Moore (*D*-Edgefield, Aiken) of Clearwater, had a complete system of floor managers and whips. The caucus existed side by side with the traditional Democratic leadership in the Senate and was more liberal than the leadership.[19]

The five African American senators formed part of the minority legislative caucus. Part of the agenda of the caucus was the creation of a majority African American congressional district following the 1990 census, a position on which the caucus was unwilling to compromise.[20] Eventually, a majority African American district was drawn largely out of the old Sixth Congressional District in the Pee Dee area as well as major sections of the upper and lower coastal plain.

The result of these changes is a Senate in which power is more dispersed and leadership is more divided when compared with the highly centralized power structure that dominated the Senate at the beginning of the 1980s. African American senator Theo Mitchell described the leadership as being more moderate, senators more individualistic, voting more independent, and perspectives more diversified. There is no longer rubber-stamp, one-man rule, and there is more give-and-take in the process.[21] But House Speaker Sheheen observed, "It was bound to happen."[22]

The House has also undergone significant change. These changes occurred mostly during the 1970s. First, longtime speaker Sol Blatt was relegated to the position of "Speaker Emeritus" in 1973. In the House, Blatt embodied in one person the same stable and dependable but perhaps autocratic rule that had been exercised in the Senate by the members of that body's senior oligarchy.[23] Blatt's replacement preceded by one year the movement to a single-member-district system of election for the House. In the 1974 House elections, fifty-two new legislators (40% of the membership) were seated.

New members and new leadership led to changes in the operation and atmosphere in the House. New House Speaker Rex Carter (*D*-Greenville) was a centrist who worked well with the more diversified membership. In addition, he instituted several reforms, including hiring a research staff, installing a computer system, providing secretarial services for members, and opening committee meetings. Internally, the body became more open, more democratic, and more decentralized in terms of decision making. Following Carter's retirement in 1980, Ramon Schwartz (*D*-Sumter) took his place and continued, for his five years as Speaker, the reformist and decentralist policies of his predecessor.[24] Since 1986, Robert Sheheen has served as Speaker.

Sheheen, a Camden lawyer first elected to the House in 1977, has exhibited a stronger leadership style than his immediate two predecessors. Although his style has been described as facilitative, he has not been unwilling to use the powers of his office to select committee members and influence the selection of committee chairs. In fact, he even agreed to the election of a Republican as House Judiciary Committee chair.

In 1990, Senator Theo Mitchell criticized House Speaker Sheheen as a man who has exercised unbridled leadership, who gets what he wants, and who reminds him of Sol Blatt. Sheheen more modestly assesses his role as Speaker. He said he decided to seek the position because he thought he "could make a contribution" and the House members believed "that a change was needed toward a more activist Speaker." When asked to compare his leadership skills with those of his predecessors, he merely said, "What I make of this job depends on the relationship I have with the House members. Comparing leaders is someone else's job."[25] Although Sheheen may exhibit stronger leadership skills than his predecessors, he is not a Sol Blatt. He is more pragmatic and generally supports legislation to broaden social programs in the state. He personifies the change in South Carolina legislative politics.

Although it may be said that the legislature has changed from a private club for conservative, rural, middle-aged white males into a body more representative of the state's population, it has been unable to make government more responsive to the needs of the state. One of the major reasons for this is that the legislature has lost its grip on the state's bureaucracy as more and more state agencies have been created with most answering only to their boards and commissions. Each group or agency develops its budget in isolation, and when legislators review them they tend to focus only on additional spending for one agency rather than challenging general spending patterns.[26]

Second, most members of the South Carolina General Assembly spend their time and energy on helping constituents work through the maze of bureaucracy or on obtaining funds for their district as opposed to focusing on broad policy issues affecting the state. A 1991 survey by the *State* newspaper of 110 members of the legislature revealed that 24 percent of the legislators named constituent service and district funding as the most important part of their jobs, while another 38 percent said constituent service and setting state policy were equally important. Only 37 percent considered setting policy for the state as their most important function.[27] Legislators see no problem in playing this role.

State senator Kay Patterson, an African American Democrat from Richland County and a retired teacher, served in the House for eleven years and has served in the Senate since 1985. Said Patterson, "[M]ost intelligent people don't give a damn 'bout policy! Constituents expect service and rightly so." Patterson said he spent five days a week in his Senate office to take calls from constituents who needed roads paved, who sought jobs in state government, and who wanted to get bureaucrats off their backs. Representative James L. Mann "Bubba" Cromer Jr. (*I*-Richland), the only independent in the legislature, named constituent service as his top priority, saying that "obviously, without (that) my tenure would be quite short."[28] Legislators know that if they can deliver service to constituents, they may be able to do whatever they want on statewide issues.

CONCLUSION

The face of the General Assembly has changed dramatically in the last twenty years. The membership has become more varied and more reflective of a mobile, economically diverse South Carolina. Committee structures and the internal operations of both houses of the General Assembly have become less inhibiting to new legislators. No longer is the state dominated by a small-county, rural white male aristocracy, oligarchy, or ring masquerading as a legislature.

The legislature has also taken a number of steps to improve its operations and facilities. The hiring of research personnel and clerical assistants and other support staff has added greatly to balanced information for legislators.

The old Wade Hampton Hotel across from the state capitol, for so long the working office facility for most legislators, was torn down in the 1980s. A new business office tower, the AT&T Building, was erected on the old hotel site. Working offices for legislators have been constructed in the State Capitol Complex.

Collectively, these changes have positive symbolic significance. Not only do they symbolize the movement of legislative politics into the professionalized modern era, they also reflect the expanding economic base of the state.

But while the membership, support services, and facilities have changed dramatically, these shifts may not have always brought anticipated results. It seems that legislators tend to concentrate more on their own constituency than on conditions in the state as a whole. Despite recent achievements in ethics and state agency restructuring legislation, interest group and agency representatives still go to great effort to have a specific influence on legislative policy decisions. To many, legislators seem unable to deal enthusiastically or independently with statewide problems. The apparent reluctance of the legislature to venture away from established policies and practices suggests a continuation of the bedrock traditionalistic political culture from the past.

A January 1992 survey of 406 registered voters revealed that only 27 percent approved of the job being done by the legislature.[29] However, the 1992 elections did not cause the wholesale changes in membership that one could expect after all the controversy of the FBI sting and after redistricting. Thus, major statewide policy initiatives are still more likely to come from the executive branch than from the General Assembly.

CHAPTER EIGHT

The Governor

Across the South, the formal powers of chief executives have typically been weak, both institutionally and politically. Limited formal powers have usually restricted the southern governor to little or no direct role over state administration,[1] and South Carolina has been no exception. South Carolina has often been identified by scholars and other observers as one of the best examples of a formally weak southern governor in a legislatively dominated state. "There is nothing to it except the honor" is how V. O. Key Jr. described the position of governor of South Carolina in 1949.[2]

A model for assessing the formal strength of a contemporary governor discusses the power of the office with respect to tenure potential, appointments, budget making, organizational authority, and veto. A strong governor exists when these characteristics are concentrated in a single chief executive; a governor is weak when there are many and varied arrangements for allocating executive powers in a state constitution. The long-standing restricted range of formal powers in the governor's office reflects South Carolina's traditionalistic political culture. Through personal and informal exercise of the powers available, recent South Carolina governors have successfully expanded the exercise of executive authority, but always under the scrutiny of a dominant, often antagonistic legislature.

FORMAL EXECUTIVE POWERS: THE SOUTH CAROLINA CASE

Schlesinger and Beyle have studied governors in the past and rated their formal powers.[3] Table 18 abstracts ratings of the powers of the South Carolina governor from the major factors used in these studies. The third column in the table assesses these formal powers in combination with a synthesis of the informal success of recent governors. The numbers and the methodology in

Table 18: Evolving Measures of the South Carolina Governor's Power

Factors	Schlesinger's (1965) Rating	Beyle's (1981) Rating	Today
1. Tenure	3	4	4
2. Appointment	1	1	3
3. Budget	1	1	3
4. Organization	1	1	1
5. Veto	3	3	4
Total	9	10	15

Scale: Very strong = 5; Strong = 4; Moderate = 3; Weak = 2; Very weak = 1.
Maximum score = 25.

the third column are thus different from the approach in Schlesinger's original work and Beyle's 1981 rating and 1990 update. Background developments and the underlying rationale for the new assessment are presented in the discussion of each formal power.

Factor 1: Tenure Potential

Tenure potential is linked to how long a governor can serve and whether a sitting governor can run for reelection. When a governor is not eligible for reelection, it weakens gubernatorial control over the legislature and the administrative bureaucracy, especially in the last two years in office. After the first two years of a governor's term, a new legislature has been elected, new candidates for governor are emerging, and the governor's original plans have been acted on by the legislature in some way. Additional policy proposals may be rejected simply on the basis that the sitting governor will not be around to implement them. A governor in this situation may easily become a "lame duck."

Generally, tenure potential for governors has increased over the last thirty years, with many states adopting the presidential succession model of two four-year terms. Many southern states, including South Carolina in 1981, went to the two-term governor, perhaps to give Democratic governors in office at the time the advantage of incumbency in their efforts to fend off increasingly potent Republican challengers. The state's first governor to serve eight consecutive years, Richard W. Riley (D-Greenville), was elected in 1978 and reelected in 1982. Now a Republican governor, Carroll A. Campbell Jr. (R-Greenville), who was elected in 1986, was reelected in 1990 to a second term. The results show the importance of tenure potential and the advantage of incumbency, since both were easily reelected.

It is also easy to suggest the growing influence of the piedmont section in statewide politics, since Riley and Campbell both come from Greenville. Although the sixteen years of governors from one county include both political parties, when the lieutenant governor (Nick Theodore, *D*-Greenville, elected 1986, reelected 1990) and the secretary of state (Jim Miles, *R*-Greenville, elected 1990) are included, some pundits readily see a "Greenville Ring" like the "Barnwell Ring" of old. If there is such a ring, it is different because it seems to symbolize metropolitan, suburban values rather than traditionalistic, rural ones. It also connects with the increasing success of the Republican party in the election of statewide officers.

Historically, there is a fear in the United States of a strong executive. Ten of the governors of the thirteen original states had one-year terms, another had a two-year term, and two had three-year terms.[4] South Carolina's constitution of 1790 granted the governor a two-year term with the office elected by the legislature. When popular election of the governor began in 1865, the governor's term of office was also extended to four years, but it was changed back to two years in 1868. The two-year term lasted until 1926, when it became a single four-year term.

Political scientists' models that assess tenure potential portray a very strong chief executive as one who has a four-year term with no limit on eligibility for reelection. In 1989, eighteen states were in this category. The next step down, a strong governor, is characterized by a four-year term with one reelection permitted. This is the most common type of tenure; it was the arrangement in twenty-six states. Three states had a moderately powerful tenure potential with a single four-year term with no consecutive reelection permitted, while two states were characterized as weak with governors serving a two-year term with no restraint on reelection.[5]

The tenure potential of governors has generally been expanded in the last thirty years, especially in the southern states. For example, in 1969 only one southern state, Louisiana, permitted its chief executive to serve a four-year term with one reelection permitted. Eight southern states, including South Carolina, limited the governor to a single four-year term with no consecutive reelection permitted. Two southern states, Arkansas and Texas, still had two-year terms with no restraint on reelection.[6] By 1991, only one southern state, Virginia, restricted its governor to one four-year term. All other southern states, including South Carolina, allowed the possibility of a second four-year term.

The movement to increase the governor's tenure potential in South Carolina was encouraged by a commission created to study improvements to the constitution of 1895. In its 1969 report, the commission recommended a second consecutive four-year term. Ten years' total tenure was possible if the governor's office became vacant just after a general election and the lieutenant governor became governor and then was elected twice as governor.

The second consecutive term constitutes the most important formal increase of gubernatorial power in South Carolina in the last half of the twentieth century. It has enhanced the influence of the governor over the budgetary process as well as in legislative decisions. It also boosts appointment power. No state agency board or commission member serves as long as eight years. Thus, the eight-year governor for the first time could participate in appointments to all the seats on an agency board or commission for which the governor had responsibility.[7]

Longer tenure creates the potential for a governor to become a more important actor in intergovernmental affairs. In particular, it allows a governor to negotiate more actively with federal agencies, to serve in leadership positions on interstate bodies dealing with various policy concerns, and to become a more important figure in regional associations of governors and in the National Governors' Association.[8]

In the long-standing and imposing tradition of legislative dominance over the governor and over executive administration in South Carolina, not all of these changes sat well with some leaders. Longtime House Speaker Sol Blatt (*D*-Barnwell) opposed the constitutional amendment that allowed the governor to succeed himself. Said Blatt,

> The governor who is in there and is allowed to succeed himself doesn't do as good a job as governor if he wasn't allowed to succeed himself. It takes the first year of his term to get acquainted with the governor's office, how many people he's got to appoint, who to appoint, how much money he has to spend; federal funds flow through his office down there in the millions. Well, he spends it—that's one year. The second year he does the job that's supposed to be done by him by arranging for the distribution of those federal funds and where they should go, he makes his appointments, and then he starts running for reelection, if you let him run for reelection, and he doesn't confine his efforts to serving the people as it was intended for him to do. Now, in the second term, he's not eligible to run for reelection as governor, but he does have an open eye looking towards Washington. And, therefore, he starts playing politics again in order to get elected to the United States Senate.[9]

State senator Glenn McConnell (*R*-Charleston), an opponent of the constitutional change, also feels that the two-term option results in the governor running for reelection instead of concentrating on where the state is heading. McConnell favors instead a single six-year term of office.[10]

Although it is too early to evaluate the impact of the two-term tenure potential, the change has clearly enhanced the South Carolina governor's potential as a state and national figure. South Carolina will soon have had the experience of two eight-year chief executives. Certainly, the formal power of the governor has been enhanced by the second term, and the actors in the process have recognized its impact on state politics and policy processes.

Factor 2: Appointment Power

A second series of twentieth-century reforms has focused on increasing gubernatorial appointment power. The assumption underlying such reforms is that governors with unilateral power of appointment are more powerful than those who must have confirmation of an appointment by either or both legislative houses. Those governors who only approve appointments rather than initiate them have even less appointive power. Those governors who are weakest neither appoint nor approve appointments but have a separate body do so—or, in some states, officials who head agencies are separately elected, not appointed.[11]

A governor usually has the challenge to coordinate state offices and agencies in order to implement legislative policies. Successful policy administration and coordination is difficult enough when the governor's office is powerful; it is even more so when state departments are diverse, functionally separated, and governed by intermediate boards, as they have been in South Carolina. South Carolina legislators in the past have typically been able to extend their policy preferences through influence over the appointment of board members, ongoing contact with those members, or even service on selected boards. The result is that legislators may have effectively operated a board or commission, usually in conflict with a governor's view.

The contemporary (although perhaps not often expressed) attitude of many legislators toward developments in the office of governor and the governor's more frequent attempts at political and administrative control of state agencies is perhaps best illustrated by the views of the late Speaker Emeritus Sol Blatt. Blatt noted in a 1982 interview,

> I never go to a Governor's office unless he invites me. I don't believe, in the 50 years I've been in the House, I have been in the Governor's office 6 times unless I was invited down there. He doesn't have me to worry him and I think

that's the way it should be. But, don't ever let the public of this State get the notion that the Governor doesn't have power. He's got too much power. What we need is not a strong executive branch of State government, but a strong legislative branch where the Governor has the right to veto.[12]

A governor's limited powers of appointment indicate the independence of state agencies from executive control. A survey of South Carolina agencies in the 1980s showed that in about one out of five cases, board members were elected by joint legislative assembly and the governor was not involved at all.[13] Another one in five appointments was made by the governor directly. Some executive appointments had limited impact; for example, one intermediate reform allowed the governor to appoint two of the twenty members of the Department of Highways and Public Transportation. In about three out of five appointments, the governor shared the appointment power with the General Assembly. Approximately one of these three appointments was with the advice and consent of the South Carolina Senate or of the legislative delegation of the jurisdiction from where the appointment was made.

In addition to the lack of accountability, numerous conflicts or potential conflicts of interest have occurred over the years. For example, in 1988 the chair of the Manufactured Housing Board, which regulates mobile-home sales, was employed by the vice-chair as a mobile-home salesperson. In 1990, the daughter of a member of the Professional Counselor's Examining Board was paid $1,700 to write a code of ethics for the board. Members of the Tax Commission, which audits tax returns, have been partners in accounting firms that file tax returns for citizens and corporations. In the same year, of the eighteen members of the State Board of Education, one was a superintendent, two were principals, one was married to a principal, and one was director of a consortium that lobbied for twenty school districts. Also, for two years the chair of the Alcoholic Beverage Control Commission was a lobbyist for resort businesses that were licensed by the commission.[14]

In addition, the boards have not been representative of the population by demographic characteristics or by proportion of population. A February 1991 review of 313 positions on 36 selected boards showed that only 20 seats (6%) were held by women. Furthermore, judicial circuits, with a size range from 105,000 people to 408,000 people, define multicounty districts from which some board members and commissioners are chosen. Finally, jobs on 5 of the state's commissions are considered political plums because they pay salaries ranging from $64,900 to $73,600 for what is usually part-time employment. Of these 23 positions, 11 were held by former legislators in July 1991.[15]

Beginning in 1991, the *State* newspaper described the members of the state's 133 boards and commissions in South Carolina as "Our 1,200 Barons" in a system of government characterized by "Power Failure," because it was not really answerable to anyone, perhaps not even to the General Assembly. The newspaper took about 150 articles in seventeen installments to tell the whole story. The varying methods of appointment made it especially difficult for observers to determine accountability for agency performance. Boards appeared as autonomous bodies, each working independently of the others in shaping public policy in narrow areas of responsibility.

In an outcome startling to many, the General Assembly in its 1993 session significantly revised the appointment arrangements for many state agencies in major restructuring legislation. The results enhance the formal, statutory appointment powers of the South Carolina governor.

Eleven cabinet-type departments were created in which the governor hires and fires the agency director. Among them are Alcohol and Other Drug Abuse Services, Commerce, and Revenue and Taxation. The governor has limited control of five other agencies. The chief executive names the directors of the departments of Public Safety and Law Enforcement and can remove them only for cause. In departments for disabilities and special needs and for natural resources, the governor names the board members, but the board members hire the agency director. In the Department of Transportation (the old Highway Department less the Highway Patrol and the Division of Motor Vehicles), the governor appoints the board chair, but the legislature appoints the board members and the board names the agency head. Coupled with these changes, longer gubernatorial tenure may allow executive policy initiatives deeper inroads into the agencies for which the governor may now appoint the director, an entire board, or the chair of a board.

The bigger reality is that the General Assembly retains control or influence over appointments to the most important state agencies and the ones that spend the most money, such as for agriculture, public education, trustees of higher education institutions, and transportation. Agency heads for Agriculture, Public Education, and the Military Department are still popularly elected, as are the attorney general, treasurer, comptroller general, and secretary of state. Even without significant appointment powers, the governor may be around long enough to make a difference by hammering away with persuasive arguments at policy decisions by legislatively run boards and commissions or independently elected executives.

Factor 3: Budgetary Power

Another reform measure is the executive budget that is centralized under gubernatorial control. In 1989, forty-four states gave the governor full budgetary responsibilities. Five states, South Carolina among them, rated a "strong" governor for budget making. Governors in these five states share responsibility with other appointees and civil servants. Two legislative committee chairs, the comptroller general, and the state treasurer are also included in South Carolina's arrangement. Texas had the weakest budget-making powers for a governor, since the responsibility was shared directly with other elected officials.[16]

Control over the budgetary process is one method by which an executive can manage administrative agencies. In a 1981 survey conducted by Glenn Abney and Thomas Lauth, state agency heads were asked to rank the budgetary influence of the governor on administrative departments in their states. The governor was ranked as the most influential entity by at least 25 percent of agency heads in all but seven states. South Carolina and Colorado were the only two states where not a single agency head cited the governor as the most influential actor in the budgetary process.[17]

In a 1981 analysis of governors' budget-making powers, the governor of South Carolina, along with governors in Mississippi and Texas, was placed in the weakest category.[18] This analysis studied the formal, legal responsibilities of the governor in budgetary matters. South Carolina's chief executive ranks very weak because the office shares budgetary powers with several other independent sources of executive and legislative strength on a separate budgeting board.

The State Budget and Control Board. It is easy to assert that the most powerful agency in South Carolina government is the State Budget and Control Board. Its form today results from a long line of shared budgetary responsibility in South Carolina.

Elected local commissions for important fiscal matters, such as care for the poor and management of roads, existed at least by the early 1800s.[19] Legislatively appointed local commissions appeared during the colonial period as well. South Carolina used a commission method in state government budgeting as early as 1870. In that year, a body called the Sinking Fund Commission was established to manage repayment of the state debt and interest. Members of the Sinking Fund Commission were the governor, the attorney general, and the chairs of the Senate Finance Committee and the House

Ways and Means Committee. In 1883, the state treasurer was added as a member.

The next major use of a commission in budgeting was the creation of a separate State Tax Commission in 1916. This body's purpose was to oversee the collection of state revenues. One reason for creating the commission was the unequal assessment ratios occurring in different counties because of the different methods used by county auditors in setting the base for the property tax. In response to taxpayer protests, the State Tax Commission was created by the legislature to ensure equalization of assessments as well as the continuation of the credibility of state revenue policies.

The 1919 creation of the Budget Commission was a more direct movement to enlarge executive control over state agency expenditures. The commission brought legislative and executive leaders together in a formal process to propose the state budget. This commission, composed of the governor and the chairs of the Senate Finance Committee and the House Ways and Means Committee, was required to meet each year after November 1. They were to hold hearings consisting of all interested parties and then report to the General Assembly in January. The broad purpose of the Budget Commission was to take the pressure for budget preparation off the legislative committees and to give a publicized, focused starting point for budget deliberations.[20]

The State Budget Commission functioned as the starting point for each annual appropriation for the next thirty years. In general, the commission tended to recommend rather than direct the budget process. It neither exercised the degree of influence that advocates had envisioned for it, nor did it end the legislative budget logjam.

The next major change in the Budget Commission occurred in 1950. The revised commission emerged as a compromise between executive reformers and legislative traditionalists who fought over control of budgetary power. Following several studies, the commission was enlarged and reorganized into a new five-member body called the State Budget and Control Board, which included two new popularly elected executive members, the state treasurer and the comptroller general. The governor remained as chair of the body and the two legislative positions on the board remained the same. Several separate boards were abolished by the creation of the new board and became part of its operation. They were the old State Budget Commission, the State Finance Committee, the Board of Claims, the Commission on the State House and State House Grounds, the Joint Committee on Printing, and the South Carolina Retirement System. All of them were absorbed into the operation of three Budget and Control Board divisions: finance, purchasing and property, and personnel administration.[21]

One major agency, the State Highway Commission, still remained largely independent of the new Budget and Control Board's jurisdiction. Also left unchanged was the state's method of budgeting. It continued to rely on a detailed, line-item, expenditure-oriented budgeting format rather than on program budgeting. In fact, the first budget submitted by the Budget and Control Board for fiscal year 1952–53 was almost five hundred pages long and included information on sixty-three state agencies.[22]

Still another major review of state government management occurred in the 1970s. In 1972, the Governor's Management Review Commission was created by Governor John C. West. This commission, composed of executives from private corporations in South Carolina, recommended a consolidation of the Budget and Control Board's divisions and the creation of the office of executive director to oversee the entire operation. The Management Review Commission was also critical of the state's continued use of incrementalism in its budgetary process. In 1978, the executive director's job was created to administer the various divisions of the Budget and Control Board. The executive director would serve at the pleasure of the board. In 1986, an internal reorganization of the board resulted in the appointment of three deputy executive directors to manage specific clusters of board functions. More recently, that number was reduced to two.

The addition of new functions to the board and the reflection of board decisions in state policies are a convenient barometer with which to measure growing deference to a more unified executive structure. For example, the board took over revenue estimating from the Tax Commission. Two units that began in the governor's office, the state personnel department and the state planning office, are now divisions of the board.

As board functions have expanded, especially since the 1960s, staff members have frequently come from the State Department of Public Education. Since education is the single largest state expenditure item, financial experts from that department have moved over to the Budget and Control Board so that basic education policies could be maintained.

Executive Influence on Budgeting Today. Although the general process for proposing budget recommendations has been consistent for decades,[23] executive influence over the budgetary process has developed under Governor Campbell. During his 1986 campaign, Campbell discussed a need for a change in the budgetary process. Campbell, who had served on the Ways and Means Committee in the United States Congress, pointed out the difficulty in planning without an executive budget and noted that the process used in South Carolina was incremental and disjointed. Following his election,

Campbell structured his staff to include a budget and finance component. Two of his senior advisors had the positions of senior assistant for finance and administration and senior assistant for budget and policy.[24]

Campbell routinely meets with Budget and Control Board members, but he submitted a separate executive budget for 1988–89. While there was resistance to the executive budget, his budget proposals were generally adopted by the board. Thus, the precedent of an executive budget was established informally, and Governor Campbell has come forth with a proposed executive budget in each subsequent fiscal year. Luther Fred Carter, former senior assistant to Campbell for finance and administration, suggested that the submission of an executive budget has made the governor a policy actor with substantive input as opposed to symbolic input. Carter's vision of an institutionalized process in which future governors would submit executive budgets was enacted into law in 1993.[25]

Philip Grose Jr., assistant executive director of the Budget and Control Board and former director of the State Reorganization Commission, has described the changes in South Carolina's budgetary process as evolutionary rather than revolutionary. Grose characterized the state's budget as being something of a composite of agency requests, built on early consensus of legislative and executive leadership.[26]

Some observers feel that the quasi-parliamentary merger of executive and legislative leadership may actually serve the public interest of the state better in the days of tight budgets than would be possible given strict adherence to the doctrines of separation of powers.[27] In fact, one claims that such budgetary practices demonstrate rather ingenious method of defusing budgetary conflict before it begins.[28] Gubernatorial vetoes are no longer surprises, because Governor Campbell tells the legislature up front what he wants through the submission of an executive budget.[29] Legislators agree.

In summary, budget reform has occurred in South Carolina, and the governor has become a more important actor in the process as a result of statutory changes, federal funding, and personal initiative. Budget reform, however, remains incomplete. Incrementalism remains the norm for both budgetary form and budgetary change.

Factor 4: Organizational Power

Since 1920, at least eight studies of the administrative structure in South Carolina have recommended a stronger chief executive with respect to organizing and managing state agencies. These studies reflected the Wilsonian view of administrative structure that would place state agencies under the unified command of the governor as chief executive.[30] Returning military veterans led by J. Strom Thurmond captured the governorship and used one of the structural studies, the Peace Commission Report in 1945, as a platform to address organizational needs. In a partial response, the legislature created a State Reorganization Commission to reduce duplication and fill gaps in state agencies.

However, the State Reorganization Commission became more of an intermediary for the legislature's interest in administrative changes than an advocate for a strong executive. Consequently, the commission has functioned regularly but largely passively. When it has come to life, it has usually made some significant recommendations that have become political fact. For example, the Reorganization Commission recommended the merger of the health and pollution agencies in the early 1970s, and called for the consolidation of alcohol and drug abuse programs for more efficient administration. More recently, the commission has made extensive studies of state government structures and operations, including a county-based demonstration of state agency service coordination.[31] It regularly conducts reviews of state agency operations to reduce costs and to discover efficiencies.

Within the executive branch, governors and agency heads have occasionally worked out new operating arrangements for more consistent state policy. For example, interagency councils were used extensively in the 1960s for informal coordination of agency operations. More integrated budgeting procedures, performance evaluation, and an emphasis on quality management are current features that may spur increased agency coordination.

The results of past reorganizing and restructuring efforts on specific state agency programs are highly varied. The 1993 restructuring legislation enhances appointment and removal powers and was a big boost to the executive branch. Although the governor does not have the organizing power—that is, the ability to abolish, revise, or create an agency—the chief executive now has the ability to hire and fire eleven agency directors and to name directors or governing board members in other agencies.

Until subsequent governors establish a record of experience in running state agencies in a more coordinated manner, the plural executive model with its divided administrative responsibilities will persist in South Carolina.

Factor 5: Veto Power

The final variable is the governor's veto power. The type of veto power varies by state and includes total bill veto, amendatory veto, item veto, item reduction veto, or, in the case of North Carolina, no veto at all. Gubernatorial vetoes have averaged approximately 5 percent nationwide; however, the rate of legislative overrides has grown nearly fivefold. The rate of increase indicates an escalation in legislative-executive conflict over legislation.[32]

Use of veto authority by a governor is usually rare because it may simply invite retaliation by the legislature.[33] South Carolina governors have used the general veto sparingly, although they have recently increased their item veto of provisos in the state appropriations bill. From 1979 to 1983, more than $150 million was struck from appropriations and bond bills by veto without being overridden. Over 250 single items were struck by Governor Campbell from the 1988 appropriations bill; none were overridden. These successful vetoes may measure the potency of informal gubernatorial power as much as formal powers.

The vetoes may also reflect a budgetary game known to all the players. Many items are often put on the budget bill as provisos, or "bobtails," which, when struck, give the legislator a bargaining chip with the governor in the future; the idea is that since the governor struck the item, the governor owes the legislator and the legislator's constituents a favor. The favor might be to let it pass in a future bill or to give in on some other project that the governor may be holding up. The vetoes also give the legislator a convenient opportunity to explain to voters that "I tried so hard, but those big interests in Columbia (or the governor's office) beat me down." In this respect, the Budget and Control Board is helpful in sharing executive responsibility with the governor, because it often issues the background studies that justify the vetoes.

The veto and its use may become more significant if partisan interests develop to prevent legislative overrides. Since it takes a two-thirds vote to override a veto, members of the governor's political party, tightly organized and voting with discipline, could block an override by the opposing party if it had more than one-third membership in either house. Following the 1992 elections, 50 of 124 House members and 16 of 46 Senate members were Republicans, but they did not always vote with the Republican governor.

The Republican governor now has an opportunity to organize partisan interests in the legislature for higher stakes. Of course, the veto is still a negative, blocking tactic, and the incentives for partisan cohesion are reduced because of local pressures on legislators. Nevertheless, the onset of more competitive political parties may have significant implications for the exercise of formal gubernatorial powers.

INFORMAL GUBERNATORIAL POWERS

Although growing stronger, the governor is still very weak overall if only formal powers are used to assess gubernatorial strength. Yet individual governors have had distinguished careers and have been able to promote significant policy achievements. The political status of the governor has really been defined as much by informal powers as by formal ones. As implied in table 18, the increasing formal powers of the South Carolina governor also suggest ever-widening responsibilities of the governor as policy formulator, chief legislator, and chief negotiator for the state in intergovernmental relationships.

Robert Highsaw maintains that governors in the South generally have "exploited their positions in order to develop command of their legislatures."[34] Gubernatorial success in South Carolina also has hinged on the credibility of individual governors with the legislature, as brief biographical sketches of recent governors indicate.

James Byrnes (D-Aiken, 1951–55) was recognized as a state leader because of national service in the U.S. House of Representatives and Senate, as a U.S. Supreme Court justice, and as U.S. secretary of state. Governor Byrnes promoted economic development and was firmly in agreement with the state's traditionalistic, conservative leaders.

During the relatively uneventful and custodial governorship of George Bell Timmerman (D-Lexington, 1955–59), the governor's primary concentration was on preserving the status quo against possible changes stemming from the *Brown* decision. This administration emphasized increased coordination of law enforcement and continued the hunt for new industry.

A more dynamic person, Ernest F. Hollings (D-Charleston), served next as governor (1959–63). Hollings had been elected to the legislature for ten years and had served as lieutenant governor prior to becoming governor. Thus, he was well versed in the art of persuasion as the key to success as chief executive. Perhaps his major accomplishment was persuading Edgar Brown (D-Barnwell), chair of the Senate Finance Committee, to support the development of a system of technical education colleges. A popular story has it that this was done one evening over a fifth of bourbon. By the end of the evening, the bottle was empty and the agreement was sealed in a handwritten paragraph.

Hollings's successor, Donald Russell (D-Spartanburg, 1963–65), a former president of the University of South Carolina, was unable to deal very fruitfully with the legislature. Nevertheless, his intellectual acumen brought dignity to the office. Two years after his election, Russell resigned and was appointed U.S. senator after the death of incumbent senator Olin D. Johnston (*D*-Spartanburg).

The next governor, Robert McNair (*D*-Allendale, 1965–71), had twelve years' legislative service. He was relatively successful in policy making because of his legislative experience, his persuasive style, and his political friendship with legislative leaders such as the aging Senator Brown. McNair led major drives for tourism development, education reform, and industrial recruitment. He also led the state through school desegregation and broad civil unrest during the late 1960s.

However, since the 1960s, changes in the legislature itself have made the governor's role as chief persuader more difficult. In particular, as the legislative body became more diversified and power vacuums began to develop first in the House and later in the Senate, governors found it increasingly important to draw on their previous legislative ties in order to enact policy. Governor John West (*D*-Kershaw, 1971–75) had served thirteen years in the Senate and had been lieutenant governor for four years. He was able to work with his friends, House Speaker Sol Blatt and Senators Edgar Brown, Marion Gressette (*D*-Calhoun), and Rembert Dennis (*D*-Berkeley), in order to pass proposals. West described his style as follows: "When I saw a piece of legislation going through that I felt was inappropriate, I would simply go to the leadership of the House or Senate and say, 'Look, fellows, please don't send that to me. Let's work out a compromise on a change before it comes.' "[35]

James B. Edwards (*R*-Charleston, 1975–79), the first Republican governor since Reconstruction, was much less successful than previous governors in his relationships with other state officials. Edwards, who had served four years in the state Senate, found his executive orders ruled illegal by the state attorney general and his appointments routinely rejected by the legislature. In addition, he was unable to gain control over state agencies' spending of federal funds. After a time, Edwards made friends with the legislative leadership. "If I hadn't developed these friendships, then I probably wouldn't have been able to accomplish anything," he said.[36]

Governor Dick Riley (1979–87) established the trademark for his administration through "single minded pursuit of a significant policy issue [education reform]."[37] This is perhaps the best illustration of a South Carolina governor using the informal powers of the office to achieve political victory. In 1983, Riley had failed to get an education reform package passed by the legislature. After the defeat of his 1983 proposal, he became singularly committed to education reform and used the office to garner the necessary publicity and subsequent political support for his reforms. In fact one observer noted, "No matter what you try to discuss with Riley, he always turned it into a forum on the education package." It was even reported that when Riley delivered a eulogy for a legislator who died during the campaign for the Education Improvement Act (EIA), he recalled how strongly the deceased had supported education reform.[38]

Riley skillfully used informal powers, such as access to mass media, political party influence, patronage, pork barrel, prestige of the office, and his personal popularity. He combined them with his interpersonal skills, bargaining ability, education, experience, energy, and ambition for successful passage of a model education reform package.[39]

Riley's efforts began with the creation of two task forces, one composed of twenty-five legislators, educators, and private sector individuals whose purpose was to design an education reform package, and a second composed of thirty-nine top leaders from the political, education, and private sectors to review the proposals and develop political support for the program. Seven public forums were then held in 1983, which were attended by over thirteen thousand people. From these came additional recommendations to the task forces. Riley also addressed the state on the state educational television network, a speaker's bureau was created to make presentations on education reform, a toll-free hot line and phone bank were created to respond to questions and to build the base of support, and an advertising fund of one hundred thousand dollars was put together to market the program.

When the legislature met in 1984, Riley's supporters skillfully maneuvered the EIA bill through the General Assembly through a point-by-point, item-by-item debate. This, combined with strong backing from the public, led to the passage of sixty-one of the sixty-four proposals, including a provision to increase the sales tax by one cent to fund the program. After it was passed by the state Senate, the EIA was signed into law in June 1984.

Riley used the same approach for day-to-day government. He nurtured support from agency boards and commissions. He held with them what he referred to as "tent meetings" to sell his budget priorities.[40] Said Riley,

> It was clear when they went out of there as to where I wanted them to go that year. . . . We'd work on these things hundreds of hours. It was not a casually done thing. The eight years I was there, the budget was framed very nearly like I requested it to be framed. Not because I told them to do it, but because I worked.[41]

State senator Glenn McConnell (R-Charleston) described Riley as a governor who was very accessible and who depended more on intensive personal contact than many other governors.[42] Senator Theo Mitchell (D-Greenville) noted that, as governor, Riley visited the legislature, was accessible, and had receptions for legislators.[43]

In contrast, Governor Campbell has utilized his staff more and has had less personal contact with legislators than did Riley. In 1990, Senator Mitchell estimated that Campbell's staff handled 90 percent of the governor's contact with the legislature and described Campbell as a recluse.[44] Senator McConnell felt Campbell's greater dependence on staff resulted in less legislative success.

House Speaker Bob Sheheen (D-Kershaw) compared the two governors in this way:

> Governor Campbell . . . has been [using] much more a chairman-of-the-board approach. He is heavily involved in economic development and is very interested in the appointments to the boards and commissions who reflect his views. He has fewer legislative initiatives . . . and he involves himself only with specific members of the House and Senate on general matters. . . . His view of the role of the governor is different. He wasn't involved with the legislative process at the state level; he came here directly from Washington. [Whereas with Riley,] his most recent work had been from the floor of the Senate, and before that, the House. Number two, the governor [Campbell] came from a highly charged partisan atmosphere [in Washington]. Everything is doled out according to party leadership and seniority. That's not the case here.[45]

CONCLUSION

Increasing demands for executive leadership have advanced the governor's potential to administer the state more independently. Previously, governors had responded personally, and they had used their new-found favor to develop greater formal capacity for governance. The governor's staff now includes special assistants for policy and budgeting; the division of administration in the Budget and Control Board has several hundred employees who administer federal programs under the governor's general supervision. In 1993, eleven cabinet-type agencies were created that the governor will be able to control directly. Never before has the executive had such administrative resources directly at its disposal.

However, the governor must still possess the ability to persuade the legislature and a diverse variety of boards and commissions to follow his policy leads. The success of a governor continues to be based more on personal qualities than on formal constitutional authority. Imitating Beyle and Schlesinger, one may say that the formal authority of the governor today rates about fifteen points, a small advancement over the historical nine- or ten-point rating.

Clearly, persuasive actions must complement the formal tools of gubernatorial power for South Carolinians to believe that a governor is successful. Widespread fear that an elected governor may be heavy-handed is probably enough to deter significant changes in the existing allocation of power among the branches and agencies of government in South Carolina.

CHAPTER NINE

Government and Policy Implementation

The agencies of South Carolina government, like its executive and judicial branches, have been dominated by the legislature. When the colonial system changed with the American Revolution, the legislature began to confront the major problems previously negotiated with the British Board of Trade. For example, the importation of slaves plunged the state into significant post-Revolutionary export deficits. The legislature stopped slave importing from 1787 to 1803 to preserve the credit of the state's economy. It promoted cotton farming by paying Eli Whitney for rights to the cotton gin so that the cotton growers in the state could have lawful access to it. A great state financed and managed network of internal canals and drainage systems was promoted by the legislature. These improvements joined the Up-Country and the Low Country by providing the transportation connections for the cotton economy.

After the stresses of secession, war, and Reconstruction, the singular dominance of the legislature was perhaps even more pronounced. Guided by inward-looking local legislative delegations, the state government did little to promote general economic renewal and social development. This reaction extended well into the twentieth century.

The legislative legacy gives South Carolina a government that operates chiefly as a network of agencies. Despite the passage of legislation in 1993 that consolidated seventy-six agencies into eleven departments for which the governor hires or fires the agency head, many major state agencies are still individually governed by a board or commission or a popularly elected head. The separate board or commission is more directly accountable to the General Assembly than to the governor for ensuring that agency responsibilities are met and that the agency is properly administered and controlled.

GOVERNING THE ECONOMIC ENVIRONMENT

At the time of the Great Depression, South Carolina was a poor state and still economically dominated by agriculture and the textile industry. Per capita income in 1929 was only 38.4 percent of the national average. Soon, significant infrastructure projects, such as improved highways and major hydroelectric facilities, began to stimulate new economic development.[1] By the post–World War II period, the state's economy was beginning to move away from agriculture toward greater variety in its manufacturing and economic base. The result has been a dramatic improvement in the living standards for residents of the state as its economy has grown and per capita income has moved closer to the national norm.

Since 1950, the per capita income in South Carolina has increased more than tenfold. In 1950, per capita income was 61.3 percent of the nation's average, and by the mid-1970s it had increased to 76 percent of the national average.[2] By 1990, per capita income topped 80 percent of the national average.[3] Although improved, the overall picture is not yet satisfactory. In 1991, median household income was the thirty-fourth highest nationally ($27,463). The poverty rate remained 2.2 percent above the national rate of 14.2 percent.[4]

Per capita income varies widely within the state. For example, in 1975 Richland County (Columbia) was $831 above the state average, while more rural Clarendon County was $1,424 below it. The increase in per capita income and the disparities within the state can be explained by the economic changes that have occurred in both industry and agriculture in the post–World War II era.

Industrial Development and Change

The stimulus for contemporary industrial and economic development was the establishment in 1933 of the forerunner of the State Development Board. It aimed to get new industry to locate in the state and to expand existing industrial operations. At the time, the textile industry made up approximately 75 percent of the industrial sector's workforce. The state's textile industry produced one-fourth of America's cloth and yarn between 1920 and 1941.[5]

In the late 1950s, the state began aggressively to recruit new and different types of industry. On April 8, 1958, the State Development Board ran a full-page advertisement in the *Wall Street Journal* with the bannerhead "South Carolina passes law reducing taxes on industry: New flexible tax law offers optional method of income tax computation to meet varying requirements of today's diverse industry.''[6] These tax incentives offered by the state included an exemption from ordinary county property taxes for five years for new industry and all capital expenditures. In addition, items on a business or manufacturer's inventory that were not offered for sale were exempted from property tax. The exemption did not forgive industries from paying school taxes, which are a large percentage of county property tax revenue.

While South Carolina had a corporate income tax, it allowed a carryforward of losses for up to seven years for new industry and up to five years for existing industry. Because of this provision, net operating losses could be deducted into the future for seven and five years respectively, which allowed industry to pay lower taxes over this period. Finally, the state provided industry with two sales tax incentives. First, industry was exempt from paying sales taxes on equipment bought to be used in the manufacturing process. Second, electricity used to operate the equipment was also exempt.

The competitive advantage of these tax incentives to South Carolina is difficult to assess in a comparative perspective. One study conducted in the 1980s ranked South Carolina twentieth out of the fifty states for tax burden on a hypothetical business, and it was estimated that South Carolina collected approximately 26.1 percent of its taxes through business, compared to a U.S. average of 30.6 percent.[7]

Another incentive for industry to locate in South Carolina was the state's "right-to-work" law, enacted in 1954. Historically the South, including South Carolina, was anti-union. Right-to-work laws attracted industry because they allowed employees to work without having to join a union. This theoretically removed the incentive for a prospective worker to join the union because he or she might still receive the same benefits without having to pay union dues. From the labor union's perspective, it made organization and negotiation with management more difficult. Without the presence of a union, management had much more discretion in the treatment of employees. At present, South Carolina's industrial labor force is less than 10 percent unionized. This is the second lowest percentage in the country, behind only North Carolina.

These various incentives have contributed to the significant growth in the manufacturing sector since the 1960s. For example, manufacturing employment in the state increased 20 percent from 1960 to 1965 and 16 percent from 1965 to 1970. Employment in the textile and apparel sectors grew by only 12 percent and 7 percent respectively during the same periods.[8]

Much of the credit for the diversification in the industrial sector must go to former governor Ernest "Fritz" Hollings. Jack Bass notes that under

Hollings "the state Development Board was transformed from a group of cronies to a scientifically oriented, business-minded agency that worked hand-in-hand with potential new industry."[9] Hollings, along with future governors Robert McNair and John West, was also responsible for creating the state's technical education system.

Under Hollings's gubernatorial leadership, the state established thirteen technical training centers around the state to help meet the needs of employees. South Carolina now has sixteen technical colleges that provide training assistance programs to help new and expanding industry to start up on a sound financial basis. Since the initiation of the technical education program, these schools have provided short-term training programs for approximately 850 manufacturing facilities and over one hundred thousand people. More and more, the technical colleges are providing college credit courses. Critics see this as a weakening of the original purpose and mission of these colleges.

A distinctive characteristic of industrial growth in South Carolina in recent years is the influx of foreign-based firms into the state. In 1956, the British-based Bowater Paper Company approached state officials about building a plant in York County if the General Assembly would lift the cap that limited foreign ownership to five hundred acres. The state responded with a law allowing foreigners or foreign corporations to own up to five hundred thousand acres.

Subsequently, a flood of foreign investment, mostly from Europe, has come into the state. Before 1960, foreign manufacturing investment amounted to $79.56 million and employed 970 people. During the 1960s and 1970s, foreign manufacturers poured $2.6 billion into the state and added 31,872 jobs. In the early 1980s, South Carolina ranked second nationwide in per capita foreign investment, and by 1986, the state ranked fourteenth among the states in terms of foreign-owned plants and property. By 1987, there were 98 foreign businesses and 250 foreign-affiliated businesses employing over 43,750 workers in the state.[10] During the 1980s, an additional $4.3 billion came from abroad and generated 23,355 jobs.[11]

In 1990, foreign investments totaled $912.6 million and made up nearly 36 percent of all new industrial capital investments. According to a study by a Greenville accounting firm, overseas investors choose South Carolina because of labor relations (few unions), transportation facilities (including the port of Charleston), living conditions and climate, joint venture opportunities, availability of space, buildings and sites, low taxes, availability of financing or financing services, and convenient air transportation.[12]

While the original foreign investment was related to the textile industry (11% historically), the present-day focus is on other sectors, including metals and machinery (30.2%), chemicals (34.7%), and paper and printing (5.2%).[13] The state achieved major national headlines in 1992 when the German automaker Bayerische Motoren Werke (BMW) announced the location of its North American assembly plant near the Greenville-Spartanburg airport. Most of the investments from abroad represent new facilities as opposed to acquisitions of American-owned firms. They also tend to pay higher wages than existing industries.

Most of the foreign-based firms are located in the Up-Country. Not counting the BMW addition, thirty-three overseas firms are located in Spartanburg County and twenty-seven in Greenville County. Historically, European countries dominate investment in South Carolina from overseas, especially Germany (28.6%), Great Britain (14.8%), France (16.2%), and Switzerland (8.1%). More recently, Japan and other Pacific rim countries have been increasing their investments in the state. Japan's historical share of foreign-affiliated investment in the state is 18 percent.[14]

Foreign investment has not been without its setbacks. In 1969, the American subsidiary of the West German dye and chemical firm Badische Anilin und Soda Fabrik (BASF) announced that it would build the largest industrial project in the state's history, a two hundred million dollar chemical-industrial complex four miles from Hilton Head Island.[15] Hilton Head developers and African American fishing boat operators formed an unusual coalition to oppose the development, protesting that it would pollute the water and air in the area. After heated debate and much adverse publicity, BASF postponed and then cancelled its building plans.

One result of the development of industry in South Carolina has been the dramatic growth of the State Ports Authority (SPA). The SPA was created by the General Assembly in the early 1940s; however, it did not begin operation until after World War II. In 1948, its first recorded year of operation, 100,000 tons of cargo passed through its facilities. By 1968, tonnage had risen to 2.2 million tons, including approximately 80,000 tons of containerized cargo. In 1991, SPA facilities in South Carolina handled over 8.3 million tons of cargo, including almost 6.3 million tons of containerized cargo.[16]

Since the late 1940s, the port of Charleston has grown to second place among container ports on the east and gulf coasts. It is now the seventh largest container port in the United States and seventeenth largest in the world.[17] Today, almost seventy shipping lines serving 109 nations use its facilities.

Domestically, the port serves twenty-seven states, although about 30 percent of its business involves South Carolina cargo.[18]

The SPA has assets of approximately $443 million and is responsible either directly or indirectly for more than fifty-eight thousand jobs, $1.23 billion in personal income, more than $5.26 billion in sales, and $166.6 million in state taxes.[19] Dollar value of port cargo activities is about equal between exports and imports, but exports have 62 percent of tonnage.

Tourism

In 1967, South Carolina created a Department of Parks, Recreation and Tourism (PRT) in order to encourage the growing tourism industry. From this beginning, tourism has developed into the second largest industry in the state.

During the 1970s, ads appeared in national publications showing beautiful scenes with the heading "South France? No, South Carolina!" During the 1980s, tourism in South Carolina grew 132 percent. In 1989, it brought in $5 billion and supported one hundred thousand jobs.[20] Approximately thirty million tourists visit South Carolina each year. Their major destinations are the coastal resort centers of Myrtle Beach (first), Charleston (second), and Hilton Head (third).

Although the largest percentage of tourists are from the neighboring states of North Carolina, Georgia, and Florida, the state is reaching out to other markets. The latest innovation has been an international marketing program that produced an increase of European visitors to South Carolina. In 1982 twenty-six thousand Europeans visited South Carolina; in 1990 they almost tripled to seventy-six thousand.[21] This included thirty-two thousand West Germans and twenty-eight thousand visitors from the United Kingdom.

As the popularity of golf has grown, so has golf-course development activity. South Carolina ranked sixteenth in the United States in the number of golf courses in 1989, with 291 courses. Almost half of them are located along the coast, with 68 in the Myrtle Beach area, 30 in Charleston, and 30 in Hilton Head. In Myrtle Beach alone, golf has gone from a $76 million industry in 1980 to a $255 million business in 1989. About two and a quarter million rounds of golf are played in the Myrtle Beach area annually, and one golf shop business in that location sells thirty-six thousand golf balls a week from March to May. The hosting of the Ryder Cup by Kiawah Island in 1991 reinforced South Carolina's image as a golfing destination, as does Hilton Head's annual Heritage Golf Classic on the Professional Golfers' Association tour. Governor Campbell's office estimates that by the year 2000, tourism should be a $10 billion industry in the state.[22]

The Military

The military has been another major employment source for South Carolina, but significant changes in military installations are planned. Approximately 119,000 military and civilian workers are currently employed at nineteen military installations statewide. The Charleston Naval Base, home port for seventy-six ships, paid about $880 million in salaries to its 26,000 military and 15,000 civilian employees in 1987.[23] Fort Jackson, a fifty-two thousand acre army training center in Columbia, has 16,300 military personnel and over 7,000 civilians for a total of more than $300 million in salaries.

In March 1993, the announcement came that almost all of the Charleston naval facilities were on the recommended closure list of the Pentagon's Base Closure and Realignment Commission. The commission voted July 25–27, 1993, to close the navy port and shipyard. It did not close the Charleston Naval Hospital, and it will add about 2,700 high-technology jobs to expand the Naval Electronic Support Center (NAVALEX) to almost 6,000 workers. The Charleston Trident Chamber of Commerce estimated a direct loss of 26,380 military and civilian jobs and about $1.3 billion in direct payroll expenses. Almost as many nonmilitary jobs would be lost in the surrounding economy.[24] Overall, the direct net job loss for South Carolina was initially estimated to be 32,689,[25] despite the fact that Fort Jackson, Shaw Air Force Base in Sumter, the Marine Corps Air Station in Beaufort, and the Beaufort Naval Hospital would gain 1,521 jobs collectively.

A state delegation, mostly Charlestonians, trekked to Washington and appeared at hearings and on national television to protest unsuccessfully the proposed closings. The governor's office and Charleston's mayor, Joseph Riley, quickly turned the community's attention toward broad-based economic developments to replace lost jobs.

Agriculture

Agriculture has also undergone major changes since World War II. From 1950 to 1975, the number of farms declined from 139,000 to 27,000 while the average size of a farm doubled to about 176 acres. Farm population declined 38 percent during the 1950s and another 66 percent during the 1960s. By 1980, only 3 percent of the state's workforce was employed in agriculture.[26] In 1987, there were 20,517 farms in the state, averaging 232 acres in size. The largest average farm size was in Allendale County (1,038 acres), the smallest in Pickens County (96 acres).[27]

For years, cotton was the dominant agricultural product in South Carolina. But cotton was not just king, it became a tyrant. Farm tenancy became the rule in the post-Reconstruction era. By 1900, approximately sixty-one of every one hundred South Carolina farmers were tenants.[28] However, as the revolution in agriculture began to affect South Carolina, there was a movement away from cotton as well as a decline in farm employment. For example, in the years before World War I and prior to the invasion of the boll weevil, cotton was grown on more than 2 million acres. By the mid-1970s, less than 100,000 acres was planted in cotton.[29]

Although there has been a small resurgence in cotton production to approximately 125,000 acres in 1989, it is no longer the dominant cash crop. Major cash crops today include tobacco, soybeans, corn, peaches, vegetables, and hay. Wood products and timber have become the state's largest cash crop.

The development of the timber industry began when several million pine seedlings were planted in South Carolina by federal Civilian Conservation Corps (CCC) workers prior to World War II. The South Carolina State Forestry Commission began to produce and distribute 30 to 40 million pine seedlings a year in the late 1940s, and by the mid-1950s, production was 110 million seedlings yearly.[30] In addition, a statewide tree farm committee was established to encourage proper growing techniques.

From this beginning, the timber industry has grown dramatically over the last thirty years. Today, South Carolina is the fifth largest tree-planting state in the nation behind Georgia, Alabama, Mississippi, and Florida. Forestry products are the state's largest cash crop. In 1989, the forest industry provided over thirty-eight thousand jobs—8.5 percent of all jobs in South Carolina—and had receipts totaling more than $530 million.[31] It is now the third largest industry in the state behind textiles and tourism. Overall, two-thirds of the state's total acreage is forestland. Commercial companies, such as Union Camp, Georgia-Pacific, International Paper, and Westvaco, own and manage an estimated 2.5 million acres.[32] Forestland covers 12,256,972 acres, 63.4 percent of the 19,320,552 acres of land in the state.[33]

ADMINISTERING SOCIAL POLICY

Overall, the South Carolina legislature has given as much attention to new social policy concerns as it has to the chronic economic policy problems. The legislature has been willing to spend more money on better schools with more school days, kindergartens, high schools for all, technical colleges, enhanced higher education, health education, hospitalization, and public assistance. However, these human services programs are implemented by a host of independently organized state agencies, as in the government of the past. At least in the minds of critics, resulting problems, such as inadequate service planning and coordination, hurt taxpayers and service recipients.

General Background

The final collapse of South Carolina's plantation system in the 1920s led to the necessity for government to take a greater interest in better health, education, and income security. Along with the growth of governmental programs came a need for good management and for political control. Public education expenditures have steadily increased and have emphasized improvements in quality. Better school facilities, improved curriculums, and more equitable financing have been the objects of recent state laws.

The expansion of health and social programs also reflects increased state reliance on the federal government. South Carolina has been a longtime beneficiary of federal grant-in-aid programs that favored the more rural and low-income states. South Carolinians were instrumental in much of the legislation. Frank Lever, a former member of Congress from Lexington County (*D,* Seventh District, 1901–19), sponsored federal legislation for grants-in-aid for county farm and home demonstration agents early in the twentieth century. United States senator James F. Byrnes (*D,* 1931–41) led South Carolina's interests in the New Deal programs and aid to military-impacted areas. Congressman Mendel Rivers (*D,* 1941–69) carried Byrnes's work forward into the 1960s through his support for military spending in the state. Federal funds were directly responsible for starting new state operating activities, such as employment security (1936), emergency relief (1933), and vocational rehabilitation (1927) as well as for the expansion of the original state boards for health and for education.

Public Education

Article XI in the 1895 constitution provided for the State Board of Education, an elected state superintendent of education, and a role for the governor as board chair. As illustrated in table 19, down through the *Brown* decision all actions were within the "separate but equal" context. The most important years were immediately after World War I, when the first significant

Table 19: Significant Twentieth-Century Milestones in South Carolina Public Education (Prior to *Brown*)

1903	Conference in Columbia on April 11 sponsored by Southern Regional Education Board to emphasize need for improved school conditions in the state and to promote political and public interest.
1907	High School Act passed; provided for state aid for secondary schools and placed them under state supervision.
1915	Local option law allowing a school district to adopt a compulsory attendance policy.
1915–1916	First agriculture teachers in public schools.
1919	Many significant improvements. Children between six and fourteen years old required to attend school eighty days a year. Schools for adults, summer schools, and county institutes allowed. Equalizing Act passed to help schools in rural areas; it guaranteed seven months of school in any district that voted an eight-mill tax, enrolled twenty-five pupils for each teacher with an average attendance of fifteen per classroom, and used the state salary schedule. Specified amounts were also provided for transportation, school buildings, libraries, high schools, and agriculture teachers.
1924	The state became the central administrative unit as opposed to local boards—a major step toward statewide uniformity. Legislation included the 6–0–1 law: the state would pay for the first six months if the district or county would pay for the additional month. Coupled with changes in financing, it was a way to tax where the ability to pay was and to spend where the children were.
1933	Constitutional provision put into effect for a general tax to guarantee a minimum term for every school. The 6–0–1 law became the 6–0–0 law, since the minimum term no longer required the additional month for district to qualify for state aid. Equitable financing not addressed again until 1970s.
1948	The Peabody Report, *Public Schools in South Carolina,* revived public interest in education after the national Depression and World War II. It recommended school construction, consolidation of school districts, state responsibility for school bus operation, and reform of school finance.
1951	Comprehensive reform under leadership of Governor James F. Brynes. Spending on African American children was double the rate of spending on white children in an effort to demonstrate that the school system was equal, though racially separate.

Sources: James Karl Coleman, *State Administration in South Carolina* (New York: Columbia University Press, 1935), pp. 114–19 and William J. Blough, "Governing South Carolina's Public Schools," in Tyer and Graham, *Local Government in South Carolina: The Governmental Landscape,* pp. 92–94.

minimum requirements were passed and financed. The 1924 policy was almost revolutionary for socially and fiscally conservative South Carolina, because it taxed areas with the ability to pay but spent where the children with the needs were. The policy eventually became submerged in the problems of segregation and the rise of other revenue sources for education.

The modernization of South Carolina's public education began in 1948 with extensive recommendations for school construction, consolidation of school districts, state responsibility for school bus operation, and reform of school finance. Many of these reforms were begun during the term of Governor James F. Brynes (1951–55) in an effort to extend the "separate but equal" policy. The first state sales tax, at 3 percent, was passed during his administration in order to finance the changes. More specifically, spending on African American children was twice the rate of spending on white children in an effort to demonstrate that the school system was equal, though racially separate. It was a flawed strategy, but it gave the state a head start on building a racially integrated public school system.

The present-day State Board of Education is managed by the state superintendent of education, a constitutional officer popularly elected to a four-year term as the administrative head of the department. A Republican challenger beat the incumbent "old-line" Democrat state superintendent in the 1990 election. The superintendent also serves as secretary to the state education board. Generally the functions of the board are to adopt rules, regulations, and minimum standards that govern the public schools. The board prescribes rules and regulations for examining and certifying teachers. It also prescribes and enforces the public school curriculum along with textbooks and instructional materials.

There are 1,100 public schools in South Carolina with more than 617,000 public school students. About two-thirds of the students use public school bus transportation. The schools employ over 42,000 staff members, including almost 2,000 principals, more than 1,000 librarians, and 35,272 teachers.[34] When custodians and lunchroom workers are added, the number is more than 62,000. About one out of three employees of state and all local governments in South Carolina work in public education.

But South Carolina's public schools are more than mere numbers. The development and improvement of public education is the highest issue on the agenda of most elected officials and administrators in the state. Quality public education is generally held as the key to state economic development.

Excellence in education has been a major theme of virtually every administration since the 1960s. For example, the McNair administration coordinated financing a comprehensive statewide public education system from kindergarten through adult education. One additional penny was added to the state sales tax in 1969, primarily for kindergartens.

Quality in public education became a major emphasis in the mid-1970s. The legislature passed the Education Finance Act in 1977 to devote additional resources to all elementary schools and also to increase state financial aid to impoverished school districts. The Basic Skills Assessment Act of 1978 required the State Board of Education to measure the effectiveness of the curriculum and to teach basic skills in the schools. In the 1979 legislative session, a teacher certification bill was passed requiring new entrance, certification, and performance standards for public school teachers.

The core of the 1984 Education Improvement Act (EIA) was a series of major "action" recommendations that targeted improvements in virtually all aspects of South Carolina's public schools. They emphasized quality controls, rewards for productivity, and higher expectations for teachers and administrators. Partnerships between schools and the community were suggested along with the repair and construction of school buildings. Most important, higher student performance levels were set, and steps were urged to strengthen basic skills. For adequate revenue, this required one more penny on the state sales tax. The legislature set the current statewide sales tax rate of 5 percent in 1984 with little opposition.

If test scores are reliable evidence, the state has moved away from its perennial "dead last" position in student achievements. *Fortune* magazine reported that South Carolina, in the six years 1984–90, raised average scores on the Scholastic Aptitude Test by forty points. This was the highest average change among the sixteen states adopting comprehensive education reforms during the period.[35] In the same article, Governor Carroll A. Campbell Jr. was featured as one of "The Ten Education Governors." The state's partnership with business to improve literacy and job training, sponsored by Campbell, was ranked as the nation's most extensive.

The 1984 EIA was in full swing as Campbell became governor in 1987. As EIA provisions were being implemented, a new task force of business, industry, education, and legislative leaders began a new review of public education policy. This group's work was named the Thompson Report after its chair, Robert L. Thompson Jr., a business leader from Springs Industries, a major textile manufacturing firm in South Carolina. Since their recommendations stretched over the entire decade of the 1990s, the legislation was called Target 2000. It became law in June 1989.

Target 2000 is a master plan for continued reform. It extends some EIA programs, expands other programs, and focuses on new policy areas. One of the major new areas is dropout prevention. This initiative will be phased in over several years with the goal of reducing the state's dropout rate by 50 percent by the year 2000. Right now, about one out of three students drops out of high school before graduation. At a current annual rate of twenty thousand dropouts, there is potential for two hundred thousand high school dropouts during the 1990s. One additional idea, still pending before the legislature, would require a school-age person to have graduated or have regular school attendance as a requirement for a driver's license.

There is also a new emphasis on programs for early childhood education for four-year-olds with significant deficiencies. In mid-1989, eighty-six of the state's ninety-one school districts had early childhood development programs, which provide a half-day class for four-year-old children who are considered by officials to be at greatest risk of school failure. The results of the programs in place show that "at-risk" children who are in the programs perform just as well academically in the first and second grades as students considered to be less at risk. Although at-risk children are not forced to attend the development program, Target 2000 requires the five remaining districts to develop such programs and provides the funds for them. A supporting education program for parents of at-risk children through age five was to be implemented in every school district by 1993–94.

Additional Target 2000 programs stress development of higher-order thinking skills and promote arts education. Workers of the future will have to do more than make simple calculations or everyday judgments. They will have to be flexible, creative, and able to apply their knowledge to solve problems. The State Board of Education is presently defining standards by which to implement such higher-level skills as analysis, synthesis, and evaluation of information.

The future quality package includes teacher training, planned textbook selection, student achievement tests in new skills areas, and arts education. By 1995–96, every district must involve students in creating art, in making informal judgments about excellence in arts, and in understanding the historical and cultural background of works of art.

To make these new programs work more smoothly, there are provisions for flexible procedures for the schools that demonstrate outstanding performance. Competitive grants are available for schools with outstanding programs for improving instruction. Teaching and school leadership are advanced through designated centers at higher-education facilities in the state.

Public education improvement in South Carolina has been extensive. It has also enjoyed considerable support from business, parents, legislators, and the general public. There may be an unspoken agreement that better education is the only feasible route to improved quality of life and to relief from poverty. Old-time small farmers around the state have been heard to say, often with a shy pride about a daughter or son now in a professional job, "Children are about the only thing that ever grew well on this old worn-out land."

Higher Education

Higher education in South Carolina is traditionally decentralized, and its institutions have long and varied customs. For example, the University of South Carolina was founded in 1801 and soon operated as South Carolina College. It was closed during secession, opened and reclosed several times subsequently, and then reopened permanently in 1906 as a university. Today, its Columbia campus is connected to a statewide system that includes four-year campuses at Spartanburg and Aiken and other two-year and specialty campuses. The USC campus at Conway became Coastal Carolina University on July 1, 1993.

The state agricultural and mechanical college, today Clemson University, was opened in 1893 and designated as a university in 1964. Clemson is the major land-grant institution and houses the state extension service and the agricultural experiment stations. It was founded in the midst of the agricultural revolt and constitutional changes of the 1890s. Governor Tillman's faction advocated the new state college by opposing the "aristocratic" forces at the university in Columbia and the "dude factory" at The Citadel, the state military college founded in Charleston in 1842. Tillman's forces also saw to it that a training school for women was moved in 1895 from Columbia to Rock Hill as Winthrop College, now Winthrop University, and that a separate, coeducational state agricultural and mechanical college was founded for African Americans in 1896 at Orangeburg. Its name was changed to South Carolina State College in 1954 and to South Carolina State University in 1992.

There are still other higher-education institutions. The Medical University of South Carolina was begun in Charleston in 1824, although it did not receive significant state financing for almost a century. The oldest institution and the first municipal college in the United States is the College of Charleston, which was founded in 1770. The city of Charleston financed it in part after 1837, and Charleston County government lent support after women were admitted in 1918. The college became private again after World War II, but it was transferred to the state in 1970. There has been talk over the years of combining the Medical University in Charleston, The Citadel, and the College of Charleston into a major, comprehensive Low Country university. The institutions work together informally at present. Of major controversy is the maintenance of the male-only policy for the undergraduate military curriculum at The Citadel.

Among other state higher-education institutions are Francis Marion University in Florence and Lander University in Greenwood. There is also a state-financed tuition assistance program for resident students who attend one of the state's many private undergraduate colleges.

The politics of higher education in the past boiled down to the presence of "alumni" clubs in the state legislature. When one major school (Clemson, Carolina, or The Citadel) received an appropriation, the others lobbied hard for parity. State senator Edgar A. Brown became known as the Clemson sponsor; House Speaker Solomon Blatt had been a cheerleader as an undergraduate and was the Carolina sponsor; The Citadel Class of 1942 became its school's advocate, counting among its members governors Hollings and West. Questions of whether the state could afford so many facilities were raised by bold observers who thought it better to concentrate resources on one great state university. Political exclusion of African Americans and women in the legislature before the 1970s tended to leave South Carolina State and Winthrop without direct legislative advocates. The development of many new institutions and the reorganization and expansion of existing ones led the legislature to create the Commission on Higher Education as a statewide coordinating body in 1967.

The primary tool of the Commission on Higher Education is planning. If the commission is against the board of trustees of a specific college or university, it makes that board's task harder with the legislature. The commission develops and annually updates the South Carolina master plan for higher education. It "centralizes, without centralizing" higher-education funding by the recommendations in its annual plan. The commission collects data and conducts research to make proposals to the legislature and to budget makers about policies, roles, operations, and the structure of higher-education institutions.

The 1984 Education Improvement Act (EIA) involves colleges and universities in three ways. One is the loan program for prospective teachers, administered by the South Carolina Student Loan Corporation. About twelve hundred college students receive loans each year in order to study needed specialties in college and then to teach in areas in the state that need them.

The second involvement is through designated centers for excellence at selected public or private colleges. For example, Clemson University is a designated center for science and math education. Both South Carolina State University and Benedict College, a private undergraduate school in Columbia, have designated centers to improve recruitment of African American teacher candidates. Third, the state Commission on Higher Education is designated by the EIA as monitor for the effectiveness of the loan and recruitment programs.

In addition to coordinating parts of the EIA, the state Commission on Higher Education coordinates, more or less, the state's institutions of higher learning. A major recent commission initiative was *The Cutting Edge* legislation of 1988, requiring all institutions to maintain minimal admissions standards. The program also encourages research and academic excellence through endowed professorships, student scholarships, a research investment fund, and more intensive planning for student academic services policies such as admissions and course transfers.

Among postsecondary institutions, only the State Board for Technical and Comprehensive Education (TEC) is exempt from the minimal admissions requirements of *The Cutting Edge*. However, the Commission on Higher Education is working with the TEC system and its sixteen colleges and thirty-two thousand full-time-equivalent students to coordinate schedules and types of courses that may be transferred from TEC campuses to four-year institutions. A vital link in the state's economic development efforts, the TEC system emphasizes skills training for high school graduates or for adults in low-paying, unskilled jobs. It also emphasizes the upward mobility of its qualified students into the senior undergraduate colleges.

Health Care

Health-care administration includes a wide range of concerns and activities. The Department of Health and Environmental Control (DHEC) provides for the public health as well as the prevention, control, and reduction of pollution. Today, DHEC has an extensive program of health services provided through 15 health district offices, 46 county health departments, and 120 clinics. These programs include control of communicable diseases, immunization programs, evaluation of health hazards, and sanitation inspection. There are separate bureaus for maternal and child health services as well as for home health services and long-term care.[36]

A Basic Health-Care Problem: The Medically Indigent. Federal cuts in Aid to Families with Dependent Children (AFDC) coupled with rising unemployment in the early 1980s deprived many South Carolinians of public or private health care. In 1985, a family had to be enrolled in the AFDC program to be eligible for Medicaid. South Carolina covered only the "poorest of the poor"—a family of four could make no more than $229 per month to qualify. Newspapers carried horror stories of poor families who made $230 or more per month but who were turned away from health-care facilities because they could not pay their bills. Federal cuts made them ineligible for Medicaid, and unemployment cost them health insurance benefits.

The South Carolina Medically Indigent Assistance Act was passed by the General Assembly in 1985, with the specific purpose of increasing the use of medical care by the poor and near poor. It aims to reduce the health-care costs that hospitals shift to paying patients in order to recover the uncollected costs of caring for the poor. The act also adds provider accountability and cost containment and establishes a medically indigent database to aid future decisions.

Access to health care for the medically indigent is boosted in three ways. First, a large number—about forty-two thousand persons—were added to the state's AFDC rolls by raising the income limits. This had the effect of increasing the number of people eligible for Medicaid and thereby enhancing their access to primary care facilities. Second, a Medically Indigent Assistance Fund (MIAF) was created that pooled county government and general hospital funds to reimburse hospitals for care to persons who were not poor enough to qualify for AFDC or Medicaid programs but who did not have any money to pay their hospital bills. In 1989 the MIAF was converted to a Medicaid expansion fund. The state Health and Human Services Finance Commission administered the MIAF, and it continues to manage the new fund. Third, hospitals were prohibited by the act from denying emergency admissions based on ability to pay or county of residence because they were assured of recovery of some funds from the MIAF. Poor women in active childbirth labor were included in the definition of emergency.

Reports near the end of 1988 showed that about one-third of the state's population (one million people) would need health services through Medicaid, or they would be medically indigent. Presently, the number of patients who pay only part of their health-care bills or nothing at all is estimated to be about the same as the number who are assisted financially by Medicaid.

The South Carolina Health and Human Services Finance Commission has a bureau of health services. Its divisions manage numerous Medicaid programs. One division deals with pharmacy services and durable medical equipment, another with hospital care and physician services. The other units manage primary care, preventive care, and eligibility requirements for Medicaid coverage. Today, an individual or family has to be enrolled in one of eleven programs, including AFDC, to be eligible for Medicaid in South Carolina. Eligibility for AFDC is determined by another agency, the Department of Social Services.

Social Services

Social services is a broad term, and many agencies can be said to provide elements of them. Among them is the Department of Social Services. In 1992, the department's separate board was abolished and it was consolidated under the direct administration of the State Budget and Control Board. Since July 1993, the department has been run by a director who works at the pleasure of the governor. The department administers a long list of categorical programs under the general headings of self-sufficiency and children, family, and adult services.

A deputy commissioner heads each group of services. The deputy for self-sufficiency has an executive assistant for such work-support programs as food stamps and the work-incentive program, an executive assistant for child support enforcement, another for economic and medical support programs, and one more for administrative and management support. The AFDC program is in this last unit. While AFDC is administered by the state, actual services are delivered by the counties, as are food assistance programs and services for children, families, and adults. The department administers adoption and birth-parent services and child support enforcement through area offices. There is a rigorous emphasis on audits, compliance with regulations, and quality, which for the agency means "knowing the specifics of one's job and doing the job right the first time."[37]

The State Agency of Vocational Rehabilitation is run by a board of seven members with seven-year terms. One is at-large and one is from each congressional district; all are appointed by the governor and confirmed by the Senate. The agency dates from the federally funded efforts to retrain disabled World War I veterans for gainful employment.

South Carolina's effort began in 1927 under the state superintendent of education with vocational training schools in Greenville and Charleston. The separate state agency was created in 1957. Today, it operates eighteen area offices and a network of evaluation and rehabilitation centers. It determines an individual's eligibility for federal social security disability payments. The agency operates cooperative programs with school districts and other institutions across the state. It also runs a residential center for persons with severe disabilities as well as two residential alcohol rehabilitation centers.[38]

A separate state agency administers programs for sightless persons. The South Carolina Commission for the Blind was created in 1966 for the purposes of preventing blindness and of rehabilitating the legally blind and persons having eye conditions that will lead to blindness. This commission has its own vocational rehabilitation department and rehabilitation center.[39] Its seven members are selected in the same manner as the vocational rehabilitation's board, except the terms are for four years.

South Carolina's alcohol and drug abuse management programs started with a facility to treat alcoholics which opened in Florence in 1962. In 1966, a Commission on Alcoholism was created, but its treatment responsibilities reverted to the State Agency of Vocational Rehabilitation for a short time. In 1971, a separate state commissioner for narcotics and controlled substances was created in the governor's office to deal with substance abuse except for alcohol. The two offices were merged in 1974 under the direction of a board composed of eleven members appointed by the governor for four-year terms, one from each congressional district and one at-large. As of July 1, 1993, the agency director will be appointed and removed by the governor.

This agency makes extensive use of statewide advisory committees and its forty-six-county network of local authorities on alcohol and other drug abuse. The state agency approves county service plans. The county authorities are required statewide under 1973 legislation and financed by the minibottle bill passed in 1972. The minibottle, like the small bottle in which liquor is sold on airline flights, is the way South Carolina authorizes the sale of hard liquor. One-fourth of the minibottle revenues goes back to counties on a per capita basis to finance alcohol and drug abuse programs.[40]

There are also separate departments for mental health and for mental retardation. Each is governed by a seven-person commission. Mental health commissioners serve five-year terms. The Mental Health Department was first created in 1821, and the State Hospital was authorized by the General Assembly in 1827. Today, the Mental Health Department has jurisdiction over the state's mental hospitals as well as over the joint state- and community-sponsored mental health clinics and centers.

Mental retardation programs were part of the Mental Health Department until 1966. Governor Richard Manning launched an investigation in 1915 into the problems of the retarded, and in 1917 a special institution was authorized for the mentally retarded. It opened in Clinton in 1920 and was named the State Training School in 1922. Today, it is called the Whitten Center. A separate training school, built first for African Americans and now called the Midlands Center, was built in 1952. There are also centers in the Low Country and the Pee Dee and a network of more than one hundred community residences.

Cooperative programs were begun with the State Department of Public Welfare (now Department of Social Services) in 1937, with the state education department in the early 1950s, and with Vocational Rehabilitation in the early 1960s. President John F. Kennedy's emphasis on mental retardation planning, the availability of federal funds, and an influential association for retarded children in South Carolina all promoted the creation of a separate department in 1967. It claims to be the first independent state agency to serve people with mental retardation in the country.[41] In the 1993 restructuring legislation, the department was renamed Disabilities and Special Needs, and now includes the Division of Autism, formerly in the Department of Mental Health, as well as the state's unit for dealing with spinal and head injuries.

One other important social services agency is the South Carolina Commission on Aging. It serves the five hundred thousand South Carolinians who are over sixty years old, and it serves more specifically the older people with the greatest social, economic, or health needs. The agency started out in 1966 as an interagency council on aging to administer federally funded programs under the Older Americans Act of 1965. It became a state commission in 1971 but was transferred to the governor's office in the 1993 state agency restructuring.

This agency uses an "aging network" to develop programs and services. The state commission coordinates the area agencies on aging. The area agencies are coordinated with the ten multicounty regional councils of government (or COGS). The area agencies are public or private organizations designated by the state commission to receive funds. The area agencies then contract with local organizations to provide access services, community-based services such as adult day care, and in-home services such as home-delivered meals. The bodies with which the area agencies contract form the third level in the "aging network."[42]

AGENCY STRUCTURE IN TRANSITION

New state agency boards are created and old ones have been renewed and redefined by the legislature in response to new program challenges or opportunites. More than half of South Carolina's existing statewide boards and commissions have been created or significantly revised since 1960.[43] The continuing flowering of these boards gives the agency governing structures wide variety in size, number, and composition. As a result, there are over one hundred separate statewide boards and commissions supervising diverse and disjointed departments and agencies in South Carolina today.

Organizationally, the state's bureaucratic agencies are typically insulated from executive leadership regardless of size or importance. Three agencies account for over half of the comprehensively budgeted expenditures of the state—the education, social services, and transportation departments—but each is organized, financed, and administered differently. The transportation department traditionally uses only earmarked funds, and the Social Services Department is primarily dependent on federal funds approved by the Health and Human Services Finance Commission. Yet other agencies also perform significant functions. Some are large, such as the agencies that provide services to or regulate private businesses. Others, such as licensing agencies, are very small and may have little, if any, state appropriations.

Observers have frequently attempted to picture the array of state agencies through an organization chart. Even the "successful" attempts are confusing to many citizens because of the way the different boards and commissions are appointed. Even though these organization charts exist and the old system was simplified somewhat by the recent restructuring, students should probably study each agency specifically. Still, some general patterns do exist among the many agencies.

Types of Agencies

Single department heads represent one type of South Carolina government agency. The state constitution contains the authority for the election to four-year terms of a secretary of state, a treasurer, an attorney general, a comptroller general, a superintendent of education, a commissioner of agriculture, and an adjutant general. Except for the superintendent of education, each of these elected department heads serves and establishes his or her agency's policies without a board or commission.

Thirteen single-headed departments will exist in South Carolina after restructuring legislation is fully implemented July 1, 1995. Among them are eleven departments for which the governor hires and fires the agency director.[44] There are two other major single-headed departments. The chief of the State Law Enforcement Division (SLED) is named by the governor to a six-year term and removed only for cause. The governor names a director to a four-year term for the Department of Public Safety, again to be removed only for cause. Public safety includes the Highway Patrol, the law enforcement division of the Public Service Commission, the public safety division from the old highway department, and other law enforcement support units.

Boards and commissions are a second approach to the organization of a state government agency. Typically, the board or commission employs the agency director, sets and implements policy under the authority granted by state law, and provides overall and even day-to-day direction of agency operations. Almost all of the functions and operations of state government are administered in this way.

Board membership may be fashioned in a variety of ways. The Budget and Control Board is an example of the control of some very significant state functions by a board of executive and legislative officials. Other boards are made up of citizens and professionals who may be full-time or part-time. The Employment Security Commission and the Public Service Commission are examples of agencies with full-time board members who serve as both policymakers and administrators. These commissions usually have a hired top administrator, but the commissioners work far more than the monthly or quarterly meeting of a typical board. They may hold policy-making sessions or quasi-judicial hearings or engage in direct administrative actions. Two agencies, formerly with full-time boards, the Tax Commission and the Alcoholic Beverage Control (ABC) Commission, will have their major functions fully consolidated into the Department of Revenue and Taxation by 1995 when administrative law judges will assume responsibility for Tax Commission cases. SLED will enforce ABC laws.

Existing boards will take over departments for Disabilities and Special Needs (formerly Mental Retardation) and Natural Resources (formerly Wildlife Department). The governor names these board members at will, but the board hires the agency director. After July 1, 1994, a reorganized Department of Health and Environmental Control (DHEC) will direct its pollution enforcement work as well as regulatory functions formerly housed in the Land Resources Commission, the Water Resources Commission, the Coastal Council, and the Mining Council. Under the new legislative arrangements, DHEC board members will be appointed by the governor, but the board will appoint the agency director. The Senate as well as the governor must approve the hiring of a specific director, and the governor may prevent the board from firing a director in office.

The board arrangement is more complicated for the Department of Transportation. The governor appoints the board chair, but legislators appoint the six board members, and the board names the executive director.

The many licensing boards are typically composed of individuals engaged in the field being licensed. The General Assembly usually lets the members of the profession or trade group determine the persons who sit on the licensing board. The administrative aspects of these boards will be managed by the head of a Department of Labor, Licensing, and Regulation to be hired and fired by the governor.

State boards and commissions are created and changed by the General Assembly through statutes that define the mission and features of the organization and the authority that appoints the board. About all that can be said regarding the structure of a board is that the sponsors of the legislation favored the organizational framework enacted at the time. Often, the structure that exists results from a negotiated agreement among the major parties at the time of the agency's creation. Upon major revisions in agency operations, the new structure is similarly negotiated.

The boards and commissions do share some general features. Most are arranged according to two basic geographic patterns: (1) membership based on the sixteen judicial circuits, which results in a large board, or (2) membership based on the six congressional districts, which produces a smaller board.

Regardless of size, often a board will have an additional member designated without regard to judicial circuit or congressional district. This statewide person may act as chairperson. The additional member may also offset or prevent the imbalance of board pursuits if a representative from one district becomes too ambitious and tries to take charge. The absence of obvious preference or bias may be necessary to promote elite cohesion and to let the board work without appearing to favor a specific person or region of the state.

Past Reorganization Efforts

Senator John Drummond (*D*-Greenwood), former chair of the State Reorganization Commission and current chair of the Senate Finance Committee, summarizes the different types of reorganization in South Carolina over the years:

(1) We have had process change, and by that, I mean we have changed the way we operate without making major changes in the structure;
(2) We have had changes in response to specific issues, and this had to do largely with the way agencies deal with each other; and

(3) We have had structural change designed to meet the needs of a given time in our history, and I think that is what we are seeing today.[45]

The impetus for recent efforts to restructure state government can be traced, in part, to the appearance of "out-of-control" management at two of the most stable agencies, the highway department and the University of South Carolina. In December 1988, the commander of the State Highway Patrol was forced from office for helping a fellow officer, the local FBI chief, avoid arrest for driving under the influence of alcohol. The president of the university resigned in May 1989 and was subsequently prosecuted for misdirecting university funds. Then came the announcement of Operation Lost Trust in August 1990. In 1992, several commissioners of the state Alcoholic Beverage Control Commission were prosecuted for taking gifts of significant value from the businesses they were regulating.

In the aftermath of Operation Lost Trust, the *State* newspaper in Columbia and other newspapers across the state carried either editorials or feature stories that called for reform through restructuring. The most extensive effort was the *State*'s "Power Failure" series that ran for nine months.[46] It was a series of in-depth studies that advocated more accountable structure and conduct in state and local government.

Political energy for comprehensive restructuring of the executive branch to improve agency governance has also come through gubernatorial leadership. In his 1991 State of the State Address, Governor Campbell emphasized accountability and announced an executive order that created a commission to study and propose a plan for comprehensive restructuring to improve state agency accountability. The governor also proposed a ten-cabinet department plan.[47]

The Commission on Government Restructuring was cochaired by Lieutenant Governor Nick A. Theodore (*D*-Greenville) and the chair of the House judiciary committee, Representative David Wilkins (*R*-Greenville). The commission had thirty-eight members drawn from the legislature, agency boards, professional educators, political organizations, and businesses. Their objectives stressed the "principles of public administration" as they began their work around March 1, 1991.

The Commission on Government Restructuring recommended a fifteen-department cabinet system and a long-term implementation timetable. It proposed that the legislature approve a 1992 referendum that would amend the state constitution by providing for up to fifteen executive departments. Also, it proposed that the referendum include questions that would allow the adjutant general, the superintendent of education, and the commissioner of agriculture to be appointed by the governor rather than elected by popular vote. The legislature did not permit the referendum.

Restructuring legislation began to gain momentum before the 1992 elections. The pattern of corruption so often decried by the governor and the media continued, with new incidents in the highway department and the Alcoholic Beverage Control Commission. A new pattern of election districts was put into place after the 1990 census. Many incumbent legislators as well as challengers ran on the restructuring theme. Forty-three first-year legislators were elected.

The momentum began to be evident through fiscal problems. State revenue estimates for the previous year were too high, just as they had been in the several prior fiscal years. The budget cuts caused by the lack of revenue gave the impression that the budget was as out of control as the structure of state government seemed to be. Reorganizing state government began to take root when House Ways and Means chairman William D. Boan (D, District 44, Lancaster County) energized the committee to connect its annual debate about increases in taxes to budget reform and increased efficiencies in government. A bill reducing the number of agencies from seventy-six to thirteen passed in special session June 14. It was signed by the governor June 18, and many provisions went into effect July 1, 1993.

CONCLUSION

The structures and functions of bureaucratic agencies need frequent updating as program tasks are revised or activities evaluated and renewed. Politicians, scholars, interest groups, and clients tend to blend the range of logical possibilities among policies and structures into a menu of choices from which political decision makers may select the most agreeable ones.

The general public, business, and political interest groups have played major roles in formulating legislative proposals for major improvements in program areas such as economic development, education, and medical indigency. Political involvement and practical necessity have undergirded public acceptance. To accept these many changes, the traditionalistic political culture has been reassured that South Carolina's reform is thoroughly monitored to prevent waste or bureaucratic overload.

The winds of change that refocused and restructured South Carolina government in the 1890s blew the Confederate war hero General Wade Hampton and his followers out of politics. The possibility of restoring a decentralized planter aristocracy went out with him, but not the ideals of a decentralized elite. Under Tillman's leadership, they were replaced by a new governing elite that maintained its influence over agency policies and functions through a divided, locally controlled governmental structure.

It will probably take a legislative revolution of Tillmanlike proportions to truly reform South Carolina agency structure. The aims of reformers stem from the application of basic principles of public administration that have been known and used for a long time, but reformers must also relate to the political realities of the day. To focus the appointment of administrators with organized responsibilities into specific functional areas, today's numerous and scattered state agencies would have to be reconcentrated and reorganized into executive, cabinet-type agencies. The legislature made a giant step in that direction in 1993, by recombining many state agencies into a smaller number of new departments. Continuing decentralization, especially in major agencies for education and transportation, maintains a challenge for advocates of streamlined governmental structures and coordinated agency functions.

CHAPTER TEN

The Judiciary

The study of state judicial systems in the South has not been a thriving enterprise.[1] In general, southern state court systems, much like their executive and legislative counterparts, have lagged behind nonsouthern states in terms of professional development. For example, Henry Glick and Kenneth Vines's 1973 study of state court systems ranked only one southern state (North Carolina) in the top thirty on a legal professionalism scale, while seven of the bottom ten states were southern.[2] In this study, South Carolina ranked forty-first.

The southern states have generally updated their judicial system structures and developed greater professionalism among judges and court managers. As these changes have occurred, their judicial systems now more closely approximate systems in other states. In particular, judicial reform gathered momentum throughout the United States during the 1960s and 1970s. Reform generally resulted in a more rational and efficient unified court structure in states across the country. South Carolina became a part of the reform movement in the 1970s.

In 1975, the South Carolina judicial system was described by the state Supreme Court as "a hodgepodge of courts, lacking in uniformity and consistency."[3] This condition resulted from the large number of independent, limited-jurisdiction courts created over the years by the General Assembly because of local demand. These courts had overlapping functions and inconsistent standards. They reflected the prevailing practice of legislative response to specific local pressures.

A 1956 study revealed extraordinary variety in South Carolina's courts. For example, the Marlboro County court could hear only civil cases with suits involving claims of seventy-five hundred dollars or less while its counterpart in Spartanburg County could handle both criminal cases and civil cases up to eleven thousand dollars. In addition, of the six types of trial courts in existence at the time (Magisterial, Municipal, Probate, Domestic Relations and Children's, County, and Circuit), not one of the sixteen judicial districts had all six types. Furthermore, the pattern of appeal varied from one judicial circuit to the next.[4]

The task of educating lawyers and judges for such diversity and the public perception of fairness across judicial circuits made the decentralized judicial system a target of reform. The first reform move took place in 1972 when voters approved a revised version of the judicial article of the state constitution. The most significant part of revised Article V was the proviso that "the judicial power of the state be vested in a unified judicial system which shall include a Supreme Court, a Circuit Court and other such courts of limited jurisdiction as may be provided by general law."[5] Other courts were allowed to operate until the article was implemented.

The result was a major political battle within the General Assembly and between the General Assembly and the Supreme Court over the creation of a new unified court system. For example, reforms recommended in a 1974 report by a special committee of the legislature were rejected by the General Assembly because they went too far. Then, in 1975, the Supreme Court struck down twenty-nine statutes passed by the General Assembly, finding that the statutes did not conform with the constitutional requirement in Article V for a unified judicial system.

In its 1975 reforms, the legislature had created new local courts, modified the functions of Probate Courts, and increased the number of state judges. However, the Supreme Court had a political mind of its own, perhaps amplified by the fact that judicial circuit boundaries were so similar to legislative representation boundaries and the feeling that only the most reputable legislators should get to serve as judges.

Finally, in 1976, the General Assembly enacted a unified court structure to become effective July 1, 1977. The legislation also stipulated that county courts and other courts inferior to the Circuit Courts be phased out by July 1, 1979, and that the jurisdiction be absorbed into the unified court system.

As this new structure was implemented, a struggle broke out between the General Assembly and the judicial branch for control over management and rule making for the unified judicial system. The centerpiece of the argument was the new Court of Appeals. It was created by the legislature on a temporary basis in 1979, and the legislature appointed four of its members to seats on the new court. The Supreme Court declared this unconstitutional, since another statute prevented a legislator from assuming a position that the legislator had helped create.

The status of the Court of Appeals wobbled along until it was approved in a constitutional referendum in 1984 and made permanent by legislative ratification in 1985. Since then, the General Assembly has given up trying to dominate management of the judicial system. There is an occasional flare-up, however. In 1993 a legislator raised questions about the travel vouchers of the chief justice of the state Supreme Court.

THE JUDICIAL STRUCTURE

The Supreme Court

The Supreme Court is South Carolina's highest court. It has a chief justice and four associate justices, all elected by the legislature for staggered terms of ten years and all eligible for reelection. The justices must be United States citizens, citizens of the state for five years, at least twenty-six years old, and licensed attorneys for at least five years. In 1994, salaries for associate justices were $97,042 ($102,148 for the chief justice). While the Supreme Court has both original and appellate jurisdiction, it generally functions as an appellate court. The court normally meets two or three weeks each month.

When the intermediate Court of Appeals first began operating in 1983, the Supreme Court reserved exclusive jurisdiction over cases on certiorari from the Court of Appeals. The Supreme Court also kept jurisdiction over five classes of appeals directly from the Circuit and Family courts. The five classes are (1) cases involving the death penalty, (2) public utility rates, (3) significant constitutional issues, (4) public bond issues, and (5) election laws.[6] Other appeals from both the Circuit and Family courts are apportioned between the Court of Appeals and the Supreme Court. The decisions of the Supreme Court are based on lower court transcripts, briefs, and oral arguments. The final function of the Supreme Court is to make rules for the unified judicial structure, to oversee admissions to the South Carolina Bar, and to discipline members of the Bar.

The workload of the state Supreme Court is exceptionally heavy. For example, in 1989 the court had a total of 1,471 cases pending, including 215 cases ready for consideration (all briefs filed), 268 cases docketed but awaiting one or more briefs, and 988 cases awaiting docketing in various stages. In 1990 the court disposed of 537 cases—359 unpublished opinions and 178 published opinions. The reversal rate of lower court decisions by the Supreme Court is almost 40 percent.[7]

Court of Appeals

Many states have recently created an intermediate court of appeals. South Carolina's Court of Appeals was initially created by Act 164 in 1979 and began operation September 1, 1983. It consists of a chief judge and five associate judges who are elected by the legislature to staggered terms of six years each. In 1994, salaries were $92,190 for associate justices and $96,060 for the chief judge. The court normally sits in panels of three, although it may sit as a whole. Its jurisdiction includes appeals on questions of law and equity arising from the Circuit and Family courts other than the five classes of cases that continue to be reviewed by the Supreme Court. The Court of Appeals was created in order to reduce the state Supreme Court's caseload. In 1990, 378 cases were scheduled for hearing during the year, and the court made 148 regular opinions and 188 unpublished rulings.

In its first seven years, the appeals court reversed, vacated, or remanded 46 percent of the cases assigned to it.[8] In general, the decisions of the three-person panels have been unanimous: in only 2.8 percent of cases has there been a dissenting opinion. Approximately 33 percent of the cases that have come before the Court of Appeals have involved private economic relations; about 25 percent involve divorce, child custody, inheritance, or probate; and 19 percent involve tort actions.[9] These are typically less interesting, more technical cases that the state Supreme Court does not wish to hear.

Circuit Courts

The Circuit Courts are South Carolina's major trial courts of general jurisdiction. They consist of sixteen judicial circuits, which range in size from two to four counties each. There are forty judges, thirty of which are elected by the General Assembly from the sixteen judicial circuits and ten of which are elected from the state at-large. Each circuit has at least one resident circuit judge who maintains an office in his or her home county. The judges serve the sixteen circuits on a rotating basis. Court terms and assignments are determined by the chief justice based upon the court administrator's recommendations. Judges serve six-year terms with a 1994 annual salary of $92,190.

Circuit Courts are divided into Civil Court, the Court of Common Pleas, and the Court of General Sessions. Civil cases exceeding twenty-five hundred dollars in value are heard by the Civil Court and/or the Court of Common Pleas, while criminal cases involving possible penalties of more than two hundred dollars or thirty days in jail are heard by the General Sessions courts.

By 1989, the number of cases filed in General Sessions courts had more than tripled since 1978, while the number of cases filed in Common Pleas courts had doubled. This resulted in a request by then–chief justice George T. Gregory Jr. for nine new circuit judgeships in 1990. He noted that South Carolina judges disposed of an average of thirty-six hundred cases each year, an increase of 50 percent over seven years earlier.[10] Justice Gregory later noted that judges had to cancel common pleas (civil court) in order to dispose of the general sessions (criminal) cases. This was due to changes in state criminal law that resulted in more trials.[11] The General Assembly approved the funding for the additional judges in 1991, raising the number of judges to the presently authorized number of forty.

Master-in-Equity

The Master-in-Equity deals with cases referred by the Circuit Court. A Master-in-Equity has limited jurisdiction but operates hearings like a regular court, except that no jury is used.[12] The jurisdiction of the Master-in-Equity is limited to matters in equity law, which is designed to provide a means by which a court can order decisions in matters not covered by ordinary legal procedures. For example, a Master may issue an injunction to prevent the sale of property over which ownership is in doubt. In some cases, Masters may conduct sales. Final orders based on reports rendered by the Masters are generally executed by circuit judges, and appeals of Masters' decisions generally go to the Circuit Court.

At present, South Carolina has twenty Masters-in-Equity. They are appointed by the governor for four-year terms with the advice and consent of the General Assembly.

The Family Court

The uniform statewide Family Court system was established in 1976. These courts have exclusive jurisdiction over cases involving domestic and family relations, including marriage, divorce, legal separation, custody, visitation rights, termination of parental rights, adoption, support, division of marital property, and change of name.[13] Family Courts also normally have jurisdiction over minors under the age of seventeen who have violated state laws or municipal ordinances. Cases involving traffic or fish-and-game law violations may be heard in Magisterial Courts, Municipal Courts, or (in the case of serious criminal charges), Circuit Courts.

The Family Court's jurisdiction corresponds with the territorial boundaries of the state's sixteen judicial circuits. It consists of forty-six judges who rotate primarily from county to county within their circuits. However, the chief justice may assign a judge to other circuits, depending on caseload requirements. Family Court judges are elected by the General Assembly for four-year terms. The 1994 salary level was $82,968. Almost all Family Court expenses are met by state funds.

The Magisterial Courts

The Magisterial Courts constitute the second level in South Carolina's court system. Magistrates are appointed for four-year terms by the governor upon the advice and consent of the Senate. In reality, the state senators choose the magistrates and the governor's approval is routine. Magistrates are not required to be attorneys and most are not. They receive their legal training through a magistrate's benchbook distributed by the state Supreme Court. There are 297 magistrates in South Carolina; the number in each county varies from 2 to 19. Their jurisdiction is countywide and extends over criminal offenses for which the penalty is a fine of two hundred dollars or less or imprisonment of thirty days or less.

The Magisterial Courts handle more cases than any other court level in South Carolina (approximately 775,000 cases). In fact, in 1989 57 percent of all dispositions were in these courts. The largest percentage of criminal cases in Magisterial Courts are traffic related (64 percent in 1989). Most criminal cases result in conviction. In 1989, 91 percent were convictions, 5 percent were nonconvictions, and 4 percent were either dismissed or transferred.[14] Magistrates are also responsible for civil cases in which the contested amount is twenty-five hundred dollars or less.

Magistrates are an important component in the early stages of the judicial process for arrested felons. Upon arrest, accused individuals are brought before magistrates for preliminary hearings. At that time, magistrates will determine if there is "probable cause" to hold the accused for trial. Magistrates also determine bail and issue arrest and search warrants.

The salaries of magistrates (which average $22,000) are paid by the counties, which are also responsible for providing them space, equipment, and staff.[15] Fines and other fees generated by these courts are partially refunded to the counties. Operating costs for Magisterial Courts just about doubled during the 1980s. They went from $7,751,995 for 1982–83 to $14,113,790 for 1989–90. Revenues increased almost 150 percent during the same period, going from $14,597,276 to $36,493,391.

Municipal Courts

A uniform system of Municipal Courts was established by legislation passed by the General Assembly in 1980. This statute repealed all other statutes that had created a variety of Municipal Courts in previous years. The municipal judges are chosen by the local governing bodies and, like magistrates, municipal judges are not required to be lawyers. The jurisdiction of Municipal Courts is narrowly defined to include only criminal offenses of both state law and municipal ordinances, not exceeding a fine of two hundred dollars or imprisonment of more than thirty days. The municipality within which the court operates is responsible for housing and funding for its court. In return, a municipality receives all its court's fines and fees.

Municipal Court filings have substantially increased during the last decade from 248,095 filings in 1980 to 394,916 in 1989. Approximately two-thirds of these cases are for traffic violations. Overall, approximately one-third of the trial court caseload for the state is handled by Municipal Courts. Operating costs for these courts have more than doubled since 1982–83. Total reported operating costs then were $2,265,120; for 1989–90, they totaled $5,714,972.[16] Revenues collected have shown a corresponding increase from $9,471,759 for 1982–83 to $20,078,166 for 1989–90.

The Probate Court

Each county has a Probate Court, with jurisdiction over marriage licenses, estates of deceased persons, guardianships of incompetents, conservatorships of estates for minors and incompetents, and involuntary commitments of mentally ill and/or chemically dependent persons.[17] Probate judges, who need not be lawyers, are elected in countywide partisan elections to four-year terms. Judges' salaries and most court expenses are county obligations.

THE DYNAMICS OF JUDICIAL CHANGE

One result of state court reform during the 1960s and 1970s was the creation of offices of court administration. The need for court administrators developed after court systems began to require sound business management practices in order to carry out their responsibilities. The office of South Carolina Court Administration was established in 1973 under the authority of the new judicial article. The article stated that the chief justice would appoint a court administrator along with the staff deemed necessary by the chief justice to assist in court operations.

The state court administrator serves as the director of the office of South Carolina Court Administration, and the office functions as the administrative staff for the chief justice. The duties of this office include the responsibility of recommending to the chief justice the scheduling of terms of Circuit Court and Family Court and the assignment of judges to preside over these terms, the supervision of the administration of the courts and their support personnel, the collection of caseload information, the analysis of proposed administrative or procedural rule changes, the conduct of mandatory legal education programs for summary court judges, and the administration of the Defense of Indigents Fund and the Judicial Commitment Fund.[18]

During its first decade of existence, the Court Administrator's office developed uniform policies concerning record keeping. Uniform records not only created a mechanism for compiling statistical data, but they have made possible the efficient tracking of cases throughout the judicial system as well.[19]

Although the reform effort has led to an explicit grant of authority to the state Supreme Court, the South Carolina General Assembly has been reluctant to relinquish its traditional role in establishing policy for the state court system. For example, in a 1979 case, the Supreme Court ruled that a statute allowing the legislature to require Circuit Court judges to preside over certain hearings held before the Public Service Commission infringed upon the judicial department and limited the chief justice's authority to use judges for judicial duty as required by Article V.[20] The chair of the Senate Judiciary Committee is said to have responded, "I think there has been a tendency on the part of the Supreme Court to carry this court reform too far."[21]

Perhaps the best illustration of the conflict between the new centralized court system and the General Assembly took place when the General Assembly, upon the recommendation of the chief justice, created the state Court of Appeals to help the Supreme Court with a growing number of appeals. Once created, the General Assembly elected four seated members of the legislature to the five-member panel. The Supreme Court, however, ruled that the appointments were illegal because of a statute that prohibited a seated legislator from being elected to an office created while serving in the General Assembly.

The Supreme Court used this decision to assert its authority over the General Assembly in establishing the creation of judicial rules and procedures. In particular, the Supreme Court found that two provisions of the statute that created the court—one that empowered the chief judge of the Court of Appeals to order circuit judges to sit with the Court of Appeals and one that allowed the Court of Appeals to prescribe the manner in which its records would be kept—were in conflict with the concept of the unified judicial system established by Article V and approved by the voters through constitutional referendum.[22]

Instead of appointing other nonlegislators as judges, the General Assembly made several other attempts to reassert its authority in the judicial field. First, it refused to allocate funds for the court's operation. Then in 1981 the General Assembly proposed legislation to create the Court of Appeals by a constitutional referendum that would have allowed the legislative body to intrude into the Supreme Court's rule-making authority. The General Assembly also proposed legislation to add seats to Supreme Court. Neither proposal passed.

A compromise was finally worked out in 1983 whereby the Court of Appeals was established by statute for a two-year period, and the voters would decide in a 1984 constitutional referendum whether the Court of Appeals would become permanent. The General Assembly also proposed the creation of a twelve-member rule-making commission to consider and propose rules of practice and procedure for the court system that would have, in effect, negated the Supreme Court's role as a centralized administrative and rule-making authority. The voters approved the appeals court and disapproved the rule-making commission. The legislature ratified the referendum and included a permanent Court of Appeals in the state's constitution on July 1, 1985.

Although a unified court system has been formally created, the South Carolina court system is plagued by a lack of financial support. A U.S. Department of Justice study ranked South Carolina fiftieth in the nation in the amount of money appropriated to operate the judicial system,[23] and South Carolina had the highest caseload per judge of any southeastern state.

Supreme Court chief justice David Harwell was elected in 1991. He immediately called for a massive budget increase for the court system, saying that it was so underfunded that justices did not even have access to a fax machine! Harwell proposed a $3.8 million budget boost to the judiciary's $27 million budget, as well as seventeen new employees to get out of the "yellow pad and pencil era."[24] Half of the proposed increase was earmarked for a computer system to modernize and make the court system more efficient. For example, this would allow the chief justice to better utilize judges throughout the state instead of having to wait for yearly reports to ascertain where problems were. In a period of general state fiscal problems, however, Harwell's requests were not met.

The state Supreme Court has been instrumental in realizing significant changes in judicial structure, but its record in judicial decision making attracts some criticism. Former chief justice of the Court of Appeals Alex Sanders summed it up as follows:

> In some cases, the Supreme Court makes law. In other cases, the Court merely applies law. In some cases, the Court invents law. In other cases, the Court discovers law. In some cases, the Court defers to other authority. In other cases, the Court does not. Who decides what the Court does and when? The Court itself decides, and that is the scary part.[25]

In late 1992, Sanders wrote about an opinion, *Langley v. Boyter,* that he composed while on the Court of Appeals. He cited more than one hundred cases from all fifty states, three territories, and seven foreign countries. He read more than three thousand pages of text materials and quoted numerous legal scholars. His final brief reduced and distilled "2,000 years of accumulated legal wisdom to 24 single-spaced pages," and yet the South Carolina Supreme Court reversed his opinion in one paragraph.[26] Most decisions of the South Carolina Supreme Court are short. An activist and scholarly court it is not.

JUDICIAL SELECTION AND COMPOSITION

South Carolina, Connecticut, Rhode Island, and Virginia are the only states featuring legislative elections for some or all of its judges. The major criticism of legislative election is that accountability is minimal, since the public has little or no role in either choosing or reelecting judges. Not all the systems are the same. In Connecticut, judicial candidates are nominated by the governor and approved by the legislature. Rhode Island does not elect trial court judges. South Carolina selects a high proportion of former legislators to judgeships.

Chief Justice David Harwell wants to modify the selection and reappointment of judges by using the South Carolina Bar to pass on judicial candidates and by adding nonlawyers to the judicial screening committee. The South Carolina Bar has suggested a merit plan that would include a screening of prospective judges by a panel of legislators, gubernatorial appointees, and lawyers. Candidates would be evaluated by the committee and rated by the Bar. The General Assembly would make the final selection, and candidates would not be allowed to campaign within the legislature for support. Chances for passage of this plan, however, are not good at the present time. Unlike the General Assembly, the judicial system has not experienced a public scandal to motivate prospective changes. Reform in South Carolina seems likely to be spurred as much by the pressure of scandal or budgetary necessity as by reform ideals. This is consistent with the traditionalistic political culture rooted in South Carolina's past.

During the 1993 legislative session, the South Carolina Bar Association rated judicial candidates on its own. In a contested race for a Court of Appeals position, the Bar rated a seated legislator as unqualified. He was narrowly defeated by Carol Conner, a seated circuit judge with five years' experience on the court. She became the first woman on the state Court of Appeals.

Today, the major criterion for selection to a judgeship appears to be service as a legislator, which may have little direct connection to the position's demands.[27] In South Carolina, the proportion of judges who have served in the legislature is exceptionally high. For example, in 1993 all five members of the state Supreme Court had served in the legislature, as had twenty-five of the forty circuit judges. The courts are also dominated by older, white Protestant males. The first woman elected to the state Supreme Court was chosen in 1988 and the first African American in 1985. The average age of the Supreme Court judges is sixty. The six-judge Court of Appeals now has one female and one African American. Their average age is fifty-five. Of the forty sitting Circuit Court justices, two are African American and one is female; their average age is fifty-one. Only one South Carolina judge, from the Circuit Court level to the Supreme Court, lists a religious preference other than Protestant.

South Carolina judges are also products of the state's educational system. Of the forty circuit judges, only six received their undergraduate education outside South Carolina, including the two African Americans. Only one graduated from a college outside the South. Thirty-eight received their law degrees from the University of South Carolina. The only non-USC-educated lawyers are the two African American judges, who hold degrees from Yale and from the now-closed law school at South Carolina State. On the six-person Court of Appeals are five South Carolina–educated undergraduates. Four of the six members graduated from the University of South Carolina Law School, one from Mercer University (Georgia), and one from Harvard. Finally, the Supreme Court consists of three persons who graduated from in-state schools. Four of the five justices received their legal training in South Carolina, three from the University of South Carolina and one from the now-closed law school at predominately African American South Carolina State College. One judge graduated from Duke University School of Law.

Thus, demographically, South Carolina judges closely correspond to the findings on the background characteristics of state judiciaries in the South. The courts are a stronghold of white, middle-aged or older, male Democrats who have close ties to the state in which they serve.

CRIME AND PUNISHMENT IN SOUTH CAROLINA

The 1970s and 1980s saw a dramatic increase in reported crime in South Carolina. Between 1970 and 1980, the state's crime rate rose from 2,067 "index crimes" per 100,000 residents to 5,439 crimes per 100,000, an increase of 163 percent.[28] By 1993, South Carolina was sentencing persons for criminal offenses at a rate of 484 state and federal prisoners per 100,000 people, the highest rate in the nation. Overall, the state had more than doubled its annual admissions rate from 5,000 inmates in the early 1980s to more than 11,000 by the early 1990s.[29] In June 1993, the prisons held 17,050 persons. Two new state prisons have been built recently at a cost of $80 million, one in Turbeville (Clarendon County) and one in Ridgeville (Jasper County). Simultaneously, the legislature balked at spending $10 million to hire correctional officers to staff them.[30]

In general, South Carolinians have adopted a "get-tough" attitude about criminals and punishment. This attitude is reflected in the treatment of the accused as well as in the incarceration rate for the state.

Indigent defendants receive counsel in one of two ways. One is by public defender corporations, which are state-approved legal offices funded through payments from a state fund. The other is by private attorneys appointed by the court and paid by the Defense of Indigents Fund. Public defender corporations are found in thirty-eight counties; eight use court-appointed attorneys.

Public defenders in the state are generally inexperienced, overworked, and underpaid. The largest percentage of public defenders are new lawyers who take the position in order to get experience. After a year or so, they leave. Because of their commitment to working long hours for low pay, lawyers remaining in public defender positions for a time are frequently referred to as "renegades."

In South Carolina, each public defender handles an average of almost five hundred cases a year, or about three hundred more than is recommended by the National Study Commission on Criminal Justice Standards.[31] According to a study by the South Carolina Bar, caseloads for public defenders in the state vary from approximately two hundred to nine hundred per person. Because of this caseload, public defenders seldom visit clients more than once or twice before they appear in court and often never meet the family of defendants until the trial. In fact, it is not unusual for public defenders to have to try two cases back-to-back in the same week of court.

In addition to the heavy caseload, the compensation for public defenders in South Carolina is among the lowest in the United States. Public defenders in South Carolina receive about half of the national average. For example, court-appointed attorneys receive ten dollars an hour for out-of-court work and fifteen dollars an hour for in-court work.[32] These figures were set in 1969. The maximum fee for death penalty cases is five thousand dollars. In December 1992, however, the state Supreme Court ruled that counties should help pay attorneys' fees in death penalty cases involving indigent defendants and that the law limiting fees to five thousand dollars governs only the state's share of the cost. Some observers feel that this will result in fewer death penalty cases inasmuch as the counties will be unable to afford the costs that may result from prosecuting a capital charge.

Support services for public defenders are also lacking. For example, in Charleston County, eleven public defenders share three investigators, one secretary, and a copying machine. The legal library is outdated and does not include sourcebooks on federal law, and no facsimile machine is available.

In 1989, a bill was introduced in the General Assembly to create a statewide public defender system, double the amount of funding, and increase the staffing by one-third. However, the legislation was not enacted. Jeffrey Bloom, president of the Public Defenders Association of South Carolina, feels that South Carolina is headed for a federal suit if the state does not revamp its public defender system. This position is echoed by former association president Patterson McWhirter. Said McWhirter, "I think it is a last resort. Nobody wants to sue their state. They want their state to do what it's supposed to do. They want to assume their representatives are responsible individuals."[33]

With the system stacked against indigent defendants it is not surprising that South Carolina has one of the highest incarceration rates nationwide. For example, in the United States in 1980 the number of prisoners with sentences of more than one year per hundred thousand residents was slightly higher than two hundred, while the figure for South Carolina was over three hundred. In addition, once imprisoned, inmates were less and less likely to have their sentences reduced by parole. For example, from the mid-1970s to 1985–86, the percentage of parole applications approved dropped from 58.4 percent to 27.5 percent.[34]

All of this has led to rapid increases in prison population and overcrowding. The average inmate population increased from 2,705 in 1971 to 8,865 in 1980. By that time, the South Carolina prisons, on average, housed 52 percent more inmates than they were designed to accommodate.[35] In addition, the prison system was receiving a net increase of 110 prisoners a month by mid-1986, more than double the projected figure. Although funding for the Department of Corrections has more than doubled over the last ten years, overcrowding may prompt continued litigation against the state's prison system.

In response to the problems of the South Carolina prison system and to a 1982 suit filed by a prison inmate, Governor Riley presented a package of proposals to the General Assembly in March 1985. His proposals were directed toward alleviating prison overcrowding, increasing support for efforts at crime prevention, and reforming sentencing.

However, an anticrime organization called Citizens Against Violent Crime (CAVE) lobbied for tougher restrictions on individuals convicted of violent crimes. For example, in its final form, the bill they supported required that persons convicted of murder in which one or more aggravating circumstances were present must receive either the death sentence or life in prison without possibility of parole until the service of thirty years (twenty for other murder convictions). Individuals convicted of a violent crime while in possession of a gun or knife may receive a nonparolable consecutive or concurrent five-year sentence. Parole hearings for inmates convicted of violent crimes would be held every other year, not annually; a two-thirds vote (not a simple majority) of the parole board would be required for approval; there would be no release on supervised furlough; there would be no release under emergency powers provisions applied to prison overcrowding; there would be no participation allowed in the community penalties plan; and there would be no reduction in sentence for taking education courses. Inmates convicted twice for violent crimes would not be eligible for parole.[36]

The result was a bill that added to prison overcrowding rather than alleviating it. Since 1986, South Carolina has had to release low-risk inmates on several occasions. Seven new prisons have been built by the state, and between bonded indebtedness and operating costs, each of these prisons may cost the state over three hundred million dollars over a thirty-year period.[37] The average cost of constructing a prison cell is about fifty thousand dollars, and the annual cost of maintaining an inmate is about twenty-five thousand dollars.[38]

While uniform sentencing guidelines for use by state judges have been explored, they have not yet been adopted. Despite the concern for the mismatch between the outflow of the judicial system and the capacity of the corrections system, progress toward better coordination between these two systems in South Carolina, as in many states, has been glacial. The state's failure to address adequately and forcefully the problem of crime and prison overcrowding will result in a continuation of a costly process for the citizens of South Carolina for the foreseeable future.

CONCLUSION

The judicial branch has experienced the least change in South Carolina and remains the most traditionalistic component of state government. The major actors in South Carolina's judicial system are entrenched in the traditionalistic political culture. The state's judges are overwhelmingly white, male, and Protestant, and they are products of the state's educational and political system. In fact, only four judges among the fifty-one judgeships from the Circuit Court level on up were educated in law schools outside the state. While women and African Americans are now beginning to be selected to judicial positions, the method of selection and the longevity of judicial tenure in South Carolina suggest that South Carolina's judicial system may experience greater institutional lag than the other branches of state government.

The development of the judicial system corresponds to similar developments in other states and also to the rapid economic development that has occurred in South Carolina over the last twenty-five years. Court filings in the Court of General Sessions have more than tripled from 1978 to 1989, while filings in the Court of Common Pleas have more than doubled during the same period. The court system is overburdened with the increase in criminal cases and yet the response to this situation has been slow. Recently retired Supreme Court chief justice George T. Gregory Jr. noted that the lack of a sufficient number of judges was the biggest problem in state courts. Justice Gregory reflected that "whatever you accomplish really is by the power of persuasion" and that "South Carolina's judicial system is the least-funded in the nation."[39]

The creation of the Court of Appeals reflects a response to modernization as well as the politicized nature of the court system in the state. While the General Assembly approved the new court in order to reduce the caseload of the Supreme Court, it fought all efforts by the state's courts to assert judicial autonomy in the state. The result was a long delay in the establishment of the Court of Appeals. On the positive side are the establishment of a unified court system and the creation of an office of court administration, resulting in greater coordination and less confusion in the operation of the court system of the state.

Despite these changes, major problems remain if the judiciary is to be prepared to meet the future. Chief Justice Harwell predicts that in the next five years the number of criminal, civil, and family court filings will double. In addition to the acquisition of a computer system, he has proposed a number of reforms for the judicial branch. Among them is the establishment of regional trial court administrators, professionals who will assist the judiciary in making the courts operate more efficiently to save judges time. Another Harwell proposal is the creation of a regional rotation for judges who can now be sent from Charleston to Greenville to hold several weeks of court. Most judges presently spend up to six months a year away from their homes. Harwell has proposed dividing the state into four regions; the Upstate, Midlands, Pee Dee, and Low Country. Under this arrangement, judges would be rotated in those districts, and one or two judges from each district would be sent to other districts for short periods of time to comply with state law. He has also proposed adding a public information office to the court and allowing cameras in the courtroom in order to bring more openness and information to the public.[40] In 1992, South Carolina first allowed cameras in the courtroom on a pilot basis. Today courtroom cameras are widespread.

The ability to modernize and reform the state's court system is largely dependent on legislative approval of the funds and personnel needed by the judiciary. If past history is any indication, such reform will be slow in coming.

Much also remains to be done in the area of corrections. Until the 1970s, prison chain gangs were common sights in South Carolina. Convicts provided local governments with an inexpensive labor force for a number of years. However, numerous scandals also resulted from the use of convict labor. In the last twenty years, South Carolina has moved to a centralized system of corrections, which has resulted in the closing of county prison camps. Despite these changes, the state still faces the possibility of federal action over its legal defense system and its prison facilities.

Crime still remains a major problem. In 1991, South Carolina ranked twelfth highest nationally in crime rate, second in incarceration rate, and thirteenth in spending for corrections.[41]

CHAPTER ELEVEN

State and Local Government

This chapter deals with two topics. First, it provides an overview of South Carolina's local government framework. South Carolina was long a highly centralized state, controlled historically by an aristocratic oligarchy that used the state legislature as its vehicle for control. The local government system is rooted in South Carolina's traditionalistic past, yet local governments have sought to break from the past in selected ways. The second topic in the chapter is a discussion of selected aspects of state-local government relations. The state retains highly centralized control of local government finances. Local governments, however, have continued to struggle for more flexibility in their authority and for more independence in their finances.

TYPES OF LOCAL GOVERNMENT

Local government assumes many forms and structures in South Carolina. The powers, duties, forms, and practices reflect the accumulation of tradition from long-standing limits on local governments. The traditional limits contrast with recent revisions in the state constitution and in statutes that have created fresh capacities and approaches for local governments to solve their problems more directly.

Since 1973, revised Article VIII of the state constitution has prohibited special laws for cities and counties, although not for school districts or for special-purpose districts. The article requires the legislature to provide through general law for the powers, duties, and forms of South Carolina city and county governments. South Carolina's local government law of 1975 is an example of a general law for cities and counties.

The 1975 law gives cities and counties greater direct responsibility for local spending decisions, personnel management, and service provision. Citizen participation and increased access to local governments are also emphasized in the redesigned state-local system. Although still legal creatures of the state, local governments are delegated more authority to deliver services without direct state supervision than ever before.

There are more than 650 local government entities in South Carolina. The county is the largest geographic unit for general-purpose local government. There are 46 counties and 272 municipal governments.[1] The state has 91 school districts and more than 300 special-purpose districts. Ten multicounty councils of government (COGs) also cover the state and bring together cities, counties, other local governments, and public service providers. COGs are important resources for cooperative intergovernmental planning, especially for land use, infrastructure, and transportation developments.

County Government

In the past, counties were dominated by the central state government, often down to their daily operations. As legal creatures solely of the state, county powers have typically been limited by state constitutions to "county purposes" such as roads, prisons, and court support.[2] South Carolina was one of many states that adhered strictly to the "county purpose" doctrine until recent years. Sometimes the legislature tried to give a county the authority to go beyond predefined county purposes, so that the county could provide some municipal-type services, such as water and recreation, needed by its residents. However, the state court did not approve these efforts because the state constitution did not expressly permit the expansion of county services beyond those specifically named purposes. Several solutions filled the gap where municipal-type services were needed but unavailable to county residents. Special-purpose service districts sprang up, cities tried and failed (or did not try) to annex in order to provide services, or people provided essential services for themselves or just did without.

As part of the broad reform of the South Carolina Constitution of 1895, the updating of South Carolina counties began with the legislative ratification of a constitutional amendment on March 7, 1973. Updating counties means reducing some detailed, centralized state requirements while strictly adhering to the "county purpose" doctrine. Ideally, an up-to-date county should be able to choose its types of services and service areas individually and to deliver varied services to specific areas in the county.

Today, a county has the potential to deliver a full range of municipal services through the powers and duties authorized under the updated state constitution. The legislature must still decide many details of how to execute these powers through general laws that apply to all counties, including the critically important decision as to whether counties should be enabled to raise significant revenue on their own through "revenue home rule." So far, the state legislature generally restricts the ability of counties to raise the revenue they need for local services; therefore, counties need additional state financing. Restrictive state fiscal control of counties demonstrates the persistence of the traditionalistic political culture in the development of South Carolina's counties.

Development of Counties. When drawing up the Fundamental Constitutions of Carolina in 1669, the owners of the colony, the eight Lords Proprietors, intended to emphasize counties.[3] Their plan was to create counties over the entire province and to create new counties as each section of territory was settled. The Lords Proprietors' design considered the county as the basic unit for local government. Within the jurisdiction of a specific county, there would be courts and administration of justice, offices to keep records of land grants, and administrators to organize elections of representatives to the legislative assembly in the colony.

Three counties were created in 1682 and named after individual Lords Proprietors: Berkeley (which included present-day Charleston), Craven (to the north of Berkeley above Awendaw Creek), and Colleton (to the south of Berkeley from the Stono River to the Combahee River). After the departure of the Lords Proprietors, a fourth county, named Granville, was staked out in 1721 below Colleton between the Combahee and Savannah Rivers. Just like the original vision, its purpose was to accommodate new settlers.

Despite early aspirations, these counties never amounted to much. Government became concentrated in Charleston, and the Berkeley County court extended its influence throughout the state. One interpretation is that Broad Street lawyers did not want to travel to the Up-Country to hold court; it was easier to collect fees from litigants if the litigants, not the lawyers, had to travel to court.[4] Although the term "county" continued to be used down through the American Revolution, it was primarily a way to locate references to land ownership and other general citizen responsibilities, such as militia organization. Counties did not develop as significant administrative service units of local government.

Another weakening in the original county design was the establishment of the Anglican Church (1706–76). The church parishes became the election districts and the effective local governments as well, with responsibilities for improving roads, registering births and deaths, and providing social services and other services often provided by counties today.

Townships were organized by the English government in the 1730s as a local government where parishes did not yet exist.[5] When the township became sufficiently populated, it would be converted into a parish with the right to elect representatives to the Assembly. The township plan stimulated much immigration into the colony from Europe. The colonial government influenced the location of settlers, the time of their settlement, and their nationality. Although the townships were not developed uniformly and many new settlers lived where they wanted, the township plan promoted increased population across the coastal plain and into the lower piedmont for several decades.[6]

After the townships faltered because of financing problems, judicial circuits came to be the statewide unit to provide state services locally. By 1789, the General Assembly had divided the "whole Province" into seven judicial districts, each with a courthouse town. Other county-type government services were provided by the former church parishes, especially in the Low Country, and by townships, especially in the Midlands. In many instances, special local commissions were created by the legislature to build a facility or deal with a special problem.

In 1785, after the American Revolution, the General Assembly again laid out counties and created county courts to judge small claims. At first, the county courts were within the larger judicial districts. By 1786, they were empowered by the General Assembly to carry out many of the duties that for so long had been centralized in Charleston. However, the district courts continued to meet at the district (not the county) courthouse towns. State justices presided over them.

By the early 1800s, most of the county courts had been transformed into district courts. The approach was a jumble; some older judicial districts were carved into smaller judicial districts approximating the county boundaries within them, while other districts were divided and still other districts were created anew. The newer, smaller district courthouses became the place to record land transfers and to probate estates. Election districts were identified in some way with the judicial district; several judicial districts were combined into an election district in some cases, and single judicial districts were divided into several election districts in other cases. Local public works and education were authorized directly by the legislature, and there was no regular system of county taxation.

The irregular structure of South Carolina local governments, along with the failure of the state to develop a dependable, centralized bureaucracy for state activities, made for unpredictable levels and quality of public services. It was truly decentralized government as envisioned in Elazar's traditionalistic model.

Politics of Constitutions and Counties. Article IV, Section 19 of the South Carolina Constitution of 1868 redesignated the judicial districts as counties. Each county was governed by an elected board of county commissioners; this board had authority over taxes and expenditures for "county purposes." Except for the limitation of purposes, this is the root of the contemporary view of county government. However, the implementation of Section 19 got caught up in the politics of Reconstruction and stalled. In 1890 the constitutional provision for county government was repealed.[7]

The subsequent 1895 constitution recognized counties again; it described specifically how a new county was to be formed or an old one altered. Counties were also required to provide for the poor and to levy a school tax. Other provisions of the 1895 constitution revived and respecified the "county purpose" doctrine. Constitutional provisions restricted the General Assembly's ability to authorize any other taxes for counties, except for limited county purposes (Article X, Section 6), and eliminated any provisions for a local governing body for the counties. This restored the traditionalistic view in full flower; a South Carolina county could do little other than provide for schools, roads, ferries, bridges, public buildings, and facilities as the state General Assembly permitted. It was a long list of duties that did not contemplate the development of cities or an orderly plan of municipal growth.

The 1895 constitution left county government in the hands of the legislature once again.[8] Unclear legal powers combined with political tensions based on fear of demands from the large numbers of poor whites and emancipated slaves led to the development of a legislative delegation that actually administered the county. County government by legislative delegation derived from law and custom originating in the colonial period. It varied greatly from county to county, perhaps resembling the post–American Revolution hodgepodge of special arrangements.

A legislative delegation at the time was composed of a state senator from each county and the members of the state House of Representatives, elected by county. Each county operated on the basis of a "supply bill" passed by the legislature as "local legislation" each year. The supply bill was actually the county's budget passed by the General Assembly as an appropriations bill for a county's revenue and expenditures.

In reality, the legislative delegation—more specifically, the county senator—governed the county because of power over the supply bill. Within both legislative chambers, all members deferred to the delegation from each county. It was government by logroll; to interfere in another county's matters was simply to ask for trouble in the bill for a member's own county. There was also an unwritten rule that a majority of the delegation from a county had to support a supply bill before it would be enacted. But the county senator had leverage: whether motivated by events, political competition, or self-direction, the county senator could veto action by the House members on the supply bill by stopping its "automatic enactment" in the Senate.[9]

The stranglehold by the delegation, or the county senator, on county government continued once the supply bill was passed. County officials were dependent on the delegation for salary level and for tenure in office. A county board, including a governing board of county commissioners, could be created, changed, or abolished by act of the General Assembly. Sometimes a new county board of commissioners only slightly different from the old one might be created because of political disagreements. New board members could even be specifically named by the legislative delegation in the supply bill. The delegation actively governed the county in every detail.

Updating County Government. The traditionalistic approach to counties through government by legislative delegations really forced two roles on state legislators. They were legislators for state purposes and legislators for county purposes. Many candidates for the legislature ran campaigns on local, not statewide, problems.[10]

Although it is not necessarily bad to run primarily on local issues, legislators frequently had to balance their involvement in local administration with their actions on statewide problems. Often, the two roles put the legislator in an awkward political vise; in human terms, it gave many legislators more than they had time to deal with. In one instance, largely because of explosive local growth erupting from World War II military operations, the Charleston County delegation permitted adoption of a local county council in 1948.[11]

Another part of the change in delegation governance came from the U.S. Supreme Court cases, such as *Reynolds v. Sims* (1964),[12] that required representation in state legislatures on a one person–one vote standard. These cases upset the neat one county–one senator pattern because some of the smaller counties did not have enough population to support their own senator.[13] Some of the more populated counties would have several senators. One person–one vote meant that county government by legislative delegation would no longer work predictably in South Carolina. Reapportionment spurred the development of some form of a county-based governing body through special legislation for about half of South Carolina's forty-six counties by 1970.

The constitutional revision committee, created in 1966, recommended new constitutional provisions for local government, including types of local government with defined powers and responsibilities.[14] The General Assembly proposed the changes for local government through constitutional referendums in the 1972 general election. They were approved by a majority of the voters and ratified by the General Assembly on March 7, 1973, as new Article VIII in today's state constitution. In June 1975, the legislation implementing part of Article VIII identified the forms of county council organization and structures from which a county had to choose by July 1, 1976.[15]

The county supply bill became obsolete through the new constitutional provision banning any new special laws for a city or county. Specific legislative delegation government of general-purpose local government was thereby diminished. Henceforward, each county had to have an active governing body or council with general powers of local government—in short, powers like that of a city council.

Municipal Government

Like counties, cities have a long and varied history in South Carolina. The original 1670 South Carolina settlement soon moved to a new area between the Ashley and Cooper Rivers. In 1672 this area was laid out as a town. The town was called Charles Town by 1679, and it became the capital of South Carolina in 1680. It was the first South Carolina city to be incorporated, June 23, 1722. It was then called Charles City and Port. The charter was the brainchild of the first appointed governor during the colonial period, Sir Francis Nicholson. Nicholson had been the lieutenant governor in New York, and students of South Carolina local government report that Charleston's charter was modeled after the charter of New York City at the time.[16]

Charleston's charter was followed by an act of the legislature in 1783. The preamble to the charter suggests that the legislature thought it necessary to create a municipal subdivision because operations in the Charleston area were simply too much for the legislature to keep up with—a fact the legislature realized for Charleston County only in the 1940s.

Because of broad changes in the nation and its economy, Charleston steadily declined with respect to the size of other American cities after 1800. Charleston was the nation's 5th largest city in 1800, but it dropped to 129th by 1940. Even today, the city itself has a population of less than eighty-one thousand despite a surrounding county population of almost three hundred thousand. An explanation based on gossip is that because of its reluctance to deal with "undesirable elements," the city was until recently only interested in expanding "west of the Ashley" where the children of the old peninsular families gradually moved into subdivisions. The state's restrictive annexation statutes may be a more plausible reason. In recent years, the city of Charleston has aggressively pursued annexation, including areas west of the Ashley, James Island, and Johns Island. It even annexed Daniel Island in Berkeley County.

Before the 1895 constitution, additional South Carolina cities were chartered individually by the General Assembly. Camden was chartered in 1791, Beaufort in 1803, Columbia and Georgetown in 1805, and so on. After 1896, municipalities were incorporated under general statutes rather than chartered by special state legislation. The incorporation procedure today is spelled out in general legislation that followed the new local government amendment in 1973.

The essential requirements for a new incorporation are ample population density, adequate distance from an existing municipality, service feasibility, and a successful election. Ample density means at least three hundred persons per square mile, except for the sea islands and coastal areas within two miles of the Atlantic Ocean. The exempted areas must have a total of 150 dwelling units or one dwelling per three acres of land. The boundaries of an existing municipality have to be at least five miles away, unless the area to be incorporated has been refused annexation, has fifteen thousand residents, or is in a county with fewer than fifteen thousand residents. The service feasibility study has to demonstrate that the municipal government is justified and that a plan to provide services exists.

The incorporation election determines (1) whether the city should actually be certified to the South Carolina secretary of state for incorporation and (2) the form of the new city government. A South Carolina city can lose its charter if it ceases to function as a city or falls below a population of fifty. There is no classification legislation for cities, and fully half of the more than 260 general-purpose municipalities in the state have a population of less than one thousand.[17]

FORMS OF LOCAL GOVERNMENT

Both cities and counties have forms of government specified by the 1975 local government law. Cities may opt for a strong-mayor or mayor-council form, a council or weak-mayor form, or a council-manager form. Counties have a council, a council-supervisor, a council-administrator, or a council-manager option. Each jurisdiction had to adopt one form by July 1, 1976, and it could not change again before July 1, 1978, if it made the 1976 decision by referendum.

For the most part, the use of a single form has been fairly consistent by each jurisdiction. Charleston has a strong-mayor form, and Columbia, Greenville, and Florence have the council-manager form. Most of the counties use a council-administrator form, although two counties, York and Greenwood, have a county manager and council. The form strengthens the manager by allowing the council to make the county treasurer and county auditor appointive rather than popularly elected offices.

STATE-LOCAL RELATIONS

The reduction of federal fiscal support for local governments in the late 1970s, and especially since the expiration of General Revenue Sharing in 1986, has generated more pressure on states to assume a greater role in financing important government services. Excluding education and welfare expenditures, South Carolina ranks thirty-second among states in per capita state aid to local governments.[18] However, local governments often provide many services, even though a state government may not allow them useful sources with which to raise adequate revenues. South Carolina is one of only six states that directly restrict how much property tax their local governments may impose or how they may spend revenue derived from it.[19]

However, the blessings are mixed. The property tax on homes is not politically popular, and the State Tax Commission assesses key industrial property. The property tax also generally lags behind economic development and is not a very dynamic source of revenue. As states assume a larger share of the state-federal financing burden, it is not clear that they will relinquish a broader fiscal responsibility to local governments.[20]

The Special Problem of State Mandates

The U.S. Advisory Commission on Intergovernmental Relations (ACIR) defines a state mandate as a legal requirement for a local government to engage in a specific activity or to provide a service that meets specified minimum state standards. The basis for the state mandate may be a constitutional provision, a statutory provision, an administrative regulation, or other legal requirement.[21] Of course, having local operations or expenditures mandated by the state bridles local decision makers. When state and local governments agree on mandated activities and how to finance them, the state rides a gentle horse, but when state mandates are disagreeable or local financing difficult, the bridle bit becomes more obvious and the local government horse begins to buck.

Along with regular local demands for increased services and activities, state mandates place real fiscal stress on local government budgets. For example, state employees deliver health and social services in local areas, but these employees must have office space and support services, such as personnel and finances, to do their job. The county has to provide offices and support because the state does not spend adequately for them.

About all that local governments in South Carolina can do to generate extra revenue is to adjust the rate on the property tax, change the rates on fees and charges, or adopt a local option sales tax. Most property tax revenues are already devoted to the public schools. Federal revenues are frozen if not declining and reduced even more when the impact of inflation is considered. At the same time, the state government is pressed between level or declining revenue and escalating statewide spending needs for health care, more prisons, increased pay for state school teachers, hazardous waste management, and economic development.

In 1986, the South Carolina Advisory Commission on Intergovernmental Relations (SCACIR) catalogued 683 mandates.[22] Often, a single mandate affected several types of local government. Counties were affected by 93 percent of existing mandates (638 mandates) and got almost the total fiscal shock from them; however, they also are the biggest recipients of state shared revenue. Municipalities were touched by 39 percent (268 mandates) and special-purpose districts by 17 percent (113 mandates).[23]

The state mandates catalog has been kept up-to-date since 1987. Generally, four specific types of state mandates are tracked: (1) active—a legal requirement for a specific activity or a service meeting state standards; (2) restrictive—for example, annexation rules that prevent rapid expansion of municipal tax and service bases; (3) traditional—activities that local governments perform because they think the state expects it; and (4) federal pass-through or federal grant requirements enforced by the state as grants administrator.

Given that continuing mandates will be fully funded only with great difficulty, the study and control of costs in specific areas, such as medical assistance for the poor or environmental control, may be equally useful. To assist in the identification of costs, the General Assembly passed a "fiscal note" bill in 1983. A fiscal note is an estimate of the fiscal impact on local government of a state mandate; it is attached to proposed legislation requiring local expenditure. The general expectation is that a fiscal note will slow down the number of state mandates. In South Carolina, however, the General Assembly has passed mandated expenditures at about the same rate before and after the fiscal note requirement.[24]

The Local Option Sales Tax

The local option sales tax (LOST) offers an alternative to the major fiscal problems of local governments: revenue weakness because of dependence on the property tax, reduced federal assistance, and the continuing cost of financing state mandates. The president of the state municipal association and mayor of Williamston identified another problem in this way: "Revenue collected by the state to be shared with local governments has been returned in full to local governments in only one year since 1975, costing local governments many millions of dollars."[25]

The LOST proposal coupled a property tax rollback of up to 63 percent in the first year with an increase of 1 percent in the sales tax in counties that gave a majority approval in the referendum. The rollback feature increases by 2 percent to a cap of 71 percent after five years. Cities and counties will share revenue after the property tax relief is funded. Also, counties that approve the local option sales tax but generate less than $2 million in revenue will get a share of the revenue from "donor" counties that produce more than $5 million. However, no county will have to redistribute more than 5 percent of its total collections.[26]

The South Carolina Merchants Association fought the proposal vigorously. The merchants especially emphasized that property tax is deductible on one's federal income tax return, while sales tax is not.[27] Local governments countered that deductibility mattered only if one itemized. The local government advocates were further hurt by the exemption of property taxes from the rollback used for public education. Public education consumes the lion's share of property tax revenue, so many voters felt that the rollback was actually small. Also, the proposal had no restrictions on future increases in the property tax base or on property tax rates.

LOST appeared as a statewide referendum on the November 1990 ballot.

However, the referendum went into effect only in the counties that approved it. The tax first went into effect in six counties July 1, 1991, since it passed in only six counties in 1990.[28] The overwhelming defeat suffered by the measure in suburban areas suggests that it came across to voters as a tax increase. The issue could be proposed again after twelve months (November 1991) by a county council if the first referendum did not pass. Nine more counties have approved the additional one-cent tax since May 1992, for a total of fifteen.[29] Charleston County is the only "donor" county among the current participants.

Interlocal Relationships

Cities and counties are general-purpose local governments that exercise their authority under broad constitutional or legislative grants of functional governmental authority. South Carolina also has about three hundred special-purpose districts that perform a specific function or a small number of related functions such as water, or water and sewer.[30]

Special-purpose districts are often fiscally independent of municipalities and counties, and their boundaries follow no specific pattern. Under the "county purpose" doctrine of state government, when an area of the county became densely settled, a special-purpose district was often the only way that citizens there could get a needed service. The legislature had to create a special-purpose district to provide a municipal-type service in the county—just so long as the district did not cover the entire geographic area of the county. If it did, then it was a part of the county and subject to county-purpose limits.

Special-purpose districts emerged as administrative commissions of a county when fees could not be adequately charged or collected to support a service. Recreation districts are an example. The county could provide recreation services by covering all of the county except for the city, which typically had a recreation department anyway. The county operations usually stayed small overall, but the county commission could legally administer the program. The legislative delegation therefore had another commission on which to place political supporters, and county residents had a city service without having to live in the city. A special property tax levy often financed the county commission's budget.

Special-purpose districts have not been a favorite of government reformers in recent decades. They are criticized for being too remote from popular control, for contributing to fragmentation and lack of local government service coordination, and for conserving lucrative revenue bases that

actually contribute to the city and county fiscal strain. They may have no capacity to provide services that are equitable, efficient, and economical for all
the neighborhoods in the countywide government. Most of the generaliza-
tions are disputed by special-purpose district advocates. South Carolina special-purpose districts recently formed a vocal and powerful lobby to protect
their interests. Because the state now has single-member representation districts for its House and Senate, the special-purpose districts are capable of a
strong voice in the areas of the state where their concentration may influence
the outcome of a legislative or local council election.

Annexation

South Carolina currently has three legally defined ways for cities to annex.
They are majority petition and election, 25 percent petition and majority
election, and 75 percent and 100 percent petition and ordinance. All are subject to preclearance under Section 5 of the U.S. Voting Rights Act of 1965,
but only the 75 percent and 100 percent petition and ordinance method may
actually be used after recent court decisions.

Under the majority petition and election method, a majority of freeholders in the area to be annexed must petition the city council. Then, voter
majorities in both the city and the area to be annexed must approve in a special election. The 25 percent petition and election method went into effect
June 7, 1988, to replace an older, constitutionally obsolete method known as
the "Three Box Method." After 25 percent of freeholders who are residents
in the area proposed for annexation file a petition, a special election is then
held within the area to be annexed. If a majority of the qualified electors in
the area approve, the council can accept it without an election within the municipality unless 5 percent of municipal residents petition for a special municipal election within thirty days' notice of the approved annexation.

The two methods are not usable because of federal district court decisions
that declare unconstitutional any municipal annexation processes in which
landowners have the sole power to initiate or block annexation elections.
Under such an arrangement, a landowner has superior rights compared to an
ordinary registered voter.

The available method is the 75 percent and 100 percent petition and ordinance method, in which 75 percent of the freeholders owning 75 percent of
the assessed valuation of the real property in the area to be annexed petition
the council. No election is required and the municipal council accepts by ordinance.[31] With these awkward voting requirements in the only approach to

annexation, it is little wonder that municipalities seldom expand their boundaries. Annexation decisions are hot political questions and annexation law reform a perennial topic of discussion in South Carolina.

Annexation problems could be due to powerful opposition to simplification or reform by special-purpose districts, the state's electric cooperatives, and taxpayer groups. For electricity distribution, South Carolina was basically carved into four utility franchise areas by the Territories Act of 1968. Duke Power, Carolina Power and Light, South Carolina Electric and Gas, and the state's seventeen electric cooperatives each have specific geographic service areas. However, twenty-one South Carolina cities are still "electric" cities that have the retail distribution of electricity within their boundaries as a municipal enterprise. When a city annexes, it is often difficult to determine the "buyout" value of the infrastructure financed and installed by the electric utility or the special-service district. In addition, if an "electric" city can take over electricity distribution from a ultility or the service area of a special district, it shrinks the revenue base of the utility or special district and may increase its rates. In either case it is likely to set off a political debate between ratepayers and advocates of city growth.

The legislature will need to sort out the competing interests and problems as it modernizes annexation provisions. For some, South Carolina's current annexation laws are too restrictive.[32] They often look across to North Carolina, where cities can take the initiative to annex based on statutorily defined standards of contiguity or of density of residents or structures.

The reform of special-purpose districts, the coordination of city and county development, and an annexation policy for local government consolidation that preserves equity positions for all interests involved are major interlocal problems in the future in South Carolina. Annexation problems may become even more complicated if the counties actively develop county special-service districts, as they are able to do under the local government law.

Consolidating Local Governments

Urbanization in South Carolina raises questions of how to organize or structure local governmental bodies so that they may operate or function productively and in a politically satisfactory way. Economic mobility and the related shifts in population and demographics have generated a pattern of suburban concentration in South Carolina just as in other parts of the country. Improvement of the split structures in local government has typically focused on the design of a metropolitan-wide government. Areawide functions could be assigned to this new government for improved efficiency. More specific or neighborhood functions could be retained by truly local or neighborhood governments.

While metropolitan-wide government is a wonderful idea in theory, two major problems usually prevent meaningful implementation of areawide reform. First, the political referendums necessary to consolidate existing structures seldom (so far *never* in South Carolina) win at the polls. Second, there is little agreement on which functions could best be assigned to an areawide government. It may be just as desirable to forget the illusion of a centralized urban government and employ more competitive, market-based solutions. Under the general model of public choice rather than the classical administrative reform model, the citizen acts more like consumers and governments more like competing businesses. The best result may come from market competition for public services, not from grand design.[33]

In March 1973, the constitutional amendment authorizing the General Assembly to pass legislation permitting local government consolidation was ratified. Almost two decades later, in March 1992, the General Assembly passed a law implementing the amendment. The bill's author, Representative Candy Waites (*D*-Richland) said, "It's really an insult to the people of South Carolina that it took the Legislature 20 years to adopt the implementing legislation."[34]

Implementing consolidation under the bill may be just as difficult as its passage. Utilities will keep the same territories they have now. Special-purpose districts and cities may opt out of a consolidated government if voters within their boundaries reject a consolidation proposal. A consolidation proposal itself will have to be initiated by a county council or by a petition of 10 percent of the registered voters in the county. A charter commission would draw the new government's plans. The commission's eighteen members must be evenly divided among appointments by affected county councils, city councils, and special-purpose districts. The commission will have one year to complete a plan that is then submitted to the voters for approval or rejection.

Cooperation on Infrastructure

Given that major changes in structures and functions are hard to achieve politically, other programs address important problems in the meantime. For example, in 1988 the South Carolina infrastructure planning project began. It is a large-scale statewide research and planning project that uses innovative technology to assist local governments in economic development. The project focuses on the evaluation of local infrastructure needs. It is a way to confront some of the regional challenges to local governments. The project is also a good illustration of the potential for state-local cooperation.

The first step in the project is the development of a GIS—geographical information system. The GIS has the purposes of managing and analyzing data so that the data can be mapped and interpreted for effective allocation of limited physical and human resources. The products of the GIS will help define county and local community infrastructure needs, especially the details of the more than 350 public water and wastewater systems.[35]

The findings of the mapping effort will help guide future infrastructure development and link infrastructure decisions to new projects that support economic growth. Presently, the State Development Board estimates that at the current rates of economic development $1.3 billion will be needed over the next fifteen years for water and wastewater needs, and $4.5 billion will be needed for highway improvements before the year 2000.[36]

The State Development Board has promoted a public-private, state-local networking approach to coordinate infrastructure development. One key network link is a university–state and local government partnership. The University of South Carolina's College of Humanities and Social Sciences computer laboratory is the central source of expertise for the GIS.

The USC college computer lab has had the technical faculty expertise to develop the system, and the faculty have trained a new generation of students versed in the technologies of mapping and data evaluation. Many of these students go on to positions in the state agencies and local governments that manage infrastructure resources, such as the State Development Board, the Water Resources Commission, or the Land Resources Commission. Clemson University's Strom Thurmond Institute of Government and Public Affairs has organized research investigations to explore the relationships between infrastructure development and economic growth. The mapping of the public water and wastewater systems was supported by a grant from the U.S. Department of Housing and Urban Development to the governor's office and to the ten councils of governments in the state.

Among local governments, a network of regional GIS centers has been developed as a way to transfer the planning information in a cost-effective manner. Regional centers are a way to get the information out to the local decision makers where it is needed and, at the same time, to involve local participants so that the application of their expertise makes the effort truly cooperative.

The model local government partnership is funded by the Appalachian

Regional Commission through the Appalachian Council of Governments.[37] The aim is to get all the major local public and private actors together, including school districts, public and private utilities, water and sewer districts, banks and lending organizations, chambers of commerce, and local economic booster clubs, as well as local developers and real estate companies. The shared data will be a means whereby the future of the multicounty area can be discussed and projected by the many players who have a part in it. A regional GIS center is being developed in each of the ten COGs, and it is expected that each center will develop a unique application of the available data. The program promises statewide cooperation in a format that is flexible enough to deal with individual jurisdictional needs.

THE PIVOTAL ROLE OF THE STATE ACIR

The South Carolina General Assembly created the South Carolina Advisory Commission on Intergovernmental Relations (SCACIR) as a permanent agency on July 1, 1984. It has twenty-one members. Eight represent the General Assembly, three represent municipalities, three represent counties, four represent the general public, and there is one member each for school boards, special-purpose districts, and the regional councils. The governor appoints each commissioner to a two-year term.

The SCACIR has worked jointly and actively with the state's associations that represent municipalities and counties in proposing new legislation for local governments. Among them have been annexation reform, authorization for cities and counties to merge selected service functions, and reform of state aid to local governments.

According to the House of Representatives' Speaker and commission member Robert Sheheen, the SCACIR is not "an intellectual exercise." It has to guide the state in making hard decisions. Sheheen observes,

> South Carolina is expected to experience a 35–40% increase in population during the next 15 years. How we cope with this growth—in terms of its demand on our tax system, our construction capabilities, and our service delivery system at both the state and local levels—is all important. Presently, we are not ready to accommodate such growth. The [SC]ACIR must anticipate the problems which are ahead of us and develop alternatives which will help us solve them.[38]

The growth issues investigated have included the proposal of the local government finance act or local option sales tax discussed above. Other reports have dealt with the cost of state and local government tax incentives to industry, with how much local governments in South Carolina depend on state and federal aid, and with definition and solutions to structural problems that might be helped through annexation reform, home rule legislation, or the consolidation of governmental services. In the ten years of its existence, the SCACIR has issued thirty-one major reports and publications.[39]

CONCLUSION

Today, South Carolinians search for the best approaches to modernizing county government and its operations, allowing increased municipal self-direction, and coordinating the multiple special-district governments. The trend is away from too much reliance on state law as a source of local government authority and away from the consideration of city, county, and special-purpose governments as just administrative arms of the state.

So far in South Carolina the General Assembly has made a beginning, but there is a full slate of issues on the future agenda. One issue is the trend away from state-mandated functions that were the major county responsibilities of half a century ago, so that counties are able to confront and finance their service priorities. A related problem is whether the cities and counties will be able to raise enough revenue locally in the "no new taxes" climate. Also, what is the best relationship between counties and cities, between counties and special-purpose districts, or among counties for efficient and effective provision of public services? Should relationships be more centralized? more market oriented? How are these changes to be implemented? Consider the following examples: (1) special-purpose districts were created by the legislature before the constitutional revision, but they still exist long after revision; they are not the same as special county taxing districts; (2) city annexation policies and actions will affect the development and political influence of neighboring cities and the surrounding county; (3) despite the recent adoption of city–county–special-purpose district consolidation procedures, practical politics suggest that they will work in only a few places; (4) planning and zoning commissions need to coordinate better with general county governments.

So far, there are only two council-manager counties in South Carolina. As counties become more capable, how will they gear up for increased administrative duties? Will the old forms be sufficient? How will the need for a stronger executive approach to county government relate to elected department heads and the variety of appointed commissions in the county? What about representation on county councils? Is the present all-at-large or all-single-member-district approach enough, or should it be mixed? What about representation after the 1990 census?

The 1975 local government law leaves many issues for study. For example, special-purpose districts and school districts were excluded from the amendment, but the changes in city and county government have strong implications for all of the special districts. School districts have a variety of forms, some with elected boards with taxing powers, others with boards appointed by the legislature. Special-purpose districts have been searching for their role in the new setup, since now counties are able to discharge functions for which the districts were created. Annexation, consolidation, local government fiscal autonomy, and state review of federal aid for local governments are continuing issues for analysis and debate.

South Carolina is an old state with a long history. The people and their state and local governments have had rich and varied experiences over more than three centuries. The present local governments reflect the historical perspective of the state, while the recent changes in local government reflect the many changes in the South Carolina of today. The key to the future of local governments is the imagination, responsibility, and judgment backing the planning and development of them.

CHAPTER TWELVE

Epilogue

The modernization of South Carolina's traditionalistic past will continue to the end of this century and beyond. What are the prospects and consequences? South Carolina is perhaps typical of "the two Souths." One part is urbanized with income and education levels above the national average; the other is rural with some of the nation's worst poverty.

Health programs, education agencies, social services, and economic development are state policy efforts that have the common goal of improving the quality of life for all the state's citizens. For example, Target 2000 is a critical education reform package that attempts to improve the chances for many children who would otherwise be trapped in the poverty culture. Legislators, boards and council members, governors and local executives, judges, and administrators provide the political and governmental directions for these ventures under constantly changing conditions.

ARENAS OF CHANGE

Underlying Economic and Social Pressures

The State Development Board continues to record higher and higher investments in new plants and higher and higher numbers of jobs in South Carolina. Even so, hard-nosed observers call South Carolina a "catch-up" situation. Many major economic changes are beyond the immediate control of the state, but they have significant implications for the state's future policies and politics.[1] The traditionalistic way of life is challenged, even potentially fundamentally changed, by the new applications of land and capital and by the economic dislocation of labor that are spawned in the state by national and global developments.[2]

Changes in national consumer patterns create new economic tensions in a traditionalistic, agricultural state such as South Carolina. Some "new frontier" market sectors, such as health services, specialty foods, or high-technology devices, are increasing in the state. The more familiar, traditional economic pursuits, such as beef and pork or lumber, are declining nationally.[3] Still, declining elsewhere or not, livestock production and timber harvests are, for many South Carolinians, improvements over former cotton fields. Critics still press for more manufacturing jobs, arguing that, since dependence on agriculture represents "a continually exploited economic frontier," today's farmers will eventually wind up in the same straits as earlier generations.

Tourism and coastal developments are vital cogs in South Carolina's economy. Tourism provides an annual financial windfall of $5.0 billion for the entire state and almost $230 million in total state tax revenue, but tourism is concentrated in the coastal counties. However, tourism is a mixed blessing, because fragile coastal environments are affected negatively in some places.

In 1988, the new Beachfront Management Act provided for regulations to control coastal development and to protect the beach and dune environment. Other than six-foot-wide wooden walkways, the act forbids construction on the ocean side of a setback line calculated from beach erosion rates. Subsequent enforcement disputes resulted in a U.S. Supreme Court case over whether the setback line violates the Fifth Amendment by taking property without payment to the owner. The petitioner argued that some expensive lots bought before the state law are now worthless because he cannot build houses on them, and the state will not pay him for the loss.[4] On June 29, 1992, the U.S. Supreme Court, in a 5–4 majority, ruled that a state must pay when it takes "all economically beneficial uses" of property unless the restriction naturally flows from the "background principles of the State's law of property and nuisance." The South Carolina Supreme Court had held that the law prevented "harmful or noxious uses" and that compensation was not constitutionally required.

At the same time that tourism and beachfront development have boomed, manufacturing jobs have been shifting abroad to nations where labor and other costs of production are less expensive.[5] Simply to keep South Carolina manufacturing workers employed at low wages will not prevent this exodus of factories and jobs. If nothing is done about it, unemployment will edge up. The loss of jobs hits particularly hard in small-town, rural areas. After North Carolina, South Carolina has the highest percentage of a state's workforce in manufacturing, and textiles is the largest component. The 1993 proposed naval base closures in Charleston compound the employment problem in a state where wages are already low.

Today, high-technology machines and even chemical or biological mechanisms often perform work that previously was done by people.[6] These applications require higher-skilled workers. They also lead to lower wages or unemployment for the part of the workforce that does not advance to high-tech skills through sound basic education and constant retraining. The "pacesetting" Japanese educational program puts more and more pressure on the "catch-up" states, such as South Carolina, "to spend more tax dollars for longer school terms and more substantive educational offerings."[7] South Carolina will need to promote and develop appropriate learning and work opportunities for its workers to prosper beyond the low-cost labor pool into jobs that require higher technical skills and pay higher wages.

The industrial sector emphasizes increased production efficiency through the new technical knowledge base and through better information.[8] The stress is on effective performance. The work enthusiasm of South Carolinians is a time-honored tradition, but it has to be more than simple effort or good intentions. In the global economy, enthusiasm will be measured against bottom-line standards of productivity. Some South Carolinians may sulk when they get laid off, but their distress may be shortened if business and government can keep them productive by creating reemployment opportunities and retraining programs. The work ethic will have to be nurtured and directed by business managers and by governmental agencies.

South Carolina's government, workers, and businesses are in constant competition for economic growth achievements. There is competition with neighboring states, especially for new jobs and new plants, because every American state today is influenced by significant increases in international trade and competition. As soon as the governor returned early in 1992 with news that the BMW automobile company was interested in a production site near the Greenville-Spartanburg airport, stories began to circulate that North Carolina and Nebraska had better deals for it. BMW has officially located the plant in South Carolina, and ground was broken to begin plant construction September 30, 1992. Cars are scheduled to roll off the assembly line in the mid-1990s.

The rates of continued decline of agriculture and textiles and the ability of the state to expand job markets are critical. These economic areas lose jobs about as fast as the State Development Board can find new ones. There is not enough small, indigenous industry to create jobs, so state agencies have to go out and look for new ones. Other significant factors influencing South Carolina's economy include more regulation of tobacco as well as changes in export markets and import policies. Free trade helps some, but not all; textile workers especially will suffer negative impacts.

The lack of economic opportunity in the past led to the emigration of significant numbers of South Carolinians, both African American and white. The exodus of some of South Carolina's best people cost the state dearly. While many will never return, current indications are that many young people are remaining in the state and that the net migration into the state will continue. From 1970 to 1980, South Carolina's population grew at a rate of 20.5 percent, almost twice the national rate of 11.4 percent. The 1990 census found that the state's inhabitants increased in number during the 1980s at about half the rate of the 1970s, 11.7 percent—still above the national population increase of 9.8 percent.

The economic and social South Carolina of 1950 is almost not recognizable as one looks back from today. The state's relatively peaceful shifts away from an agriculturally based economy and a racially segregated society are truly remarkable to many who have lived through the changes.

Underlying Political Pressures

Political forces join economic and social pressures to stimulate interest in orienting the structures and actions of state governments toward improved policy responsiveness and greater bureaucratic accountability. Changing economic and social conditions mean that politics and government will have to change along with business and labor to keep up.

One political push stems from the popular perception of the need for states to perform their functions more productively. General interest has grown since the mid-1960s in reorganized state governmental structures and operations as a way to achieve better state government.[9] An uncoordinated executive branch may inhibit governmental policy initiatives and administrative actions necessary to deal with changing conditions. Governmental performance may be blunted by a diffused, divided administrative structure that allows bureaucratic specialists to become so preoccupied with their individual objectives that they lose incentives to cooperate with elected officials on broader goals. Reorganization may improve state government efficiency, effectiveness, and economy by making elected executives as powerful in fact as citizens think they are.

Another push comes from the perception that government is somehow different from business and needs to be restructured so that it is more like business.[10] Government always struggles to be efficient—that is, to provide the most return in programs and services for tax dollars spent. State governments must demonstrate effectiveness by winning citizen approval, and they must be economical—that is, cost as little overall as possible. When restructured along business principles, so the theory goes, state government should be able to perform better.

The renewal of state legislatures is a third political force ushering in improved state agency administration.[11] Part-time, "ol' boy" legislators have been tested by the impact of reapportionment and more intense public scrutiny. The new breed of legislator is more professional and wants a stronger, more effective legislature. The contemporary legislator understands that effective administration is necessary if new legislative mandates for change are to be implemented.

Yet another political force is the willingness of state governors to be leaders on critical issues.[12] It is also possible that the legislature may better solve state problems if it is able to deal with one responsible administrator, especially a governor, who may be held accountable while being in charge of state administrative operations. Governors need good state government administration to help define major problems for appropriate political solutions.

Politically, South Carolina today is very much a two-party state. The support of old-line Democrats for presidential candidates such as Thurmond, Eisenhower, Goldwater, Nixon, Reagan, and Bush demonstrates Republican dominance in presidential elections. Since the 1960s, Republicans have become powerful in most of the state's urban areas, while Democrats are still strong in the rural counties. The only problem for the Democrats is that most of the people live in the urban counties, and these are the rapid-growth areas in the state.

An important departure from Democratic dominance of state government has been the election of Republican governors in 1974, 1986, and again in 1990 and the election of a Republican superintendent of education, and secretary of state, commissioner of agriculture. The 1986 gubernatorial election was won by a very organized state Republican party. The victory has led to an enhanced image for the state's GOP leaders. While there has not been meaningful development of cohesive party structures in the legislature, the number of Republican legislative representatives is the highest ever, so two-party adversarial debate is more possible than before.

South Carolina's current leaders struggle with the challenges of internal political change as well as external pressures emerging from the state's competition with other states and with countries and markets around the globe. The ongoing question is whether the existing legislatively dominated state will be as responsive to these changing conditions and demands as a more executive-centered agency governance structure might be.

A CHALLENGING FUTURE

Contemplation of South Carolina's future continues to raise new political issues and governmental problems that give the reader an incentive for continued study and action. The most ambitious citizen effort to define the state's future was the Commission on the Future of South Carolina. Lieutenant Governor Nick Theodore (1987–present), cochair with Governor Campbell, maintained that South Carolinians needed to "design their own fate instead of being the victims of change, as we have been so often in the past. We need a blueprint for the future as we move forward into the next century."[13]

The commission's 1989 blueprint was quite reformist, but it was only one blueprint. Not everybody agreed with its conclusions or endorsed its recommendations. The commission focused generally on the environment, education, the economy, and government. These areas provide a convenient backdrop with which to focus a brief but wider discussion of key future issues and concerns.

The Environment

Future urban development is inevitable. Urbanization will strain South Carolina's highway system and its traditionalistic political culture. Land utilization plans, scarce water reserves, regulations that control economic growth, beachfront management, and mass transit are alien terms to most South Carolinians today, but they may be household words tomorrow.

South Carolina's current environmental issues center on nuclear waste disposal and hazardous and toxic waste regulation. South Carolina has twenty-four toxic waste sites on the Superfund's national priorities list. This ranks it sixteenth in the country. Regulated nuclear waste disposal, even though governed by interstate compact, is an ongoing political issue.

Some say that in the past the state had a tendency for "casual acceptance" of nuclear, hazardous, or toxic waste. The image of "casually selling the state" to the waste industry persists for some. In 1992 a national television network featured Hampton County as the medical waste incineration capital of North America. The television commentary illustrated the constant trade-offs that underlie state hazardous waste policy. These trade-offs apply to the nuclear waste problem as well. On the positive side are the creation of new jobs, solutions for rural poverty, and more state and local government revenue. On the negative side are the potential for environmental and transportation accidents, fear for the adequacy of state and local government regulations, and increased costs for state and local supervision of waste sites.

The Economy

South Carolina has moved from agriculture and textiles to a diversified manufacturing economy. It is presently moving into a postmanufacturing era where the trade, service, and financial sectors are becoming more important. Between 1980 and 1990, South Carolina lost over thirty-seven thousand jobs in the textile industry. Richard Ellson projects that by the year 2000, only 6.4 percent of the state's workers will be in textile-mill product employment, compared to 32 percent in 1950. For manufacturing as a whole the comparable figures are 18 percent and 46 percent respectively. Ellson estimates that South Carolina could gain half a million jobs (a 2.2% annual increase) from 1985 to 2000. The largest increases will be in wholesale and retail trade, services, government and finance, insurance, and real estate.[14]

Despite this projected growth, one of the underlying problems facing South Carolina is how to spread economic development to rural areas. Rural counties tend to be characterized by low-wage manufacturing firms and farming. Although South Carolina experienced a net increase in private sector employment from 1978 to 1985 of 134,143 jobs, only 10,442 of these (7.8%) were in the thirty-one nonmetropolitan counties. Per capita income in these counties was 28 percent below per capita income in the metropolitan areas.[15]

Explanations given for the economic slowdown in these rural areas include international factors (which have led to diminished farm export demand and less low-wage manufacturing employment), a shift to a service economy (for which rural areas are ill suited), deregulation (which has increased the cost of doing business in the rural areas for banks and the transportation industry), and changes in agricultural distribution networks (which have resulted in farmers seeking fuel, fertilizer, and supplies from larger cities).[16] The future of small towns is vitally important for development, but that future is in doubt. Their economies could be boosted by small business development, homegrown and minority job opportunities, improved transportation connections to major cities, and improved regional cooperation in economic development.

South Carolina has the potential for dramatic economic development, but there is a continuing debate about what kind of development. High-tech, higher-value economic development interests have generally won out over heavy-industry advocates. Before comprehensive economic development can take place, the state must improve the level of education and skills of the workforce and improve the capacity for long-term planning, financing, and implementation of economic development programs.[17]

The People

If South Carolina is to have an "economic miracle," it will have to be through the improvement of its people—its human capital—via education. The state's economy will no longer improve if cheap labor continues as its major resource. The state's workers must compete in minds and skills with educated, trained, and hard-working citizens from other states and from countries around the world. A redesigned tax structure may also help, because the state's traditional reliance on the sales tax imposes direct burdens on the poor, the very ones who face the toughest economic and educational problems. A reformed tax system may also help this state generate adequate revenues for needed services, attract and retain desirable industries to enhance the economic base, and more equitably distribute tax burdens to encourage fairness.[18]

Education is the most important solution for uplifting the people. Six out of ten prison inmates in South Carolina are high school dropouts. In 1980, one of four South Carolinians over twenty-five years of age had completed less than eight years of school. When analysis of recent results is available, the proportion will not have changed greatly. If eight years of school is a measure of literacy, then only about 75 percent of the adult workforce in South Carolina can read and write effectively. The achievement of total adult literacy is the highest priority for the governor and legislative and business leaders as they pursue developments for an economically competitive state. Longer-term concerns for education stress improved school system governance and more efficient administration.

Longer-term concerns for the people also involve living conditions and health and human services. South Carolina's social service agencies, public and private, face extraordinary challenges. Housing for some South Carolina residents resembles the "shanties" seen in the poorest countries abroad.

The state has one of the highest rates of teen mothers on welfare in the nation. More than half of South Carolina's AFDC payments go to households headed by women who were mothers before they were twenty years old. In 1988, South Carolina ranked third highest in the country in infant mortality (12.3 deaths per 1,000 live births) and first in the percentage of low-birth-weight babies (9%).[19]

The state needs to coordinate its administrative capacities to get better information about human needs, to run its agencies more effectively and more cooperatively, and to blend public sources with private ones. Mental health and aging policies are critical areas for constant evaluation and improvement. More day care centers for children and the aging would improve access of workers, especially women, to the job market. Women are often kept away from work opportunities by family responsibilities in a traditionalistic society. State leadership and the cooperation of businesses and others will be instrumental in reducing the many barriers to a more competitive workforce and in promoting a healthier, happier population.

The Government

Today, some critics assail a governmental structure that is so decentralized that one official literally does not know what another is doing. Even the best state and local governmental structures have to be reexamined periodically. Today, pressures for better government come from federal government cutbacks and from demands for more efficiency, and because a smoothly functioning system of state and local governments is crucial to economic development.[20]

For some observers, conditions in South Carolina are ripe for change in the design, framework, and functioning of statewide governmental institutions.[21] Change may be necessary partly because the world is managed increasingly by executives. Some urgency may be contributed by the embarrassing federal indictment and conviction of several state legislators on charges of selling their votes on pending legislation. More broadly, South Carolina's three centuries of devotion to legislative dominance may have created perceptions that encourage citizens to look for a more effective state government.

The primary restraint on modern governance has been the 1895 state constitution that reinstituted a legislatively run executive branch as a way to control the governor. Fresh from Reconstruction experiences with stronger governors from out-of-state and from the reinstatement of the antebellum planters as governors, 1890s agrarian reformers arranged to keep the governor weak. The agrarians took on the veneer of colonial aristocrats to give credibility to their oligarchic control of the state's economy and its society.

A constitutionally weak executive, along with a powerful but decentralized legislature, was the best way to control a governor who might be elected against the wishes of a narrow political elite. Whether serving narrow interests or promoting broader values in government, a state governor today strives to set the administrative agenda for state operations and to direct the agencies implementing it.

External change has forced a more fluid political environment that has made the roles of governing boards and commissions less stable. Now, state reorganization as a means to control bureaucratic independence and to promote accountability in government are themes of structure and operations that will be much discussed in the future. Previous administrative reform of South Carolina's governmental structure has focused on the need to arrange executive authority clearly and effectively.[22] Yet difficulties in the political realities of establishing more uniform administrative structures in place of the divided and scattered arrangements for commissions and agencies have persisted for most of the twentieth century.[23] Competing ideals of reform such as public choice or market models must be weighed along with the classical administrative approaches.

Whether immediately successful or not, the challenges to legislative dominance will continue. Some have advocated a constitutional convention. The governor and leading citizens have conveyed, with some success, the call for extensive statutory changes and state agency reorganization. The legislative role in agency governance through commissions for major agencies, the formal and informal strengthening of the governor's powers so he or she can actually be a chief executive, and the increasing unification and modernization of the judicial system are major focal points for state government of the future.

Questions about the structure and function of local governments are also on the future agenda. South Carolina's local government traditions all too often reflect the agricultural, small-town past. Furthermore, the urbanization of the state is uneven. The General Assembly will have to consider how to finance state mandates for local governments as well as considering a renewed annexation procedure; a coordinated energy distribution policy for the state's public utilities, electric cooperatives, and municipalities; clarification of the role of special districts; and provision of independent revenue sources for municipal governments. The politics of "friends and neighbors" from the past may indeed be transformed as these issues are resolved. The underlying political tensions may create sharp differences among neighbors who may turn out to be just as competitive as they are friendly.

Continued urbanization and changes in workplace skills without an accessible, affordable, and accountable system of government promise to maintain or even to worsen the differences in family resources. Developing the future ability for South Carolinians of all backgrounds, especially the isolated rural and central-city poor, to gain access to an improved lifestyle is the most critical need.

The future promises a continuation of the entrenched traditionalistic political culture, but the recent and rapid changes in the state's economy and in the attitudes and achievements of its people suggest more favorable conditions for fresh approaches to persistent problems. The state and its people have much more power than they realize to mold their shared and individual destinies. Every person has a stake in finding mutually acceptable ways to agree on future political objectives and in making the changes necessary to realize them.

CHAPTER THIRTEEN

Suggestions for Further Reading

The study of South Carolina government and politics ranges from European roots to contemporary controversies. All along the way are inviting characters and challenging problems. The colonial period, interaction between African American and white settlers and between settlers and Native Americans, antagonisms between residents in internal geographic sections, the state's role in the United States, or major current economic problems suggest just a few of the topics a student of South Carolina government might investigate for study or read about for pleasure.

The study of South Carolina's political history, political institutions, and governmental processes is served by a wide range of sources that provide a vast body of information. There are rich studies of historical periods, biographies, anthropological and sociological studies, political studies, archives, data sets, and manuscript collections for the serious student.

In the sections that follow, illustrations of these many sources are provided. The reader must remember that the listings here are not intended to be exhaustive; they are examples selected by the authors to illustrate major types of sources and examples of each type.

GENERAL

Libraries

Among the major libraries of materials on South Carolina are the State Department of Archives and History, the South Carolina State Library, the South Carolina Historical Society's Collection in Charleston's Fireproof Building, the South Caroliniana Library Collection at the University of South Carolina, and university and college libraries' collections around the state.

State Department of Archives and History. The South Carolina Archives and History Commission governs the department. The commission is composed of the heads of the history departments at The Citadel, the University of South Carolina, Clemson University, and Winthrop University and representatives from the South Carolina Historical Society, the American Legion, and the South Carolina Historical Association.

The department keeps the noncurrent archives of state government. The holdings include records from before the permanent colonial settlement in 1670. The contemporary Archives Department was created in 1968 for the purposes of historic preservation, historical services, and records management. It stems directly from older state agencies such as the Public Record Commission of South Carolina, created in 1891 to obtain copies of South Carolina records in the British Public Record Office, and the South Carolina Historical Commission, created in 1894.

The archives contain many valuable materials not available elsewhere. Among major collections of records are legislative journals from 1692 and acts from 1691; Executive Council journals from 1671 and governors' papers from 1860; treasury records from 1721; land records (plats and grants) from 1731; wills, estate inventories, and similar records of the secretary of the province and state from 1671; military service records from the American Revolution, the War of 1812, the Mexican War, and the Civil War; and county records. A reference collection is also available that includes published reference works, bibliographies, archival guides, and monographs on South Carolina history.

The South Carolina State Library. The South Carolina State Library is the official depository for publications issued by state agencies, boards, and the General Assembly, and it contains a large collection of South Carolina state publications. The documents contain unique research information relating to South Carolina and the operation of state government.

The South Carolina State Library also maintains collections of publications relating to the history of the state and to contemporary problems. It is a rich resource of books, pamphlets, newspapers, periodicals, indexes, and related materials on South Carolina. The library is also an official depository for United States government publications and receives about 50 percent of available documents.

The State Library's computerized catalog contains information about the library's collection of books and other materials. *New Resources,* a monthly publication, highlights recent additions to the library's collection that are of interest to students of state government. It is the closest thing to a printed master list of state documents available.

The South Carolina library network is coordinated by the State Library. The network links public library headquarters in all forty-six counties and most academic, technical, college, and special libraries to the South Carolina State Library. Access to all of the resources of the State Library are available through this network.

State University Libraries. The major student and research libraries at the state's major higher education institutions, the College of Charleston, The Citadel, Clemson University, South Carolina State University, the University of South Carolina, the Medical University of South Carolina, and Winthrop University have long-established resources for the researcher. Each houses special collections—for example, the University of South Carolina's Thomas Cooper Library has a rare book collection that includes an emphasis on the Scottish poet Robert Burns. Clemson University Libraries' Special Collections include the papers of governor and United States senator Ben Tillman, state senator Edgar Brown, and United States senator Strom Thurmond.

Students of South Carolina history and politics will find the University of South Carolina's South Caroliniana Library an indispensable resource. Located on the university's historic Horseshoe, it houses extensive collections of manuscripts, published works, newspapers, and audiovisual records, documenting every phase of the life of the state, past and present. A separate division of Modern Political Collections is devoted specifically to documenting modern government in South Carolina. Its holdings include the papers of individuals such as United States senators Olin Johnston and Fritz Hollings, congressmen William Jennings Bryan Dorn and John McMillan, former governor Robert McNair, and state legislators Solomon Blatt, Rembert Dennis, and Isadore Lourie. The papers of Dennis, Hollings, and McNair are all being processed and will not be available publicly until processing is completed. The Modern Political Collections also includes records of the League of Women Voters and both the Democratic and Republican parties of South Carolina. The division is also engaged in an extensive oral history project. Members of the library's friends organization, the University South Caroliniana Society, receive an annual publication describing acquisitions received over the preceding year. The library is currently under the direction of Dr. Allen Stokes. Dr. Stokes is the author of *A Guide to the*

Manuscript Collection of the South Caroliniana Library, 1982, which describes the library's entire manuscript holdings at the time.

Journals and Books

A very useful journal devoted to South Carolina studies is *South Carolina Historical Magazine,* published by the South Carolina Historical Society. The society is a widely recognized and very prestigious resource for the study of South Carolina, and it emphasizes careful research and peer review of its published articles. The professional historians of the state are organized as the South Carolina Historical Association. The papers read at its annual meetings are published in the association's *Proceedings.* Scholarly articles that include or occasionally emphasize South Carolina as an object of study are found in a variety of journals in disciplines such as political science and sociology. Magazines emphasizing popular history are published intermittently: *Sandlapper: The Magazine of South Carolina* is one example.

Among the most useful books are general histories of South Carolina. The standard history for generations has been David Duncan Wallace, *History of South Carolina,* 4 vols. (New York: American Historical Society, 1934). Most major libraries in the state have a copy, and book hunters avidly look to purchase the out-of-print set, which is now quite expensive. The University of South Carolina Press makes available a one-volume, condensed version, D. D. Wallace, *South Carolina: A Short History* (Chapel Hill: University of North Carolina Press, 1951; Columbia: University of South Carolina Press reprint, 1961), that is less expensive and contains most of the substance of the larger work. As was the necessity of the day, volume 4 of the larger collection is a volume of printed biographies sold to finance the publication of the three scholarly volumes. Professor Wallace was a historian trained at Vanderbilt University who taught for generations at Wofford College in Spartanburg and whose interpretations are still a departure point for many contemporary treatments.

Other general histories exist. Edward McCrady, *History of South Carolina under Proprietary Government, 1670–1719* (New York: Macmillan, 1897) is a very detailed political, social, and institutional history of the period as viewed by a South Carolina advocate. Yates Snowden, *History of South Carolina,* 5 vols. (Chicago: Lewis Publishing, 1920), is an entertaining but glorifying history of the state.

Among more contemporary histories is Lewis Jones, *South Carolina: One of the Fifty States* (Orangeburg, S.C.: Sandlapper Publishing Company,

1985). While written as a school history to replace the traditional, dated versions in use, this volume is appealing to the general reader as well. The scholarship is extensive, well documented, incisive, and presented in an attractive style. Jones, a Wofford College professor, also has an earlier book, *South Carolina: A Synoptic History for Laymen* (Columbia, S.C.: Sandlapper Publishing Company, 1971), that is a compilation of articles that originally appeared in *Sandlapper Magazine*. The revised edition of the synoptic history was published in 1987. It includes a helpful reading list (pp. 289–95).

Another recent school history is Archie Vernon Huff Jr., *The History of South Carolina in the Building of the Nation* (Greenville, S.C.: Alester G. Furman III, 1991). Huff is a faculty member at Furman University who continues the tradition of a school history for the state's students begun by William Gilmore Simms in 1840. The most recent study of contemporary South Carolina is Walter B. Edgar, *South Carolina in the Modern Age* (Columbia: University of South Carolina Press, 1992). Another history of recent South Carolina is Ernest McPherson Lander Jr., *A History of South Carolina, 1865–1960* (Chapel Hill: University of North Carolina Press, 1960).

South Carolina celebrated its Tricentennial in 1970. As a part of the celebration and renewed interest in its historical past, several scholarly booklets and monographs on past events, themes, and periods were published by the University of South Carolina Press. Two widely used volumes that emerged during this time are Elmer D. Johnson and Kathleen Lewis Sloan, *South Carolina: A Documentary Profile of the Palmetto State* (Columbia: University of South Carolina Press, 1971), and Ernest M. Lander Jr. and Robert K. Ackerman, *Perspectives in South Carolina History, the First Three Hundred Years* (Columbia: University of South Carolina Press, 1973). The documents in the first book are supported by excerpts from major commentaries in the second one. Together they make a very useful essential library on the background of South Carolina.

South Carolina's long and varied history has been a fertile ground for biographies. Biographies range from laudatory directories, in which one often purchased an entry, to truly scholarly studies. Among scholarly studies of the state's more important and colorful political leaders is David Duncan Wallace, *Life of Henry Laurens* (New York: Putnam, 1915). Among his many roles, Laurens was president of the Council of Safety, a Revolutionary-era state governing body, and of the Continental Congress as well as a diplomat who was imprisoned in the Tower of London and exchanged for Lord Cornwallis.

There have been numerous scholarly biographies of John C. Calhoun with varying interpretations over the years, including Arthur Styron, *The Cast-Iron Man: John C. Calhoun and American Democracy* (New York: Longman, Green, 1935); Richard Nelson Current, *John C. Calhoun* (New York: Washington Square Press, 1963); and Margaret Coit, *John C. Calhoun: American Portrait* (Boston: Houghton Mifflin, 1950; Columbia: University of South Carolina Press, 1991). Citing one biography as authoritative will lead to a lively intellectual discussion. The collected works of John C. Calhoun are published in a continuing series, Clyde N. Wilson (ed.), *The Papers of John C. Calhoun* (Columbia: University of South Carolina Press). Professor Wilson has a helpful bibliography on Calhoun: Clyde N. Wilson, *John C. Calhoun: A Bibliography* (Westport, Conn.: Meckler, 1990). A useful collection of Calhoun's works is Clyde N. Wilson, *The Essential Calhoun: Selections from Writings, Speeches, and Letters* (New Brunswick, N.J.: Transaction Publishers, 1991).

South Carolina's military traditions have generated many studies of warrior/leaders. A brief selection of Revolutionary-era subjects includes Hugh F. Rankin, *Francis Marion: The Swamp Fox* (New York: Crowell, 1973); Robert D. Bass, *The Gamecock: The Life and Campaigns of General Thomas Sumter* (New York: Holt, 1961); and Alice N. Waring, *Fighting Elder: Andrew Pickens, 1739–1817* (Columbia: University of South Carolina Press, 1962).

Two interesting studies of leading figures in plantation life and conflicts are Carol Bleser, *The Hammonds of Redcliffe* (New York: Oxford University Press, 1981), and Elizabeth Muhlenfeld, *Mary Boykin Chesnut: A Biography* (Baton Rouge: Louisiana State University Press, 1981). An important book about the Civil War is C. Vann Woodward (ed.), *Mary Chesnut's Civil War* (New Haven: Yale University Press, 1981). Another important pre-Confederate life is described in John B. Edmunds Jr., *Francis W. Pickens and the Politics of Destruction* (Chapel Hill: University of North Carolina Press, 1986).

Of Confederate military leaders, General Wade Hampton III is probably the most noted. One tribute to him is Manly Wade Wellman, *Giant in Gray: A Biography of Wade Hampton of South Carolina* (New York: Scribner, 1949). There are histories of the various Confederate regiments from South Carolina that include sketches of officers. An interesting Reconstruction-period biography is Lillian A. Kibler, *Benjamin F. Perry: South Carolina Unionist* (Durham, N.C.: Duke University Press, 1946).

Among more contemporary biographies and studies of political careers is Francis Butler Simkins, *Pitchfork Ben Tillman, South Carolinian* (Baton

Rouge: Louisiana State University Press, 1944). James F. Byrnes has two autobiographical books, *Speaking Frankly* (New York: Harper, 1947) and *All in One Lifetime* (New York: Harper, 1958).

Biographical studies of individual African American South Carolinians are scarce. The story of an important national educator who was a native of the state is Benjamin E. Mays, *Born to Rebel: An Autobiography* (Athens: University of Georgia Press, 1977). A poignant autobiographical statement about the experiences of a young African American in the 1960s is Cleveland Sellars with Robert Terrell, *The River of No Return: The Autobiography of a Black Militant and the Life and Death of SNCC* (New York: William Morrow, 1973).

A recent biography of a major political figure is Nadine Cohodas, *Strom Thurmond and the Politics of Southern Change* (New York: Simon & Schuster, 1993).

Some single books help develop feeling for special aspects of the state. Chapman J. Milling, *Red Carolinians* (Chapel Hill: University of North Carolina Press, 1940) is an intriguing treatment of South Carolina's Native Americans and their relationships with increasing numbers of white settlers. Warren B. Smith, *White Servitude in Colonial South Carolina* (Columbia: University of South Carolina Press, 1961), is a study of indentured servants. George C. Rogers Jr., *Charleston in the Age of the Pinckneys* (Norman: University of Oklahoma Press, 1969), is a thoroughly scholarly study of South Carolina at its highpoint of influence in American history. Lacy K. Ford's *Origins of Southern Radicalism: The South Carolina Upcountry, 1800–1860* (New York: Oxford University Press, 1988) treats a significant force in the state's political, economic, and social development with thoughtful insights. Perspectives of Southern workers are included in Tom E. Terrill and Jerrold Hirsch (eds.), *Such As Us: Southern Voices of the Thirties* (Chapel Hill: University of North Carolina Press, 1978). The best recent collection of essays about South Carolina is David R. Chesnutt and Clyde N. Wilson (eds.), *The Meaning of South Carolina History: Essays in Honor of George C. Rogers, Jr.* (Columbia: University of South Carolina Press, 1991). Rogers is a preeminent historian who has written numerous books on South Carolina and South Carolinians.

There are many books about African American slavery, often with competing points of view. One study that gives a view of the contribution of slaves to the economic development of the South is Asa H. Gordon, *Sketches of Negro Life and History in South Carolina*, 2nd ed. (Columbia: University of South Carolina Press, 1971). Another that examines master-slave relations before the secession is Carol Bleser, *Secret and Sacred: The Diaries of James Henry Hammond, a Southern Slaveholder* (New York: Oxford University Press, 1988). Other revealing studies emphasizing social conditions of slavery in South Carolina are Charles Joyner, *Down by the Riverside: A South Carolina Slave Community* (Urbana: University of Illinois Press, 1984), and Leland Ferguson, *Uncommon Ground: Archaeology and Early African America, 1650–1800* (Washington, D.C.: Smithsonian Institution, 1992).

Two readable commentaries are Ben Robertson, *Red Hills and Cotton: An Upcountry Memory* (New York: Knopf, 1942), a description of life in early twentieth-century Up-Country South Carolina, and W. J. Cash, *The Mind of the South* (New York: Knopf, 1941). Cash came from the Blacksburg, South Carolina–Shelby, North Carolina, area and gives a provocative interpretation of a "southern" perspective. It is useful for insight into and for contrasts with contemporary conditions.

The truly serious student would best study South Carolina in the context of the southern region and the nation. One of the best starting points is the ten-volume series *History of the South* published by Louisiana State University Press. South Carolinians played many prominent roles in the development of the region and in national affairs and they are referred to often in this series. The first volume is Wesley Frank Craven, *Southern Colonies in the Seventeenth Century*, (Baton Rouge, 1949). The last volume in the series is by Greenville, South Carolina, native and University of North Carolina history professor George Brown Tindall, *Emergence of the New South, 1913–1945* (Baton Rouge, 1967).

The emergence of contemporary southern politics is treated in two seminal books by Earl Black, former University of South Carolina political science professor now at Rice University, and his brother Merle Black of Emory University. They are *Politics and Society in the South* (Cambridge: Harvard University Press, 1987) and *The Vital South: How Presidents Are Elected* (Cambridge: Harvard University Press, 1992). Another volume on regional politics as seen through the eyes of a native who served in the Nixon White House is Harry S. Dent, *The Prodigal South Returns to Power* (New York: John Wiley & Sons, 1978).

A seminal work on the South Carolina constitution is Professor James Lowell Underwood's four-volume series published by the University of South Carolina Press. The first volume deals with the relationship of the legislative, executive, and judicial branches. Volume 2 treats local self-government; volume 3 is a study of church and state, morality, and self-expression.

The fourth volume covers the struggle for political equality, emphasizing the evolution of voting rights in the state. Professor Underwood is a member of the University of South Carolina Law School faculty.

Important updates on South Carolina in the regional context include Chester Bain, "South Carolina: Partisan Prelude," in William C. Havard, *The Changing Politics of the South* (Baton Rouge: Louisiana State University Press, 1972), pp. 588–637; Jack Bass and Walter DeVries, "South Carolina: The Changing Politics of Color," in *The Transformation of Southern Politics: Social Change and Political Consequences since 1948* (New York: Basic Books, 1976), pp. 248–84; Neal R. Peirce, "South Carolina: Fossil No More," in his *The Deep South States of America: People, Politics, and Power in the Seven Deep South States* (New York: W. W. Norton, 1974), pp. 380–435; and Alexander P. Lamis, "South Carolina: No Place for 'Wild Men'?" in his *The Two-Party South* (New York: Oxford, 1984), pp. 63–75.

REFERENCE WORKS

Almanacs, Directories, and Atlases

A very popular one-volume treatment is the reissued *South Carolina: The WPA Guide to the Palmetto State,* with a new introduction by Walter B. Edgar (Columbia: University of South Carolina Press, 1988). The Federal Writers' Project (FWP), a part of President Franklin Roosevelt's New Deal, produced separate guides for many states in the late 1930s and early 1940s. Typical sections treat the natural setting, Native Americans, history, travel, agriculture, industry and labor, education, religion, recreation, and folklore. There is a section on the principal cities and towns, their history, and interesting facts about them. It is a good way to travel the state by armchair and to learn its basics.

The Legislative Manual is an indispensable source of information about South Carolina generally and its government and politics. It is published by the clerk of the South Carolina House of Representatives and has information on all state legislators as well as state agencies. The Office of Research for the House of Representatives also publishes *Legislative Update and Research Reports,* a summary and overview of major bills and issues as they are considered by the House.

The State Data Center publishes the annual *South Carolina Statistical Abstract,* a compendium of facts on South Carolina's social and economic development, manufacturing outputs, imports and exports, construction, housing activity, business and industry, wholesale and retail trade, employment, banking and finance, income, taxes, education, climate, recreation, and population. It is as close to a general-purpose reference work as one may find in the state.

The state offices and their employees are listed in the State Budget and Control Board's *Telephone Directory,* sold to the public at newsstands. Virtually every association in the state publishes a directory of its leading members and its major activities. Among them are the South Carolina Press Association, the South Carolina Municipal Association, and the South Carolina Association of Counties. Reporters, newspapers, and television stations, as well as county and city council members and department heads, are listed along with their telephone numbers. The State Development Board publishes an almanac of South Carolina businesses that is a good guide to the location of major economic activities in the state.

The authoritative geography of the state is Charles F. Kovacik and John J. Winberry, *South Carolina: The Making of a Landscape* (Columbia: University of South Carolina Press, 1989). It treats physical, historical, and contemporary aspects of South Carolina's landforms, the uses to which they have been put, and the implications for the state's economy and society. An especially attractive feature of this book is its emphasis on the visual landscape and its many changes over the decades.

Bibliographies and Listings

Two authoritative and comprehensive bibliographies that relate to the study of topics in South Carolina history are J. H. Easterby, *Guide to the Study and Reading of South Carolina History, Topical Lists* (Columbia: Historical Commission of South Carolina, 1949), and Lewis P. Jones, *Books and Articles on South Carolina History,* 2nd ed. (Columbia: University of South Carolina Press, 1991). Each inventory includes a list of major books, journal articles, bulletins, and booklets with helpful annotations. Both follow a chronological format and identify major topics for each significant historical period. Years that define the periods often overlap so that topics may be treated separately and thoroughly. Easterby, for example, has bibliographic entries for "Secession from the British Empire, 1765–1783" and for "Transition from Colony to State: Constitutional Developments, 1773–1790." Professor Jones's selections and comments on recent books and journal articles serve as a model for students to develop future bibliographies.

George C. Rogers Jr. and C. James Taylor have comprehensively catalogued events in the state's history in *A South Carolina Chronology, 1497–1992* (Columbia: University of South Carolina Press, 1993).

STATE DOCUMENTS (GENERALLY AVAILABLE IN THE STATE LIBRARY)

Legislative Branch

The *Journal of the South Carolina House of Representatives* and the *Journal of the South Carolina Senate* are issued daily during legislative sessions and report the business and selected roll calls of each body. Significant debate is summarized and some reports are also included.

Executive Branch

Acts of South Carolina are published by number and in an annual volume. Laws are periodically collected into the *South Carolina Code* and annual updates are published for the code.

The *South Carolina State Register,* a chronological collection of all agency rules and regulations, is published by the Legislative Council under the state administrative procedure act. Annually, the rules and regulations of the state are updated in a special supplement to the *South Carolina Code.*

Each agency issues an *Annual Report.* The annual report typically includes budget data, program performance data, and general information about the agency. They are available from the agency or from the State Library. Many agencies also publish special newsletters.

Judicial Branch

Case reports are available informally from the state Supreme Court and from the intermediate Court of Appeals. The *Annual Report* of the judicial branch includes a description of the state court system and information about its current operations.

RESEARCH CENTERS AND DATA SOURCES

Research Centers

The special research centers in the state are so numerous that any listing is destined to be incomplete. Major research centers are connected with the state's universities. Clemson University houses the Strom Thurmond Institute of Government and Public Affairs, which engages in a variety of social and public policy studies. The College of Charleston's Institute for Public Affairs and Policy Studies engages in research related to its surrounding area.

The University of South Carolina's research centers include institutes for southern studies, public policy, business and economic research, geological investigations, and the state archaeologist. Among them, for example, usc's Institute for Southern Studies offers a program of study for an undergraduate minor in southern studies or South Carolina studies, and it conducts research through an active program for Institute Fellows and Associates. The usc College of Business Administration's *Business and Economic Review* is widely read by the state's business leaders. The Institute for Public Affairs houses numerous policy research centers and distributes *South Carolina Public Policy Forum* within civic, governmental, and business circles. Coastal Carolina University has a research center for the study of South Carolina folklore. The publications and newsletters of each center are influential in a variety of settings locally, across the state, and elsewhere.

Coastal zone and marine wildlife interests are pursued by the University of South Carolina's Baruch Institute and many state agencies. The South Carolina Sea Grant Consortium holds many conferences and publishes a variety of studies as well as *Coastal Heritage,* a newsletter. *South Carolina Wildlife* is a popular subscription magazine published by the Department of Wildlife and Marine Resources that features scenic photography.

A recent series of four edited volumes published by the University of South Carolina's Bureau of Governmental Research and Service (now the Institute of Public Affairs) is a useful reference compilation of articles on South Carolina government by scholars, researchers, and administrators from across the state. They are Luther F. Carter and David S. Mann (eds.), *Government in the Palmetto State* (1983); Charlie B. Tyer and Cole Blease Graham Jr. (eds.), *Local Government in South Carolina,* 2 vols. (1984); and Charlie B. Tyer and S. Jane Massey (eds.), *Government in the Palmetto State: Perspectives and Issues* (1988). Carter and Mann have also written an update of the 1983 book, *Government in the Palmetto State: Toward the Twenty-First Century* (1992).

Public Opinion Surveys

The major statewide public opinion survey is the University of South Carolina's Institute for Public Affairs annual South Carolina Survey. It was only recently initiated, but it promises to be an ongoing source for scientific survey information about the state in general. Dr. Robert Oldendick directs the survey. Other occasional surveys are conducted by polling experts for mass media organizations.

Numerous surveys are undertaken on special issues by advocacy groups or on local matters by local media. Of special interest always are the various campaign polls during the primaries and elections. The results of these polls are usually reported in newspapers or on television.

Voting Return Information

Before the 1960s, South Carolina was exclusively a Democratic party primary state. As a result, most election outcome information was filed at the individual county level. The results may be learned in newspapers or through archival research. One source for general results of these primaries is Frank E. Jordan Jr., *The Primary State: A History of the Democratic Party in South Carolina, 1896–1962* (Columbia, S.C.: Privately printed, n.d.). County-by-county primary results are not included.

Beginning in 1968, detailed voting return information has been published in the annual report of the State Election Commission. The commission reports registration data, primary results by county, and general election results by precinct for all counties in the state.

Campaign Contribution Information

There is no single state source for campaign contribution information. Information required to be filed is available in the offices of the secretary of state, the clerk of the state Senate and the clerk of the state House of Representatives, the State Ethics Commission, and the Federal Election Commission in Washington. The federal commission has information about candidates for federal office in the state, such as the United States Congress.

Demographic, Economic, and Fiscal Data

The South Carolina State Data Center is the primary source for demographic, economic, and fiscal data about the state. It is a cooperative effort of the State Budget and Control Board's Division of Research and Statistical Services and the South Carolina State Library. The State Data Center was created in March 1981 through an agreement with the United States Bureau of the Census; it serves as a clearinghouse for Bureau of the Census information and products. The center receives, processes, and distributes census data. It creates population estimates and projections and provides assistance on sources of data, census concepts and definitions, and interpretation and use of census data. Data are made available in printed reports, diskettes, computer tape, and computer-generated maps. In addition to producing the *South Carolina Statistical Abstract* described above, the center also collects and maintains revenue and expenditure data from municipal and county governments.

Economic indicators for the state are defined and maintained by the University of South Carolina's College of Business Administration and the Labor Market Division of the South Carolina Employment Security Commission. The most comprehensive recent study of the state's economy was conducted by the Division of Research, College of Business Administration, University of South Carolina. Funded by the Liz Claiborne Foundation, *South Carolina: An Economy in Transition* (1987) analyzes the economic and human resource implications of state policy decisions.

Newspapers

Day-to-day accounts of life in South Carolina are recorded in the state's numerous weekly newspapers as well as the major ones. Among the large newspapers are the *State* (Columbia), the *Greenville News,* the *Charleston Post and Courier,* the *Florence Morning News,* and the *Spartanburg Herald-Journal.* The South Carolina section of North Carolina's *Charlotte Observer* is also read widely by regular political observers.

Dissertations, Theses, and Student Research

Each university houses the advanced and selected research of its students. The University South Caroliniana Library on the University of South Carolina Horseshoe in Columbia is the respository for all dissertations and theses completed by University of South Carolina students. Many studies in this collection treat the history and current policy concerns of South Carolina.

Notes

SERIES INTRODUCTION

1 *Rurban* designates "a settlement pattern of large belts of relatively small cities, towns, and rural areas populated by urbanites engaged in traditionally urban . . . pursuits, but living lives that mixed city and small town or rural elements." Daniel J. Elazar, *American Federalism: A view from the States,* 3rd ed. (New York: Harper and Row, 1984), p.126.

CHAPTER ONE

1 Elazar, *American Federalism,* p.109.
2 See Elazar, *American Federalism,* pp.114–22 for a more detailed explanation.
3 John Kincaid, "Political Cultures of the American Compound Republic," *Publius: The Journal of Federalism* 10 (Spring 1980): pp.1–15.
4 Donald W. Meinig, *The Shaping of America: A Geographical Perspective on Five Hundred Years of History* (New Haven: Yale University Press, 1986).
5 Bernard Bailyn, *The Ideological Origins of the American Revolution* (Cambridge: The Belknap Press of Harvard University Press, 1967), p.248.
6 The crop-lien system developed during Reconstruction because of the scarcity of money and the absence of banks. A farmer often did not have enough cash to operate until a crop could be harvested and sold, so farmers bought necessary goods and farm supplies at a country store on credit from the storekeeper. To make sure the debt was repaid, the storekeeper took a lien, or right to collect payment, on the future crop. See John D. Hicks and George E. Mowry, *A Short History of American Democracy,* 2nd ed. (Boston: Houghton Mifflin, 1956), pp.518–21.
7 The Great Awakening was a series of religious revivals that originated in New England and spread through the colonies in the mid-eighteenth century. See William J. Cooper Jr., and Thomas E. Terrill, *The American South: A History* (New York: McGraw-Hill, 1991), pp.68–70.

8 "Cosmopolitans" and "locals" are terms used by social scientists to describe tensions within a contemporary organization. Cosmopolitans follow the standards of a profession and the judgments of leaders in the profession regardless of where they are located. Locals build up their position in the organization rather than the profession, and they are more committed to the employing authority than to the profession. See, for example, Alvin W. Gouldner, "Cosmopolitans and Locals: Toward an Analysis of Latent Social Roles—I," *Administrative Science Quarterly* 2 (1957): 281–306, and Robert K. Merton, "Patterns of Influence: Local and Cosmopolitan Influentials," in his *Social Theory and Social Structure* (Glencoe, Ill.: Free Press, 1957), pp.393–95.

9 "Ol' boy" is a term that is frequently used in South Carolina to describe the intense networking of a small number of "connected" persons who run the state. In South Carolina, state legislators, lobbyists, and selected agency heads may be the best examples. These "ol' boys" often exhibit the aristocratic manners of traditionalistic political culture, perhaps reminiscent of English club politicians. For other observers, "ol' boys" may be more of a "bubba" network. "Bubba" is a regional nickname that sometimes has pejorative connotations of crudeness, lack of restraint, ham-handedness, and roughness in political conduct, especially if it is pronounced "bubber." An example from the past is a group of legislators that called itself "The Fat and Ugly Caucus." Caucus members prided themselves on how much personal consideration they could wring from lobbyists when conducting legislative business.

10 The colonial settlement and land-use patterns are treated extensively in David D. Wallace, *South Carolina: A Short History* (Columbia: University of South Carolina Press, 1961). Underlying political developments and political trends are discussed with perceptive insight by Chester Bain, "South Carolina: Partisan Prelude," in William C. Havard (ed.), *The Changing Politics of the South* (Baton Rouge: Louisiana State University Press, 1972), pp.588–637, and by Laurence W. Moreland, Robert P. Steed, and Tod A. Baker, "Regionalism in South Carolina Politics," in Luther F. Carter and David S. Mann, *Government in the Palmetto State* (Columbia: University of South Carolina Bureau of Governmental Research and Service, 1983), pp.5–26.

11 The discussion of South Carolina's geography is patterned after John Winberry and Charles Kovacik, *South Carolina: A Geography* (Boulder, Colo.: Westview, 1987).

12 Winberry and Kovacik, *South Carolina: A Geography,* pp.21–22.

13 South Carolina, *Statistical Abstract* (Columbia: State Budget and Control Board, 1991), pp.292, 304–5, and *South Carolina State Data Center Newsletter* (State Budget and Control Board) 11, no.1 (Winter 1991), p.2.

14 South Carolina, *Statistical Abstract* (Columbia: State Budget and Control Board, 1992), p.288.

15 South Carolina, *Statistical Abstract,* 1992, p.3.

16 South Carolina, *Statistical Abstract,* 1992, p.296.

17 Bain, "South Carolina: Partisan Prelude," pp.560–65.

18 *Statistical Abstract,* 1992, p.196. In January 1992, the counties were Allendale (59.4% African American), Bamberg (50.1%), Clarendon (50.1%), Fairfield (51.2%), Hampton (52.0%), Jasper (53.8%), Lee (55.4%), McCormick (52.0%), Orangeburg (52.7%), and Williamsburg (58.4%). Overall, African American voters comprised 25.1 percent of the state's registered voters.

19 By United States Census definition, persons living in densely populated areas and in places with populations of at least twenty-five hundred outside densely populated areas are classified as urban. The percentages used here are from South Carolina, *Statistical Abstract,* 1992, p.313.

20 As defined in the 1990 United States Census, an area qualifies as a Metropolitan Statistical Area (MSA) if it has a city of fifty thousand inhabitants or if it has an urbanized area of fifty thousand with a total metropolitan area population of at least one hundred thousand. The MSA is one or more urban counties along with adjoining counties that share a close economic relationship. The designation is valuable because it defines a market area in which businesses may potentially operate profitably. A potential disadvantage of the MSA designation is the loss of federal funds intended for the development of isolated areas.

21 South Carolina, *Statistical Abstract,* 1992, p.291.

22 South Carolina, *Statistical Abstract,* 1992. p.288.

23 Ernest M. Lander Jr., *A History of South Carolina: 1865–1960,* 2nd ed. (Columbia: University of South Carolina Press, 1970).

24 South Carolina, *Statistical Abstract,* 1992, p.147.

25 South Carolina, *Statistical Abstract,* 1992, p.158.

26 *Brown v. Board of Education* 347 U.S. 483 (1954) reversed the "separate but equal" doctrine, in force for South Carolina's public schools since 1896. A year later, *Brown II, Brown v. Board of Education* 349 U.S. 294 (1955), ordered school boards to proceed to dismantle the dual school system "with all deliberate speed."

27 Wallace, *South Carolina: A Short History,* pp.616–17.

28 John G. Sproat, "'Firm Flexibility': Perspectives on Desegregation in South Carolina," in Robert H. Abzug and Stephen E. Maizlish (eds.), *Race and Slavery in America: Essays in Honor of Kenneth M. Stampp* (Lexington: University Press of Kentucky, 1986), pp.164–84.

29 Ira Sharkansky, "The Utility of Elazar's Political Culture: A Research Note," *Polity* 2 no. 1 (Fall 1969), p.66–83; quote from p.68.

30 See, for example, Ellen M. Dran, Robert B. Albritton, and Mikel Wyckoff, "A Measurement Model of Political Culture: Operationalizing the Concept," a paper presented at the annual meeting of the Midwest Political Science Association, Chicago, April 1989; and John Kincaid and Joel Lieske, "Political Subcultures of the American States: State of the Art and Agenda for Research," a paper presented at the annual meeting of the American Political Science Association, Washington, D.C., August 1991.

31 See, for example, Robert L. Savage, "Patterns of Multilinear Evolution in the American States," in John Kincaid (ed.), *Political Culture, Public Policy and the American States* (Philadelphia: Institute for the Study of Human Issues, 1982), pp.25–58; Nicholas P. Lovrich Jr., Byron W. Daynes, and Laura Ginger, "Public Policy and the Effects of Historical-Cultural Phenomena: The Case of Indiana," in ibid., pp.176–206; and Robert L. Savage and Richard J. Gallagher, "Politicocultural Regions in a Southern State: An Empirical Typology of Arkansas Counties," in ibid., pp.207–21.

32 Details of the analysis discussed are in Cole Blease Graham Jr., "Differences in Political Culture: A Microanalysis," a paper presented at the annual meeting of the American Political Science Association, Washington, D.C., 1988.

33 Typical counties are picked by the authors from inspection of a factor analysis by county. No attention is given to potential differences within the county or the potential for significant distortions in the groupings. About all that can be said is that counties similar to the typical examples chosen by the authors on the basis of the factor analysis are similar to each other overall. By contrast, the counties in any other clusters are different.

34 South Carolina, *Statistical Abstract,* 1992, p.314.

35 Bob Bestler, "Horry Panel Looks ahead Two Decades," *Sun News,* Myrtle Beach, S.C., January 24, 1993. The convention was chaired by Coastal Carolina University faculty member Edgar Dyer.

36 The "Renaissance Weekend" is the creation of Phil Lader, Hilton Head Island homeowner and former president of Sea Pines Resort. Lader was an unsuccessful candidate for governor and served as president of Winthrop University in South Carolina, was president of Australia's first private university, and was recently appointed by President Bill Clinton as deputy director for management at the U.S. Office of Management and Budget. For more than a decade, Lader and his wife have invited other families to Hilton Head for an "off-the-record" discussion of current issues and problems. Bill and Hillary Clinton have attended for many

years. See Dave Moniz, "Clintons Put Hilton Weekend on the Map," *State*, Columbia, S.C., January 3, 1993, 1B, 7B.

37 See, for example, the discussion of contrasts in Greenville, South Carolina, by Alan Ehrenhalt, *The United States of Ambition* (New York: Times Books, Random House, 1991), chapter 8, "The Awakening of the Innocents," pp.85–104.

CHAPTER TWO

1 "Golden Age" is a term that describes the prominence of Charles Town (later Charleston) merchants and Low Country rice planters from about 1740 to 1800. See Lewis P. Jones, "The Golden Age," in his *South Carolina: A Synoptic History for Laymen* (Columbia, S.C.: Sandlapper Press, 1972), pp.76–89, and George C. Rogers Jr., *Charleston in the Age of the Pinckneys* (Norman: University of Oklahoma Press, 1969).

2 See the discussion in Louis Hartz, "The Feudal Dream of the South," in his *The Liberal Tradition in America* (New York: Harcourt, Brace and World, 1955), pp.145–200.

3 See James Lowell Underwood, *The Constitution of South Carolina*, Vol. 1: *The Relationship of the Legislative, Executive and Judicial Branches* (Columbia: University of South Carolina Press, 1986), pp.7–9.

4 See V. O. Key Jr., "South Carolina: The Politics of Color," in his *Southern Politics in State and Nation* (New York: Vintage, 1949), pp.130–55.

5 E. D. Johnson and K. L. Sloan, *South Carolina: A Documentary Profile of the Palmetto State* (Columbia: University of South Carolina Press, 1971), pp.10–11.

6 Ibid., pp.34–39.

7 Wesley F. Craven, *A History of the South*, Vol. 1: *The Southern Colonies in the Seventeenth Century, 1607–1689* (Baton Rouge: Louisiana State University Press, 1949), p.341.

8 Description from John Langdon Weber, *History of South Carolina* (Boston: Ginn and Company, 1891), pp.17–19. The several histories from the 1890s are dated by contemporary standards, but they catalog many events and developments in more detail than present histories permit.

9 Basic description in John A. Chapman, *School History of South Carolina* (Richmond, Va.: Everett Waddey, 1895), pp.35–37.

10 Lewis P. Jones, *South Carolina: One of the Fifty States* (Orangeburg, S.C.: Sandlapper Press, 1985), p.311.

11 Ibid.

12 W. Hardy Wickwar, *Three Hundred Years of Development Administration in*

South Carolina (Columbia: University of South Carolina Bureau of Governmental Research and Service, 1970), pp.63–67.

13 Henry Alexander White, *The Making of South Carolina* (New York: Silver, Burdett and Co., 1906), pp.156–57.

14 Wallace, *South Carolina: A Short History,* p.324.

15 The sport has long since been outlawed, but the "Fighting Gamecocks" is the mascot of the University of South Carolina. Francis Marion University, in General Marion's area of operations, claims "Patriots" as the name for its athletic teams.

16 Jones, *South Carolina: One of the Fifty States,* p.332.

17 David Ramsay, *History of South Carolina* (1809), in Johnson and Sloan, *South Carolina: A Documentary Profile,* p.430.

18 Elazar, *American Federalism,* p.46.

19 Numbers are from Wallace, *South Carolina: A Short History,* p.341.

20 Primogeniture means that the oldest child, usually a son, has the right to inherit the complete estate of one or both parents. This practice sanctions a traditionalistic elite.

21 Wallace, *South Carolina: A Short History,* p.344.

22 Ibid., p.345.

23 Rogers, *Charleston in the Age of the Pinckneys.*

24 Wallace, *South Carolina: A Short History,* pp.533–34.

25 Charles E. Cauthen, *South Carolina Goes to War, 1860–1865* (Chapel Hill: University of North Carolina Press, 1950), pp.201–16.

26 Wallace, *South Carolina: A Short History,* p.563.

27 Willie Lee Rose, *Rehearsal for Reconstruction* (New York: Oxford University Press, 1964).

28 Wallace, *South Carolina: A Short History,* pp.563–64.

29 Susan Bowler and Frank T. Petrusak, "The Constitution of South Carolina: Historical and Political Perspectives," in Carter and Mann, *Government in the Palmetto State* (1983), p.29.

30 Francis B. Simkins and Robert H. Woody, *South Carolina during Reconstruction* (Chapel Hill: University of North Carolina Press, 1932), p.109.

31 William J. Cooper Jr., *The Conservative Regime in South Carolina, 1877–1890* (Baltimore: Johns Hopkins University Press, 1968).

32 George B. Tindall, *South Carolina Negroes, 1877–1900* (Columbia: University of South Carolina Press, 1952).

33 Columbus Andrews, *Administrative County Government in South Carolina* (Chapel Hill: University of North Carolina Press, 1933).

34 Ralph Eisenberg, "The Logroll, South Carolina Style," in Richard T. Frost (ed.), *Cases in State and Local Government* (Englewood Cliffs, N.J.: Prentice-Hall, 1961), pp.155–63.

35 David D. Wallace, *The South Carolina Constitution of 1895*, Bulletin No. 197 (Columbia: University of South Carolina Press, 1927), pp.119–25.

36 Robert H. Stoudemire, "Constitutional Revision and the Task Ahead," *University of South Carolina Governmental Review* 17, no.1 (1975): 1–4.

37 Council of State Governments, *Book of the States*, 1960–1961 (Chicago: The Council, 1961).

38 Robert H. Stoudemire, "The S.C. Constitutional Revision Report," *University of South Carolina Governmental Review* 12, no.2 (1975): 1–4.

39 Ibid.

40 See Harry C. Martin and Donna B. Slawson, "The Expanding Role of the State Constitution," *Intergovernmental Perspective* 15, no.3 (Summer 1989): 27–29.

CHAPTER THREE

1 James M. Banner Jr., "The Problem of South Carolina," in Stanley Elkins and Eric McKitrick (eds.), *The Hofstadter Aegis: A Memorial* (New York: Knopf, 1974), p.60.

2 Ibid., p.61.

3 See, for example, Carol Bleser, *Secret and Sacred: The Diaries of James Henry Hammond, A Southern Slaveholder* (New York: Oxford University Press, 1988), for a discussion of racial and social interaction in a plantation setting.

4 See discussion in Alfred G. Smith Jr., *Economic Readjustment of an Old Cotton State: South Carolina, 1820–1860* (Columbia: University of South Carolina Press, 1958).

5 Ben Robertson, *Red Hills and Cotton: An Upcountry Memory* (New York: Knopf, 1942; Columbia: Reprint with introduction by Lacy K. Ford Jr., University of South Carolina Press, 1991), pp.19–20. Robertson observes that the romantic notion of "The People" easily deteriorates into narrow political interests.

6 The authors are indebted to Professor Daniel J. Elazar for his guidance in the interpretation of Calhoun's writings.

7 Richard C. Hofstadter, *The American Political Tradition* (New York: Vintage, 1948), p.68.

8 See Richard K. Cralle (ed.), *The Works of John C. Calhoun* (New York: D. Appleton, 1851–56), Vol. 1.

9 David Walker, *Toward a Functioning Federalism*, (Cambridge, Mass.: Winthrop, 1981), pp.47–48.

10 For a focused discussion of the "Civil Rights Revolution," see chapter 26 in Cooper and Terrill, *The American South: A History,* pp.700–738.

11 Daniel J. Elazar, "The Shaping of Intergovernmental Relations in the Twentieth Century," in John Kincaid (ed.), *Annals of the American Academy of Political and Social Science* 359 (May 1965): 10–22.

12 *Smith v. Allwright* 321 U.S. 649 (1944); *Gomillion v. Lightfoot* 364 U.S. 339 (1960).

13 *South Carolina v. Katzenbach,* 383 U.S. 301 (1966).

14 John J. Harrigan, *Political Change in the Metropolis,* 4th ed. (Glenview, Ill.: Scott, Foresman, 1989), p.122.

15 South Carolina Election Commission, *Annual Report, 1988–1989,* pp.415–37. Note: The annual numbers cited in the text do not occur in the same month.

16 South Carolina, *Statistical Abstract,* 1992, p.196.

17 *Statistical Abstract of the United States* (1992). Table 455: Federal Aid to State and Local Governments—Selected Programs, by State: 1990, p.283.

18 *Statistical Abstract of the United States* (1992). Table 25: Resident Population—States: 1970 to 1991, pp.22–23; table 505: Federal Funds—Summary Distribution, by State: 1990, p.324.

19 *Statistical Abstract of the United States* (1992). Table 531: Department of Defense Contract Awards, Payroll and Civilian and Military Personnel—States: 1990, p.324.

20 Richard L. Cole, Carl W. Stenberg, and Carol S. Weissert, "Two Decades of Change: A Ranking of Key Issues Affecting Intergovernmental Relations," *Publius: The Journal of Federalism* 13 (Fall 1983): 113–22.

21 South Carolina Legislative Audit Council, *A Study of the Impact of Federal and Other Funding on Legislative Oversight* (Columbia: South Carolina General Assembly, 1977), p.10.

22 Philip G. Grose, "Budget Reform in South Carolina: A Historical Perspective," in Charlie B. Tyer and S. Jane Massey (eds.), *Government in the Palmetto State: Perspectives and Issues* (Columbia: University of South Carolina Bureau of Governmental Research and Service, 1988), p.197. These major joint committees are the Joint Bond Review Committee, the Joint Appropriations Review Committee, and the Joint Committee on Health Care Planning and Oversight.

23 William V. Moore, interview with L. Fred Carter, September 18, 1989.

24 Richard C. Kearney, "Radioactive Waste Compacts: States Move Ahead," *State Government News* 30, no.9 (September 1987): 6–7.

25 108 S.Ct. 1355 (1988). Baker is James Baker, United States secretary of the Treasury at the time of disposition of the suit. The action was originally filed when

Donald Regan was Treasury secretary and may be seen in some articles as *South Carolina v. Regan.*

26 Public Law 97–248; 96 Stat. 324. Effective date was July 1, 1983. TEFRA is an amendment to specific provisions of the Internal Revenue Code, 1954.

27 See John J. Keohane, "*South Carolina v. Regan:* The New Federalism Drives Out the Old," *Municipal Finance Journal* 5, no. 1 (Winter 1984): 3–44, espe- -cially pp. 7–32, for a review of the historical arguments.

28 See "S.C. Municipal Bond Suit Attracts Support," *State,* Columbia, S.C. (May 8, 1984), 12A:1–2.

29 Margaret R. Wrightson, "The Road to *South Carolina*: Intergovernmental Tax Immunity and the Constitutional Status of Federalism," *Publius: The Journal of Federalism* 19 (Summer 1989), p. 52.

30 According to Louis Fisher, the states realized that the briefs in state-initiated cases, often prepared by a state attorney general, were being "outmatched" in le- gal arguments before the United States Supreme Court. As a result, a State and Local Legal Center was established in Washington, D.C., in 1983 "to coordinate strategy, sharpen advocacy skills, and prepare amicus briefs." Louis Fisher, *Constitutional Structures: Separated Powers and Federalism,* Vol. 1 of *American Constitutional Law* (New York: McGraw-Hill, 1990), p. 395.

31 *Chisholm v. Georgia,* 2 U.S. (2 Dall.) 419 (1793).

32 Elder Witt, "States and Localities at the Supreme Court: High Stakes, No Ap- peals," *Governing,* 1, no. 1 (October 1987): 19.

33 Saundra K. Schneider, "South Carolina, FEMA, and the Response to Hurricane Hugo," *South Carolina Forum* 1, no. 2 (April/June 1990): 16–23.

34 Public Law 93–288, Disaster Relief Act of 1974. Public Law 100–707 is an amendment, the Stafford Disaster Relief and Emergency Assistance Act of 1988.

35 Saundra K. Schneider, "FEMA, Federalism, Hugo, and 'Frisco," *Publius: The Journal of Federalism* 20 (Summer 1990): 97–115; quote from p. 107.

36 Jon Pierce and Edwin C. Thomas, "Disaster Preparedness Planning: Lessons Learned from Hurricane Hugo," *South Carolina Forum* 1, no. 2 (April/June 1990): 24–30.

37 Elliott Mittler, "The Plight of State Legislation Mandating Building Codes in South Carolina," a paper presented at the American Society of Civil Engineers' meeting, Charleston, S.C., September 1990.

38 Quoted in Dan B. Mackey, "Intergovernmental Focus: Spotlight on the South Carolina ACIR," *Intergovernmental Perspective* 11, no. 2/3 (Spring/Summer 1935): 6.

39 Daniel J. Elazar (*American Federalism*) maintains that major public problems

have been dealt with at national, state, and local governments since the time of American Independence without much regard for the federal structure. Most of these issues reflect the following concerns:

> (1) the essential character of the problems raised by each concern; (2) the essential distribution of authority and power between the federal government and the states; (3) the essential operational relationships between the two; (4) the essential subareas of subconflicts within each area, where any exist; (5) the essential position of the states as states, if the individual states take any position, in regard to the concern or any of its subareas; (6) the important interests aligned on various sides; and (7) any special considerations that should be weighed when viewing the specific issues involved (p.32).

40 Ann O'M. Bowman and Richard C. Kearney, *The Resurgence of the States* (Englewood Cliffs, N.J.: Prentice-Hall, 1986).

CHAPTER FOUR

1 Key, *Southern Politics*, p.131.

2 Earl Black and Merle Black, *Politics and Society in the South* (Cambridge: Harvard University Press, 1987), p.51.

3 321 U.S. 649 (1944).

4 *State,* Columbia, S.C., April 7 and April 14, 1944, quoted in Lander, *A History of South Carolina,* p.170.

5 Lander, *A History of South Carolina,* p.172.

6 Ibid., p.173.

7 Key, *Southern Politics,* p.150.

8 Black and Black, *Politics and Society,* p.52.

9 Jack Bass and Walter DeVries, *The Transformation of Southern Politics* (New York: Basic Books, 1976), pp.25–26.

10 Neal B. Peirce, *The Deep South States of America* (New York: W. W. Norton, 1974), p.397.

11 "Why a Democratic Senator Turned Republican," *U.S. News and World Report* (September 28, 1964): 84.

12 Alex Lamis, *The Two-Party South* (New York: Oxford University Press, 1984), pp.65–66.

13 Poll in the *State,* Columbia, S.C., 1986, reported in Cole Blease Graham Jr., "Partisan Change in South Carolina," in Robert H. Swansbrough and David M.

Brodsky (eds.), *The South's New Politics* (Columbia: University of South Carolina Press, 1985), p.171.

14 One problem with the Mason-Dixon Poll was that it did not provide the respondent with the "independent" alternative. Rather, the respondent had to make this assertion. The result may be a larger percentage of individuals who chose a party loyalty based on being presented only two alternatives.

15 *Charleston News and Courier,* October 30, 1990.

16 William V. Moore, "Party Development in South Carolina: County Chairmen Revisited," a paper presented at the annual meeting of the South Carolina Political Science Association, Florence, S.C., April 1, 1989, pp.18–19.

17 Key, *Southern Politics,* p.670.

18 Black and Black, *Politics and Society,* pp.59–66.

19 *Charleston News and Courier,* October 30, 1990.

20 Michael A. Maggiotto, "South Carolinians' Political Attitudes," in Tyer and Massey, *Government in the Palmetto State,* pp.141–66.

21 Moore, "Party Development," pp.10–11.

22 *Charleston News and Courier,* October 30, 1990.

23 Ibid.

24 Michael A. Maggiotto, "Parties and Elections in Local Government," in Charlie B. Tyer and Cole Blease Graham Jr. (eds.), *Local Government in South Carolina: The Governmental Landscape* (Columbia: University of South Carolina Bureau of Governmental Research and Service, 1984), p.208.

25 William V. Moore, interview with Vaughn Howard, Charleston County Republican party chairman, December 1990.

26 Maggiotto, "Parties and Elections," p.209.

27 South Carolina *Code of Laws* (1976), Sec. 7–11–20.

28 *State,* Columbia, S.C., February 14, 1988.

29 William V. Moore, interview with Mike Burton, Executive Director of the South Carolina Republican party, July 1991.

CHAPTER FIVE

1 Alexander Heard, *A Two Party South?* (Chapel Hill: University of North Carolina Press, 1950), p.58.

2 Key, *Southern Politics,* p.296.

3 Donald Fowler, *Presidential Voting in South Carolina* (Columbia: University of South Carolina Bureau of Governmental Research and Service, 1966), p.40.

4 Ibid., p.60.

5 Peirce, *Deep South States,* p.400.

6 Fowler, *Presidential Voting,* p.62.

7 Ibid., p.119. Republican success under these conditions suggests white backlash to Democratic party positions in counties with large numbers of unregistered African-American citizens.

8 Bass and DeVries, *Transformation,* p.27.

9 Fowler, *Presidential Voting,* p.122.

10 Bass and DeVries, *Transformation,* pp.25–26.

11 Peirce, *Deep South States,* p.32.

12 John P. Frank, *Clement Haynesworth, the Senate and the Supreme Court* (Charlottesville: University Press of Virginia, 1991).

13 Numan V. Bartley and Hugh D. Graham, *Southern Politics and the Second Reconstruction* (Baltimore: Johns Hopkins University Press, 1975), pp.173–74.

14 Lamis, *The Two-Party South,* p.69.

15 Julian Ian Fraser, *Republicanism in the Palmetto State: 1945–1986,* an honors thesis presented for Modern History and Politics, University of South Carolina, 1987, p.29.

16 Lamis, *The Two-Party South,* p.70.

17 Fraser, *Republicanism,* p.22.

18 ABSCAM refers to the 1979 "Arab Scam" in which Federal Bureau of Investigation agents posed as Arab sheiks and succeeded in buying promises of influence and favors from a few members of Congress, including Representative Jenrette.

19 Peirce, *Deep South States,* p.401.

20 Bass and DeVries, *Transformation,* p.262.

21 Bartley and Graham, *Southern Politics,* pp.152–53.

22 Fraser, *Republicanism,* p.28.

23 Lamis, *The Two-Party South,* p.72.

24 Ibid., p.73.

25 Peirce, *Deep South States,* p.400.

CHAPTER SIX

1 The conservatives organized as an all-white political party, the Democrats, after Reconstruction when the Republican party collapsed in the state. The conservatives were called, often sarcastically, "Bourbons," after the French royal house that was deposed by the French Revolution. When restored to post-revolutionary rule, the French royal house was said not to have changed from the ways of the past. By implication, the label "Bourbon" suggested that South Carolina conser-

vatives had the same political policies after Reconstruction that they had had before the Civil War.

2 Key, *Southern Politics,* p.155. Both of these bills supported labor unions. The "check-off" would authorize payment of union dues as a deductible item on a paycheck, thereby ensuring regular payments. The "closed shop" would restrict employment to union membership. South Carolina textile leaders were against any support for labor unions.

3 Peirce, *Deep South States,* p.411.

4 David S. Mann, "Mr. Solomon Blatt: Fifty Years in the South Carolina State Legislature," a paper presented at the University of South Carolina Symposium on South Carolina, Aiken, S.C., March 1–2, 1985.

5 Peirce, *Deep South States,* p.418.

6 *State,* Columbia, S.C., January 26, 1986.

7 Lewis P. Jones, *South Carolina: A Synoptic History for Laymen,* rev. ed. (Orangeburg, S.C.: Sandlapper Publishing, 1987), p.268.

8 Robert Botsch, "Interest Groups in South Carolina: The Triumph of the New South or Where Have All the Planters Gone?" Unpublished manuscript, p.12.

9 South Carolina, *Statistical Abstract,* 1992, p.65.

10 Walter B. Edgar, *History of Santee-Cooper, 1934–1984* (Columbia, S.C.: R. L. Bryan, 1984).

11 A cooperative is a business enterprise owned jointly by an association of users of its facilities or services. Cooperatives were formed in rural areas as a way to distribute electric power generated by a federal or state agency. See, for example, Clyde T. Ellis, *A Giant Step* (New York: Vintage, 1966). In many areas of South Carolina today, a specific co-op's service area may be in a suburb or a small town grown large.

12 *Charleston News and Courier,* September 10, 1989.

13 *Charleston News and Courier,* February 16, 1990.

14 *Charleston News and Courier,* April 23, 1990.

15 *State,* Columbia, S.C., August 11, 1991.

16 The agency representative justified attendance as a favor to help out a legislator who had to leave committee meetings every day by 4:00 P.M. in order to get home in time to feed his cows before dark. The representative told the legislator what happened after he left.

17 *State,* Columbia, S.C., August 11, 1991. State government employed 85,455 persons in 1989. Local governments combined totaled 125,962 employees, but the largest grouping, local school districts, included 77,620. The largest corporate site is the Westinghouse Savannah River Company, which had 24,000 employees as of December 1990. It is far larger than the Charleston Naval Shipyard's 8,100

employees or E. I. DuPont de Nemours & Company's Kershaw Count May Plant with 2,319 employees. South Carolina, *Statistical Abstract,* 1992, pp.70, 152.

18 For 1974–86, see Botsch, "Interest Groups in South Carolina." For 1987–89, see *Charleston News and Courier,* September 10, 1989. For 1990–91, see *State,* Columbia, S.C., July 14, 1991.

19 *Charleston News and Courier,* September 10, 1989.

20 Ibid.

21 *State,* Columbia, S.C., May 23, 1984.

22 William V. Moore, interview with state senator Glenn McConnell (*R*-Charleston), February 1990.

23 This and following quotations from *Charleston News and Courier,* March 12, 1990.

24 John V. Crangle, "Common Cause Research Report: Campaign Finance—South Carolina 1988 General Assembly Elections," a paper presented at the annual meeting of the South Carolina Political Science Association, Aiken, S.C., April 1990, pp.5–10.

25 Ibid., pp.7–8.

26 Ibid.

27 *Code of Laws of South Carolina, Annotated, 1976* (annual update, revised 1986), title 2, chap. 17, sec. 10.

28 *Charleston News and Courier,* February 5, 1990.

29 Ibid.

30 *Charleston News and Courier,* September 10, 1989.

31 Crangle, "Common Cause Research Report," p.5.

32 18 *U.S. Code Annotated* 1951 (1984). The *Code* section is known as the Hobbs Anti-Racketeering Act or the federal antiextortion law.

33 *Charleston News and Courier,* September 22, 1990.

34 *State,* Columbia, S.C., March 10, 1991.

35 Ibid.

36 Ibid.

37 William V. Moore, interview with Ron Fulmer, (*R*-Charleston), April 1991.

38 William V. Moore, interview with L. Fred Carter, April 1991.

39 *State,* Columbia, S.C., February 18, 1991.

40 William V. Moore, interview with Ron Fulmer, April 1991.

41 William V. Moore, interview with Robert Barber (*D*-Charleston), April 1991.

42 Ibid.

43 *State,* Columbia, S.C., February 18, 1991.

44 *State,* Columbia, S.C., July 21, 1991.

45 *Charleston News and Courier,* August 21, 1990.

46 *Charleston Post and Courier,* March 16, 1991.

47 *Charleston News and Courier,* March 14, 1991.

48 *Charleston News and Courier,* March 28, 1991.

49 *State,* Columbia, S.C., September 24, 1991.

50 Ibid.

51 *Charleston Post and Courier,* October 7, 1991.

52 *Charleston Post and Courier,* October 2, 1991.

53 *Charleston Post and Courier,* October 7, 1991.

54 South Carolina, *Legislative Manual* (Columbia: South Carolina General Assembly, 1992), pp.180–81.

55 Clive S. Thomas and Ronald J. Hrebenar, "Interest Groups in the States," in Virginia Gray, Herbert Jacob, and Robert B. Albritton, *Politics in the American States: A Comparative Analysis,* 5th ed. (Glenview, Ill.: Scott, Foresman/Little, Brown, 1990), pp.123–58. The other states in the dominant category are Alabama, Alaska, Florida, Louisiana, Mississippi, New Mexico, Tennessee, and West Virginia.

56 Ibid.

57 *Charleston News and Courier,* July 11, 1991.

CHAPTER SEVEN

1 Key, "South Carolina: The Politics of Color," p.151.

2 Ibid., p.154.

3 See William D. Workman Jr., *The Bishop from Barnwell: The Life and Times of Senator Edgar A. Brown* (Columbia, S.C.: R. L. Bryan, 1963), pp.99–129, especially pp.100–101. Workman was for many years the editor of the *State,* a newspaper in Columbia, and a member of the state's 1966 constitution revision study committee. He was also an unsuccessful Republican candidate for United States senator and for governor.

4 Bass and DeVries, *Transformation,* p.277.

5 Mann, "Mr. Solomon Blatt," pp.7–8.

6 William D. Workman Jr., "The Ring That Wasn't," in Ernest M. Lander Jr., and Robert K. Ackerman (eds.), *Perspectives in South Carolina History* (Columbia: University of South Carolina Press, 1973), p.393.

7 Cole Blease Graham Jr., and Kenny J. Whitby, "Party-Based Voting in a Southern State Legislature," *American Politics Quarterly* 17, no.2 (April 1989): 8.

8 *Charleston Post and Courier,* October 29, 1992, p.3B.

9 *Charleston News and Courier,* April 8, 1990.

10 Crangle, "Campaign Finance."

11 The resolution sets a final adjournment so that the legislature will not meet again until the formal date for a new meeting. It is called a "sine die" resolution, or one without a specific date for a future meeting. Legislators commonly pronounce it "sign-a-die."

12 Steven H. Haeberle, "The General Assembly and the Legislative Process," in Carter and Mann, *Government in the Palmetto State* (1983), p.94.

13 Ibid., p.97.

14 William V. Moore, interview with Glenn McConnell, February 1990.

15 *Charleston News and Courier,* February 23, 1975.

16 William V. Moore, interview with Glenn McConnell, February 1990.

17 *Charleston News and Courier,* February 26, 1990.

18 David S. Mann, interview with House Speaker Robert Sheheen (*D*-Kershaw), April 1990.

19 William V. Moore, interview with Glenn McConnell, February 1990.

20 William V. Moore, interview with state senator Theo Mitchell (*D*-Greenville), March 1990.

21 Ibid.

22 David S. Mann, interview with Robert Sheheen, April 1990.

23 Glen T. Broach, "Reform and Function: Continuity and Change in the South Carolina General Assembly," a paper presented at the annual meeting of the South Carolina Political Science Association, Aiken, S.C., April 1990.

24 Ibid.

25 David S. Mann, interview with Robert Sheheen, April 1990.

26 *State,* Columbia, S.C., May 5, 1991.

27 *State,* Columbia, S.C., January 14, 1992.

28 Ibid.

29 *Charleston Post and Courier,* January 28, 1992.

CHAPTER EIGHT

1 Robert B. Highsaw, "The Southern Governor—Challenge to the Strong Executive Theme," *Public Administration Review* 19 (1959): 7–11.

2 Key, *Southern Politics,* p.150.

3 J. A. Schlesinger, "The Politics of the Executive," in J. Jacob and K. Vines (eds.), *Politics in the American States* (Boston: Little, Brown, 1965), pp.207–37; Thad L. Beyle, "Governors," in Virginia Gray, Herbert Jacob, and Kenneth Vines (eds.), *Politics in the American States,* 4th ed. (Boston: Little, Brown,

1983), pp.180–221; and update by Beyle in Gray, Jacob, and Albritton, *Politics in the American States,* pp.201–51.

4 Beyle, "Governors," 1983, p.194.

5 Thad L. Beyle, "Appendix, Formal Powers of the Governor," in Gray, Jacob, and Albritton, *Politics in the American States,* p.568.

6 Diane Blair, *Arkansas Politics and Government* (Lincoln: University of Nebraska Press, 1988), p.136.

7 Cole Blease Graham Jr., "The Evolving Executive in South Carolina," in Tyer and Massey (eds.), *Government in the Palmetto State,* p.180.

8 Beyle, "Governors," 1983, p.196.

9 Mann, "Mr. Solomon Blatt," p.33.

10 William V. Moore, interview with Glenn McConnell, February 1990.

11 Beyle, "Governors," 1983, p.197.

12 David S. Mann, "Mr. Solomon Blatt: Fifty Years in the South Carolina State Legislature (An Oral History)." Unpublished Manuscript, p.333.

13 Harold B. Birch, "South Carolina State Government Administrative Organizations: The Orthodox Theory of Administration Reexamined," in Carter and Mann, *Government in the Palmetto State* (1983), pp.115–35; information from table on p.123.

14 *State,* Columbia, S.C., July 14, 1991.

15 Ibid.

16 Thad L. Beyle, "Appendix, Formal Powers of the Governor," (1990), p.570.

17 Glenn Abney and Thomas P. Lauth, *The Politics of State and City Administration* (Albany: State University of New York Press, 1986), pp.42–43.

18 Beyle, "Governors," 1983, p.456. In the assessment of gubernatorial powers in 1989, Beyle breaks the index into two parts, the budget-making power of the governor and the legislative budget-changing authority. Under this scheme, South Carolina's governor scores a 4 on the 5-point scale, but only five other states score as low. The 4 points mean that the governor shares the responsibility with others. On the legislative budget-changing authority, South Carolina scores 1 point along with forty-six other states. See Beyle, "Governors, Appendix B," 1990, pp.570–71.

19 James Lowell Underwood, "The Journey toward Local Government," in his *The Constitution of South Carolina,* Vol. 2, (Columbia: University of South Carolina Press, 1989), pp.18–19.

20 Graham, "The Evolving Executive," p.172.

21 South Carolina, *Journal of the Senate,* January 10, 1950.

22 South Carolina State Reorganization Commission, *The Budget Process in South Carolina: A Management Study* (Columbia: The Commission, 1985), p. A-47.

23 J. Samuel Griswold, "The State Budget and Control Board," in Luther F. Carter and David S. Mann (eds.), *Government in the Palmetto State: Toward the Twenty-First Century* (Columbia: Institute of Public Affairs, University of South Carolina, 1992), 143–48.

24 William V. Moore, interview with Luther F. Carter, September 18, 1989.

25 Ibid.

26 Grose, "Budget Reform in South Carolina," p.203.

27 John Dempsey and Samuel M. Hines Jr., "Management and Administration in South Carolina State Government," in Carter and Mann, *Government in the Palmetto State* (1983), p.150.

28 Bernard T. Pitsvada, "The Executive Budget—An Idea Whose Time Has Passed," *Public Budgeting and Finance* 8 (Spring 1988): 90.

29 William V. Moore, interview with L. Fred Carter, September 18, 1989.

30 Woodrow Wilson felt that government would work best if it worked more like a business. Wilson wrote about the conduct of governmental operations during the 1880s, a time during which American corporations were rapidly developing new approaches to management. He advocated the concentration of power in a single authority at the top of a hierarchical structure. Woodrow Wilson, "The Study of Administration," *Political Science Quarterly* 2 (June 1887): 197–222.

The highly integrated and centralized administrative structure required a strong chief executive. Reform studies have generally recommended more integration and coordination of South Carolina's divided administrative structure with the governor as the centerpiece.

31 South Carolina State Reorganization Commission, *Overview, South Carolina Human Services Demonstration Project* (1978), and *South Carolina Human Services Demonstration Project: A Report on the Final Conference* (1983).

32 Beyle, "Governors," 1983, p.201.

33 Thomas R. Dye, *Politics in States and Communities,* 4th ed. (Englewood Cliffs, N.J.: Prentice-Hall, 1981), p.161.

34 Highsaw, "The Southern Governor," pp.7–11.

35 *State,* Columbia, S.C., May 19, 1991.

36 Ibid.

37 Richard C. Kearney, "How a 'Weak' Governor Can Be Strong: Dick Riley and Education Reform in South Carolina," in Thad L. Beyle (ed.), *State Government: CQ's Guide to Current Issues and Activities, 1988–89* (Washington, D.C.: Congressional Quarterly Press, 1988), p.132.

38 Ibid., p.130.

39 Ibid., p.127.

40 "Tent meetings" refers to the practice of itinerant evangelists who pitch a tent in an open lot or field in order to hold a religious revival.

41 Kearney, "How a 'Weak' Governor," p.127.

42 William V. Moore, interview with Glenn McConnell, February 1990.

43 William V. Moore, interview with Theo Mitchell, March 1990.

44 Senator Theo Mitchell became the Democratic party's nominee for governor in the June 1990 primary and subsequently lost to Campbell in the November general election.

45 David S. Mann, interview with Robert Sheheen, April 1990.

CHAPTER NINE

1 See, for example, Edgar, *History of Santee-Cooper.*

2 Richard W. Ellson, "The Changing South Carolina Economy from 1950 to the Present," in Tyer and Massey, *Government in the Palmetto State,* p.229.

3 South Carolina, *Statistical Abstract,* 1992, p.253.

4 Steve Piacente, "Dollars Decline As Number of Poor Rises," *Charleston Post and Courier,* September 4, 1992, p.1A.

5 Ellson, "The Changing South Carolina Economy," p.227.

6 Lander, *A History of South Carolina,* pp.215–16.

7 Susan M. Walsh and Craig M. Wheeland, "Tax Incentives for Industrial Economic Development," in Cole Blease Graham Jr., and Charlie B. Tyer (eds.), *Local Government in South Carolina: Problems and Perspectives* (Columbia: University of South Carolina Bureau of Governmental Research and Services, 1984), p.162.

8 Ellson, "The Changing South Carolina Economy," p.238.

9 Quoted in Peirce, *Deep South States,* p.418.

10 *Charleston News and Courier,* July 2, 1989.

11 South Carolina, *Statistical Abstract,* 1992, p.77.

12 Ibid.

13 South Carolina, *Statistical Abstract,* 1992, p.77.

14 Ibid., p.78.

15 Peirce, *Deep South States,* p.424.

16 South Carolina, *Statistical Abstract,* 1992, p.330.

17 *Charleston News and Courier, Business Review,* May 2, 1989.

18 *Charleston News and Courier,* May 23, 1989.

19 Ibid.

20 *Charleston News and Courier,* February 2, 1990.

21 Ibid.

22 Ibid.

23 *Charleston News and Courier,* July 7, 1987.

24 Peter Applebome, "When Saving Navy Money Costs Jobs," *New York Times,* July 5, 1993, A7: 1–3.

25 *Charleston News and Courier,* March 13, 1993, 1A.

26 Jeffrey R. Clements, *Roles and Relationships: South Carolina Government in the Year 2000* (Columbia: South Carolina Advisory Commission on Intergovernmental Relations, January 1987), p.11.

27 South Carolina, *Statistical Abstract,* 1992, p.23.

28 Lander, *A History of South Carolina,* p.107.

29 *Charleston News and Courier, Business Review,* June 27, 1989.

30 Ibid.

31 *Charleston News and Courier, Business Review,* December 4, 1990.

32 Harold B. Birch, "Growth and Development in South Carolina," in Tyer and Massey, *Government in the Palmetto State,* p.277.

33 South Carolina, *Statistical Abstract,* 1992, p.31.

34 South Carolina Department of Education, *Annual Report,* 1988–1989, p.53.

35 Ann Reilly Dowd, "How Washington Can Pitch In," *Fortune* 121, no. 12 (Spring 1990): 53–63; statistics on p.58.

36 South Carolina Department of Health and Environmental Control, *Annual Report,* 1988–1989.

37 South Carolina Department of Social Services, *Annual Report,* 1988–1989.

38 South Carolina Vocational Rehabilitation Department, *Annual Report,* 1988–1989, pp.12–15.

39 South Carolina Commission for the Blind, *Annual Report,* 1988–1989, pp.6–9.

40 South Carolina Commission on Alcohol and Drug Abuse, *Annual Report,* 1988–1989, pp.10–13.

41 South Carolina Department of Mental Retardation, *Annual Report,* 1988–1989, pp.30–40.

42 South Carolina Commission on Aging, *Annual Report,* 1988–1989, pp.1–4.

43 South Carolina *Legislative Manual* (Columbia: South Carolina General Assembly, 1982), pp.294–403.

44 These departments are (1) Alcohol and Other Drug Abuse Services, (2) Commerce, (3) Parks, Recreation and Tourism, (4) Revenue and Taxation, (5) Labor, Licensing and Regulation, (6) Corrections, (7) Health and Human Services, (8) Insurance, (9) Juvenile Justice, (10) Probation, Parole and Pardon Services, and (11) Social Services.

45 John Drummond, Remarks to the South Carolina Executive Institute (Columbia, S.C.: 1991), pp.4–5. Unpublished manuscript.

46 Described in Walter B. Edgar and Cole Blease Graham Jr., "State Government Reform in South Carolina," a paper presented at the 1992 Citadel Symposium on Southern Politics, Charleston, S.C.

47 Carroll A. Campbell Jr., *State of the State Address,* Columbia, S.C., 1991, and "Restructuring State Government," *South Carolina Forum* 2, no.1 (January–March): 33–36.

CHAPTER TEN

1 Ronald G. Marquardt, "Judicial Politics in the South: Robed Elites and Recruitment," in James F. Lea (ed.), *Contemporary Southern Politics* (Baton Rouge: Louisiana State University Press, 1988), p.243.

2 Henry Glick and Kenneth Vines, *State Court Systems* (Englewood Cliffs, N.J.: Prentice-Hall, 1973), p.12.

3 Steven W. Hays, Steve Dillingham, and Nancy Wolfe, "The Judicial System in South Carolina," in Carter and Mann, *Government in the Palmetto State* (1983), pp.151–52.

4 Ibid.

5 Ibid., p.154.

6 South Carolina Judicial Department, *Annual Report, 1989* (Columbia: State Budget and Control Board, 1990), p.7.

7 Bradley T. Farrar, "Decision-Making on the South Carolina Intermediate Court of Appeals," a paper presented at the annual meeting of the South Carolina Political Science Association, Aiken, S.C., April 1990, p.18.

8 Ibid.

9 Ibid., p.25.

10 *Charleston News and Courier,* December 5, 1989.

11 *Charleston News and Courier,* January 20, 1990.

12 Judicial Department, *Annual Report,* p.10.

13 Ibid., p.8.

14 Ibid., p.104.

15 Steven W. Hays and Hillary McDonald, "The Criminal Justice System in South Carolina," in Tyer and Graham, *Local Government in South Carolina: The Governmental Landscape,* p.193.

16 Judicial Department, *Annual Report,* p.181.

17 Judicial Department, *Annual Report,* p.9.

18 Ibid., p.11.

19 Hays, Dillingham, and Wolfe, "Judicial System," p.158.

20 Ibid., p.159.

21 *State,* Columbia, S.C., January 1980, quoted in Hays, Dillingham, and Wolfe, "Judicial System," p.159.

22 Hays, Dillingham, and Wolfe, "Judicial System," p.162.

23 *Charleston Post and Courier,* December 16, 1991.

24 *Charleston Post and Courier,* November 13, 1991.

25 Personal correspondence, Judge Alex Sanders to William V. Moore, March 11, 1993.

26 Alex Sanders, "A Judge's Swan Song," *South Carolina Lawyer* (November/December 1992): 37–41; quote is from p.40.

27 Ann O'M. Bowman and Richard C. Kearney, *State and Local Government* (Boston: Houghton Mifflin, 1990), p.286.

28 The United States Bureau of Justice Statistics uses these offenses to compile the Crime Index: (1) murder and nonnegligent manslaughter, (2) forcible rape, (3) robbery, (4) aggravated assault, (5) burglary, (6) larceny-theft, (7) motor vehicle theft, and (8) arson. Arson was added as the eighth offense in 1978. See *Sourcebook of Criminal Justice Statistics,* 1990: 710. Also see Phil Jos and Mark E. Tompkins, "Crime and Corrections in South Carolina: The Problem of Prison Overcrowding," in Tyer and Massey, *Government in the Palmetto State,* p.101.

29 L. Douglas Dobson, "Toward the Future," in Carter and Mann, *Government in the Palmetto State: Toward the Twenty-First Century* (1992), pp.157–70; statistics from p.166.

30 *Charleston Post and Courier,* June 21, 1993, p.3B.

31 *Charleston Post and Courier,* November 11, 1990.

32 Ibid.

33 Ibid.

34 Jos and Tompkins, "Crime and Corrections," p.104.

35 Ibid., pp.102–6.

36 Ibid., p.115.

37 Ibid., p.121.

38 Dobson, "Toward the Future," p.166.

39 Barbara Martin, "Once a Judge," *State,* Columbia, S.C., March 2, 1992.

40 *Charleston Post and Courier,* December 10, 1991.

41 "State Yearbook, 1993," *Governing* (February 1993), p. 38.

CHAPTER ELEVEN

1 The latest municipal government is the city of James Island, created January 1993.

2 W. Hardy Wickwar, *The Political Theory of Local Government* (Columbia: University of South Carolina Press, 1970), pp.27–29.

3 A general monograph on the historical development of South Carolina counties is Andrews, *Administrative County Government in South Carolina*.

4 Wallace, *South Carolina: A Short History,* p.118.

5 Jones, *South Carolina: A Synoptic History for Laymen* (1987), pp.52–63.

6 Wallace, *South Carolina: A Short History,* p.148, and chapter 19, "Settling the Lower Middle Country, 1732–1760," pp.149–56.

7 William J. Blough, "Local Government in South Carolina," in Carter and Mann, *Government in the Palmetto State* (1983), p.168.

8 George R. Sherrill, "South Carolina," in Paul W. Wager (ed.), *County Government across the Nation* (Chapel Hill: University of North Carolina Press, 1945), p.425.

9 Eisenberg, "The Logroll, South Carolina Style," pp.155–63.

10 The practice of "staking" illustrates the local emphasis in some past campaigns. Supporters, especially for a senatorial candidate, would go to unpaved country roads and "stake them out" pretending to be highway department survey crews. This would lead citizens to believe that the state would pave the road if the candidate were successful. Without political parties, it was necessary to be nominated in the primary, since there were no opponents in the general election. Successful senators often controlled large amounts of county paving funds and could shift the funds around in the county at will. They could blame it on the big government in Columbia if the roads were not paved as promised in some areas of the county.

11 Robert H. Stoudemire, "Charleston County Governmental Organization," *University of South Carolina Governmental Review* 6, no. 4 (1959): 1–4.

12 377 U.S. 533 (1964).

13 On the low end of the spectrum in 1970 was McCormick County with about 8,000 people and Allendale and Calhoun with about 10,000. On the upper end are Charleston and Greenville with almost 250,000. Under the delegations system, each county had one state senator regardless of its population.

14 South Carolina Committee to Make a Study of the South Carolina Constitution of 1895, *Final Report* (Columbia, S.C.: The Committee, 1969).

15 The forms are council, council-supervisor, council-administrator, and council-manager.

16 George R. Sherrill and Robert H. Stoudemire, *Municipal Government in South Carolina* (Columbia: University of South Carolina Bureau of Governmental Research and Service, 1950), p.6.

17 In some states, cities are classified according to size. Larger cities usually have greater range to determine revenues and service solutions to local problems

through their city council or mayor. The smaller cities often have more specific requirements or limits.

18 Jonathan Walters, "Cities Have a Simple Message for States This Year: Set Us Free," *Governing* 5, no.4 (January 1992): 40–43.

19 Michael A. Pagano, "State-Local Relations in the 1990s," in John Kincaid (ed.), "American Federalism: The Third Century," *Annals of the American Academy of Political and Social Science* 509 (May 1990): 97. The other states are Connecticut, Georgia, Maine, New Hampshire, Vermont, and Wisconsin.

20 Steven B. Farber, "Federalism and State-Local Relations," in E. Blaine Liner (ed.), *A Decade of Devolution: Perspectives on State-Local Relations* (Washington, D.C.: Urban Institute Press, 1989), p.45.

21 Advisory Commission on Intergovernmental Relations, *State Mandating of Local Expenditures,* Report A-67 (Washington, D.C., July 1978), p.2.

22 Janet M. Kelly, *State Mandated Local Government Expenditures and Revenue Limitations in South Carolina, Executive Summary* (Columbia: South Carolina Advisory Commission on Intergovernmental Relations, June 1988).

23 South Carolina Advisory Commission on Intergovernmental Relations, *State Mandated Local Government Expenditures and Revenue Limitations in South Carolina,* Part 4, S. Jane Massey and Edwin Thomas (Columbia: The Commission, 1988), p.32.

24 Kelly, *Executive Summary,* p.6.

25 Marion W. Middleton, "Why South Carolina Local Governments Need a Local Option Sales Tax," *South Carolina Forum* (April–June 1990): 47.

26 Steven D. Gold and Sarah Ritchie, "State Policies Affecting Cities and Counties: Important Developments in 1990," *Public Budgeting and Finance* (Summer 1991): 37.

27 Jim Hatchell, "The Local Option Sales Tax: A Deal for Industry and Homeowners," *South Carolina Forum* (April–June 1990): 49.

28 The six counties were Charleston and five rural counties—Colleton, Hampton, Jasper, McCormick, and Marion. Charleston will redistribute funds to all in this original group but Colleton.

29 These counties are Abbeville, Allendale, Bamberg, Chester, Edgefield, Florence, Lancaster, Marlboro, and Saluda. Votes to adopt the tax have lost in other counties.

30 Charlie B. Tyer, "The Special Purpose District in South Carolina," in Tyer and Graham, *Local Government in South Carolina: The Governmental Landscape,* pp.75–89.

31 Mike Easterwood, "The Municipality and South Carolina Government," in Tyer

and Graham, *Local Government in South Carolina: The Governmental Land-scape*, pp.24–25.

32 South Carolina Advisory Commission on Intergovernmental Relations, *The Future of Municipal Annexation in South Carolina*, text by Andrew G. Smith (Columbia: The Commission, May 1991).

33 As general background on the public choice approach, see, for example, A. F. MacKay, *Arrow's Theorem: The Paradox of Social Choice* (New Haven: Yale University Press, 1980); Mancur Olson, *The Logic of Collective Action: Public Goods and the Theory of Groups* (1965; 2nd ed., Cambridge: Harvard University Press, 1971); or James M. Buchanan and Gordon Tullock, *The Calculus of Consent* (Ann Arbor: University of Michigan Press, 1962). A general discussion is David Schmidtz, *The Limits of Government: An Essay on the Public Goods Argument* (Boulder, Colo.: Westview, 1991).

34 Quoted in Jeff Miller, "Merger Bill Finally Goes to Governor," *State*, Columbia, S.C., March 31, 1992, p.7A.

35 Richard E. Greer, "Infrastructure Project Involves Cooperation," *Economic Developments* 4, no.8 (June 1990): 1.

36 Ibid., p.8.

37 The Council is composed of Anderson, Cherokee, Greenville, Oconee, Pickens, and Spartanburg counties, located in the northwest corner of the state.

38 Quoted in Dan B. Mackey, "Intergovernmental Focus: Spotlight on the South Carolina ACIR," *Intergovernmental Perspective* 11, no.2/3 (Spring/Summer 1985): 7.

39 South Carolina Advisory Commission on Intergovernmental Relations, *Tenth Anniversary Year Report*. Columbia: The Commission, 1990.

CHAPTER TWELVE

1 See the discussion in W. H. Phillips et al., *South Carolina: An Economy in Transition* (Columbia: University of South Carolina College of Business Administration, The Liz Claiborne Foundation, 1987), pp.5-32–5-54.

2 See, for example, articles on the economic squeeze on South Carolina's African American farmers (Pat Butler, "Losing a Way of Life" and "In Economic Squeeze, Farmer Lives on Hope," *State*, Columbia, S.C., December 28, 1991. According to Butler, by 1987 South Carolina's African American farmers had lost 90 percent of the land they held in 1984. The squeeze is also discussed in "South Carolina's Rural Life: Can It Be Saved?" *Coastal Heritage* 6, no.6 (Spring 1992): 2–8. Published by the South Carolina Sea Grant Consortium, the article notes the calculation by Professor James Hite, Clemson University, that more than two-

thirds of South Carolina's farmers depend on some form of nonfarm income in order to stay in operation.

3 Russell L. Ackoff, Paul Broholm, and Roberta Snow, *Revitalizing Western Economies* (San Francisco: Jossey-Bass, 1984).

4 *Lucas v. South Carolina Coastal Council,* No. 91–453, 60 LW 3609, 1992.

5 Robert H. Hayes and William J. Abernathy, "Managing Our Way to Economic Decline," *Harvard Business Review* (July/August 1980): 67–77.

6 David L. Birch, *Job Creation in America* (New York: Free Press, 1987).

7 John Shannon, "Federalism's 'Invisible Regulator'—Interjurisdictional Competition," in Daphne A. Kenyon and John Kincaid (eds.), *Competition among States and Local Governments* (Washington, D.C.: Urban Institute Press, 1991), p.120.

8 Martin N. Baily and Alok K. Chakrabati, *Innovation and the Productivity Crisis* (Washington, D.C.: Brookings Institution, 1988).

9 James L. Garnett, *Reorganizing State Government: The Executive Branch* (Boulder, Colo.: Westview, 1980), and Thad L. Beyle, "The Executive Branch: Organization and Issues, 1986–87," in *The Book of the States,* Vol.27 (Lexington, Kentucky: The Council of State Governments, 1988), pp.47–50.

10 G. W. Downs and P. D. Larkey, *The Search for Government Efficiency: From Hubris to Helplessness* (New York: Random House, 1986).

11 Alan Rosenthal, *Legislative Life: People, Process and Performance* (New York: Harper and Row, 1981), and Alan Rosenthal, *Governors and Legislatures: Contending Powers* (Washington, D.C.: Congressional Quarterly Press, 1990), especially chapter 3, "The Resurgent Legislature."

12 Larry Sabato, *Goodbye to Good-time Charlie: The American Governorship Transformed* (Washington, D.C.: Congressional Quarterly Press, 1983).

13 Commission on the Future of South Carolina, *Final Report* (Columbia: The Commission, 1989), p.4. Much of the following discussion is based on the report.

14 Ellson, "The Changing South Carolina Economy," pp.247–48.

15 Mark Henry and Georgann McMullen, "The Rural Economy in South Carolina: Prospects and Problems," in Tyer and Massey, *Government in the Palmetto State,* pp.250, 258.

16 Ibid., pp.263–64.

17 Ibid., p.268.

18 A comprehensive review of the state tax system is *Financing Government in the Palmetto State: A Study of Taxation in South Carolina* (Columbia: South Carolina Advisory Commission on Intergovernmental Affairs, February 1991).

19 South Carolina, *Statistical Abstract,* 1992, pp.6–7.

20 Steven D. Gold, *Reforming State-Local Relations: A Practical Guide* (Denver: National Conference of State Legislatures, 1989), pp. 1–9.

21 See, for example, a series of essays by Walter B. Edgar and Cole Blease Graham Jr.: "Legislature Has Been Dominant throughout S.C. History," *State*, Columbia, S.C., August 26, 1990; "Hydra-headed Monster of State Government Clumsy, Costly," *State*, August 29, 1990; and "It's Time to Change State's Horse-and-Buggy Constitution," *State*, August 31, 1990.

22 See, for example, the discussion in Robert McC. Figg Jr., "State Reorganization in South Carolina," *South Carolina Law Quarterly* 3, no. 133 (1950): 133–41.

23 Birch, "South Carolina State Government Administrative Organizations."

Index

Abney, Glenn, 145

adjutant general (military department), 54, 144, 176

African Americans: criticisms of Operation Lost Trust, 110–11; and economy, 160, 220; education policy, 166, 170–71; 1895 backlash, 38–39; immigration, xxv; as judges, 196; population, 12–13, 19, 26, 67; post–Civil War conditions, 35–36; public service, legislative, 122–24; on Republican party, 73; slavery, 46, 49; social position, 14–15, 47, 64; support for Democrats, 74, 77–78, 83–84; voter registration, 12, 51–53, 74, 80, 82; voting, 36–37, 39, 65–66, 68–71, 81, 83, 87, 92, 97

Agnew, Spiro, 92

agriculture, 26, 162–63, 218–19; commissioner, 97, 144, 176, 180

Aiken: city, 88, 169; county, 10, 13, 87, 92, 98

Alabama, 68, 82, 163

alcohol 42–43. *See also* state agencies and boards, Alcoholic Beverages Control Commission, Alcohol and Other Drug Abuse Services; mini-bottle

Allendale County, 12, 19, 163

American Revolution, 9, 23, 27, 30–31, 46, 156, 201; development of state constitutions, 27, 29

Anderson County, 13, 96

annexation, 12, 210–11, 215–16

aristocracy, 4, 7, 24, 31–33, 38

Arizona, 12, 82

associations, lobbying activities, 101–5, 208

at-risk students, 168–69

attorney general, 144, 176

Atwater, Lee, 77

Bamberg County, 85

Bandy, Lee, 68

Banner, James M., 46

Barber, Representative Robert, 112

Barnwell, county, 92, 120–21; waste site, 57–58, 103

Basic Skills Assessment Act (1978), 167

Bass, Jack, 67, 92, 158

Beachfront Management Act (1988), 218

Beasley, Jerry, 106
Beaufort: city, 162, 205; county, 18, 96
Berkeley County, 13, 18, 25, 90, 96, 98, 200, 205
Beyle, Thad L., 138–39, 155
Black, Earl, 127
Black Codes, 35–37, 39
Blatt, Speaker Solomon, 100, 120–21, 134–35, 141–44, 152, 170
Blough, William J., 165
Boan, Representative William D., 180
Board of education. *See* state agencies and boards, Education
bonds, municipal (bearer bonds), 58–59, 184; rating, 101
Bourbons, xxv, 100
British military, 29–30
Brown, Senator Edgar, 100, 120–21, 132, 151–52, 170
Brown v. Board of Education, 14, 68
Bryan, Senator James E., Jr., 113, 133
Buchanan, Patrick, 78
budget: bobtails, 150; line-items, 147
bureaucracy, xxix-xxx, 176–81
Burton, Mike, 78
Bush, Gwen, 86
Bush, President George, 70, 77, 84–85, 221
Buzhardt, J. Fred, 83
Byrd, Harry F., 81
Byrnes, Governor James F., 14, 68, 79, 151, 164, 166

Cabinet-type departments, 144, 154, 156, 176–81
Cabot, John, 23
Cabot, Sebastian, 23
Calhoun, John C., xvii, 21, 47–50, 64
Calhoun County, 10

Camden, city, 205
campaigns, 109, 114–16, 127
Campbell, Governor Carroll A., Jr., 73, 93–96, 139, 140, 150, 154, 167, 179, 222; as congressional candidate, 89–91; role in budgets, 147–48; role in elections, 77–78, 84–85
Caribbean, trade with, xxiii
Carnell, Representative Marion, 126
Carter, L. Fred, 112, 148
Carter, President Jimmy, 61, 83–84, 99
Carter, Speaker Rex, 135
Cave, Daisy, 44
Charles Town (Charleston), 25–26, 29–30, 204
Charleston (city), xxiii, 4–5, 7, 9, 31, 47, 55, 76, 82, 98, 103, 169, 173, 197, 201; economic activity, 159–61; local government, 205–6; as place for constitutional meetings, 33–35; population, 12–13
Charleston (county), 13, 81, 90, 94, 96, 98, 100, 169; government, 203–4; islands, 205; political party, 75–76
Charleston newspapers, 34, 70, 105
Chase, John, 92
Cherokee County, 12–13
chief justice, state Supreme Court, 188–90
Christian Coalition, 75, 91
churches: Anglican, 4, 25, 29, 200; Congregationalist, 5
Citadel, The, 169–70
cities, 198–99, 205–6, 209, 215–16
Civil Rights, Act of 1964, 51; amendments to U.S. Constitution, 35; national policy, 51–54; new laws in 1870s, 35
Civil War, xviii, xxiii, xxxi

Civilian Conservation Corps (CCC), 163

Clarendon County, 157

Clinton, city, 13, 174

Clinton, President Bill, 18, 77, 85

Clyburn, U.S. Congressman James, 91

coastal plain, 7–10, 18, 201

Cobb, Ron, 110–11

Coleman, James Karl, 165

Colleton County, 25, 200

colonization, xv; settlers, 3; South Carolina, 24–27, 200

Colorado, 12, 145

Columbia, 13, 31, 33–34, 54, 82, 88, 98, 117, 134, 162; government, 205–6

Common Cause, 105, 107, 109, 118

Commons House, 23–28

commonwealth, xvi, xxvi, xxix

comptroller general, 144–45, 176

Confederate Constitution, 33–34

Congressional elections, 86–92

Connally, John, 84

Connecticut, xviii, 74, 191

Conner, Judge Carol, 192

consolidation of local governments, 211–12, 215–16

Constitution, state: of 1790, 28, 31–33; of 1861, 33; of 1865, 34–36; of 1868, 28, 36–37, 202; of 1895, 28, 38–45, 199, 202, 225

constitutional revision, of 1895 Constitution, 28, 40–45, 62, 204

constitutionalism, xviii-xxi

Corbett, Representative Kenneth S., 108

corporations: advertisements by state development board, 57; importance to state economy, 100, 159, 163, 219

corrections, 194–97

cosmopolitans, 5

cotton, 13, 33, 49, 64, 156, 163

councils of governments, (COGs) 199, 214

counties, 37, 119, 198–202, 204, 206, 209, 215–16; legal doctrine, 199–200, 202, 209; reform 203; supply bill, 39, 202–4

county party chairpersons, 70, 72–73

Courson, Senator John, 107

courts, state, 182–90, 196

Crangle, John, 107

Crawford, Leon, 87

crime, 197

Cromer, James L. Mann "Bubba", Jr., 136

crop-lien system, 4, 34, 65

Cunningham, Robert, 86, 88, 92

Daniel, E. Bart, 111

Daniel, Lieutenant Governor Mike, 93, 95, 134

Davis, Confederate President Jefferson, 34

Davis, Congressman Mendel, 89

defense: base closure, 162; federal department, 55

Democratic party, xviii, 38, 54, 64–66, 69–74, 76–79, 81–82, 98–99, 122–24, 127, 221

Dennis, Senator Rembert, 126, 132–33, 152

Dent, Harry, 83

Derrick, Congressman Butler, 91

DeVries, Walter, 67, 92

Dewey, Thomas E., 66, 79

Dixiecrats, 66, 68–69

Dole, U.S. Senator Robert, 77, 85

Dorchester County, 13, 18, 90, 96

Dorn, Congressman William Jennings
    Bryan, 54, 93–94
Drake, Dwight, 105
Drummond, Senator John, 178
Dukakis, Michael, 77, 84–85
Duke, David, 78
dynamic counties, 16, 17, 18–20

early explorers, 23–24
economics, 6, 13–14, 105, 157, 217–
    20, 223–24; economic develop-
    ment, 57, 157, 159, 217, 223–24.
    See also state agencies and boards,
    Development Board
Edens, J. Drake, Jr., 68
Edgefield County, 10, 12–13, 19, 84
education: dropouts, 168–69, 224; Edu-
    cation Finance Act (1977), 131, 167;
    Education Improvement Act (1984),
    128, 152–53, 167–69, 170–71. *See
    also* state agencies and boards, Edu-
    cation
Educational Television Commission,
    117
Edwards, Governor James B., 84, 93–
    94, 152
Eisenhower, President Dwight D., 68,
    79, 81, 221
Elazar, Daniel J., 3, 15, 62
elections: district structure, 201; for
    governor (table), 93; laws, 184; out-
    comes, 79–99; for president
    (table), 81
elitism, xxix, 4, 100
Ellson, Richard, 223
environmental administration. *See* state
    agencies and boards, Health and En-
    vironmental Control

ethics: committee, 190, 128–29; legisla-
    tion, 114–16; reform, 113–16; regu-
    lations, 118
executive budget, 145, 147–48

Fairfield County, 88
farm: owners, 65; population, 162; ten-
    ants, 65, 67, 163
federal aid, 55–56, 206–8, 215; Aid to
    Families with Dependent Children
    (AFDC), 172–73, 225; general reve-
    nue sharing, 206
Federal Bureau of Investigation (FBI),
    110–11, 179
Federal Emergency Management
    Agency (FEMA), 60–61
federalism, xvii, 60–63; cooperative
    federalism, 51; dual federalism, 48,
    59; state-centered, 21, 48–49, 50
Florence, city, 13, 170, 206; county, 12,
    19
Florida, xxxi, 25, 40, 161, 163
foreign investment: business, 159–60;
    tourism, 161
forests, 9–11, 163. *See also* state agen-
    cies and boards, Forestry Commis-
    sion
Fowler, Donald, 81–82
Freedman's Bureau, 34
frontier, xxi–xxiv
Fulmer, Representative Ron, 111–12
Fundamental Constitutions, 21, 23–28,
    200
fundamental orders, xviii
Future: commission, 222; government
    structure, 225–26; population, 224–
    25; the economy, 223–24; the envi-
    ronment, 222–23

General Assembly, 27; activity, 131; committees, 128–30, 132–33; major changes, 133–37; oversight, 130–31; processes, 127–29; resources, 129–30; *See also* legislators; legislature

Geographical Information System (GIS), 213–14

geography, 7, 8, 9–11

geology, 7, 8, 9–11

Georgetown, 205

Georgia, xv, xix, xxiv, xxxi, 13, 25, 60, 74, 82–83, 124, 161, 163

Gephardt, Richard, 77

Gerald, J. Bates, 79

Gilbert, Senator Frank, 110

Glick, Henry, 182

Glover, Senator Maggie, 124

Goldwater, Senator Barry, 68, 82, 88, 221

golf, 18, 161

Gore, Vice President Albert, 77

Gottman, Jean, xxii

governor, 29; administration of grants, 56; appointment power, 139, 142–44; budget power, 139, 145–48; formal powers, 138–39, 155; informal powers, 151–55; office in South, 138, 140, 151; organization power, 139, 148–49; removal powers, 43; staff, 154; tenure potential, 139–42; term limits, 40, 42, 139–42; veto power, 37, 40, 139, 148–50

Governor's Management Review Commission, 147

Graham, George, 95

Grand Strand, 18, 57

Great Depression, 62, 157

Great Society, xviii, 62

Greene, General Nathaneal, 30

Greenville (city), 12–13, 82, 98, 160, 173, 197, 206, 219

Greenville (county), 13, 81, 87, 91, 94, 96, 98, 160

Greenwood: city, 170; county, 206

Gregory, Justice George T., Jr., 186, 196

Gressette, Senator Marion, 41, 126, 130, 132–33, 152

Grose, Philip, Jr., 148

Haeberle, Steven, 129

Hamilton, Alexander, 48

Hampton, General Wade, 180

Hampton County, 103, 222

Harley, Governor J. E., 120

Harris, Representative Patrick, 126

Hart, Gary, 77

Hartnett, Congressman Thomas, 86, 88–89, 95–96

Harwell, Chief Justice David, 190–91, 197

Haskell, Colonel A. C., 38

Haskins, Representative Terry, 127

Hawaii, xx, 55, 74

Haynsworth, Clement, 83

health administration. *See* state agencies and boards, Health and Human Services Finance Commission, Health and Environmental Control

health care, 171–73; interest groups, 104

Heath, Sir Robert, 24

Heller, Max, 89

Hicks, Jay, 112

higher education, 37, 103, 169–71

Highsaw, Robert, 151

Highway Patrol, 144, 177, 179

highways and public transportation. *See*
    state agencies and boards, highways
    and public transportation
Hilton Head Island, 18, 69, 90, 160–61
historical sketch: constitutions (table),
    28; major periods (table), 22; public
    education (major events), 165
Hofstadter, Richard, 48–49
Holderman, James, 104
Holland, Congressman Kenneth, 91
Hollings, U.S. Senator Ernest F., 14,
    54, 99, 151, 170; as governor, 158–
    59; as senatorial candidate, 86–87
home rule: amendment, 198–99, 204,
    212; legislation, 216
Horry County, 12, 18, 98
House members demography, state,
    122–24
Huguenots, xxiii, 5, 15
Humphrey, Hubert, 83
Hurricane Hugo, 9, 60–61

ideology, 71–73
immigration, 5, 34. *See also* population
independent voters, 54, 69
individualistic political culture, xxvii,
    5–6
industrial development, 6, 101, 157–59,
    219. *See also* state agencies and
    boards, Development Board
infrastructure, 212–14
Inglis, Congressman Robert, 91
interest groups: impact of Operation
    Lost Trust, 111–12; methods, 105–8;
    profile, 101–5; reforms, 112–16; reg-
    ulation, 108–9; spending, 107–8
intergovernmental relations, 46; fiscal,
    54–56; state advisory commission
    on, 61

interstate compacts, 57–58
interstate highways, 13, 57
intrasectional conflicts, xxv

Jackson, President Andrew, 49
Jackson, Jesse, 77
Jacksonborough Legislature, 30
Japan, 160, 219
Jasper County, 12, 19
Jefferson, President Thomas, 48
Jenrette, Congressman John, Jr., 89–
    90, 92
Jim Crow system, 39, 52
Johnson, President Lyndon B., 81
Johnson, President Andrew, 34
Johnston, Senator Olin D., 65, 86–87,
    91, 152
judges, 185–87, 192, 193, 196
judicial system: circuits, 143; districts,
    31, 183, 201; fragmentation, 182–
    84; reform, 183–84, 188–91, 196–
    97; in the South, 182

Kemp, Jack, 85
Kennedy, President John F., 81, 175
Key, V. O., Jr., 64, 66–67, 71, 100,
    119, 138–39
Kiawah Island, 161
Kincaid, John, 3
kindergartens, 167
King of England, 24
Kohn, Robert, 115

Lamar (city), 92
Lamis, Alex, 94
Land, Senator John, 107, 113
land-grant colleges, 169
Lauth, Thomas, 145

law enforcement. *See* crime; state agencies and boards, Law Enforcement

Lee County, 12, 19

Legislative Audit Council, 56, 130–31

legislators: career patterns, 124–26; demography, 121–24; general characteristics, 221; salaries, 127–28; work, 131–32, 136

legislature: budget committees, 145–47; delegations, 39, 119–21, 202–4; information system, 130; powers, 32, 35, 47; service, 125–26

Lever, Congressman Frank, 164

Lexington County, 13, 87–88, 92, 94, 98, 164

licensing boards, 178

literacy tests, 39

lobbyists 102–5, 107–16, 118

local government, 39, 43; forms, 206; home rule, 131–32; types, 198–99

local option sales tax (LOST), 208–9

Locke, John, 24

Long, Senator J. M., 107

long ballot, 43–44

Lords Proprietors, 24–25, 200

Louisiana, xx, xxv, xxxi, 82, 124, 140

Lourie, Senator Isadore, 113, 134

Low Country, 7–10, 20, 29–33, 35, 47, 80, 95, 100, 156, 170, 175, 207

Madison, James, 48

Maggiotto, Michael, 71

Mann, Congressman James, 89

Manning, Governor Richard I., 174

manufacturing jobs, 14, 218–20, 223

Marion, General Francis, 30

Marion County, 84–85

Marlboro County, 19, 84–85, 182

Marshall, Justice John, 48

Marx, Karl, 49

Massey, S. Jane, 71

Maybank, U.S. Senator Burnet R., 120

Mays, Representative Marshall, 86

McConnell, Senator Glenn, 106, 116, 132–33, 141–42, 154

McCormick County, 94

McGovern, U.S. Senator George, 83, 88

McKay, Representative Woodrow M., 106

McMaster, Henry, 86, 88, 97

McMillan, Congressman John, 89, 92

McNair, Governor Robert E., 152, 159; education policy, 166–67; governor's election, 92–93

media, 116–17

Medicaid, 63, 104, 172–73

mental retardation, 174–75

Metropolitan Statistical Area (MSA), 12–13

middle class 65, 67–69, 72, 82

Miles, Secretary of State Jim, 140

military facilities, 10, 18, 55, 63, 162

minibottle, 43, 174. *See also* alcohol

Mississippi, xxiv, 82, 85, 145, 163

Mitchell, Senator Theo, 93, 97, 106, 134–35, 154

Moore, Senator Tom, 134

moralistic political culture, xxvii-xxix, 4–5

Morrah, Senator Bradley, 86–87

municipal government, 186, 188, 204–6

Myrtle Beach, 12, 161

Napier, Congressman John, 90

Negro Citizens Committee, 65

New Deal, xviii, xxv, 50, 62, 67, 164

New England, xviii, xx, xxv-xxvi, 4–
   5, 11, 49
New South, 84, 217
newspapers, 117, 144, 172
Nicholson, Sir Francis, 204
Nixon, Julie, 92
Nixon, President Richard, 68, 83, 221
nominating primaries, 76–77; Super
   Tuesday, 77
North Carolina, 13, 34, 45, 58, 124,
   150, 161, 182, 218
North Charleston (city), 12

Oconee County, 96
Older Americans Act (1965), 175
one-party politics, 64–66
Operation Lost Trust, 110–11, 114, 116,
   118, 125
Orangeburg: city, 88, 169; county, 10

palmetto tree, 9
Parker, Senator Marshall, 86–87
parole, 195–96
Passailaigue, Senator Ernest L., Jr., 97,
   114
Patterson, State Treasurer Grady, 58
Patterson, Senator Kay, 136
Patterson, Congresswoman Liz, 91–92
Peace Commission Report (1945), 149
Pee Dee region, 89, 134, 175, 197
Peirce, Neal, 81
Perry, Governor Benjamin F., 34–35
Pickens, General Andrew, 30
Pickens County, 13, 96, 163
Political Action Committees (PACs),
   108, 127
politics: change, 65; competition, xxx;
   conditions, 220

political culture, xxvi-xxx, 3–6, 15–16,
   19–21, 46
political factions, xxx, 21, 30, 64
political parties, xxvii, 74–76; dealignment, 69, 73, 78; loyalty oath, 66;
   organization, 75–76; realignment,
   73, 78; two-party system, 66
political rings: Barnwell, 120–21, 140;
   Greenville, 140
poll tax, 37, 53
population, 6, 11–13, 67, 220; migration, xxii. See also immigration
ports. See state agencies and boards,
   Ports Authority
"Power Failure," 116, 144
prisons, 194–97; incarceration rates,
   194–96
property tax, 44, 206–10
protective tariff, 49
public education, 6, 37, 43, 164–69,
   208. See also state agencies and
   boards, Education, higher education
public opinion polls, 69–73, 118
public safety. See state agencies and
   boards, Public Safety
public utilities, 102–3, 106, 184; in
   cities, 211
Purvis, Melvin, 86

racial integration, 14–15
Ramsay, David, 30
Ravenel, Charles "Pug," 86–87, 89,
   94
Reagan, President Ronald, 50, 62, 84,
   221
Reconstruction, 4, 34–38, 50, 51, 68,
   156, 163, 202
redistricting, 125–27, 133, 180
Reese, Senator Glenn, 111

republicans, types of, 67–69

regionalism, xx-xxvi

Renaissance Weekend, 18

representation, 32, 33, 35–39, 126–27, 204, 216; county-based, 39; single-member districts, 126–27, 133

Republican party, xviii, 67–79, 81–82, 86, 98–99, 122–24, 127, 134–35, 221; presidential primary (1988), 85

restructured state government 144, 149, 156, 175–81, 220. *See also* state agencies and boards, Reorganization Commission

Reynolds v. Sims, 203

Rhett, Robert Barnwell, 34

Rhode Island, 191

Richland County, 10, 13, 65, 81, 94, 98, 157

Riley, Governor Richard W., 61, 93, 94, 105, 139, 140, 162, 195; style as governor, 152–54

rivers: Ashley, 5, 204–5; Black, 9; Combahee, 200; Cooper, 103, 204; Coosawhatchie, 9; Edisto, 30; Wateree, 10; Santee, 9, 103; Stono, 200

Rivers, Congressman L. Mendel, 54, 164

Roberts, U.S. Justice Samuel J., 59

Robertson, Ben, 48

Robertson, Pat, 75, 77, 85

Rock Hill (city), 13, 169

Rogers, Joseph, 92–93

Roosevelt, President Franklin D., 67

Russell, Judge Donald, 151–52

rust belt, xxvi

Sanders, Judge Alex, 191

Schlesinger, J. A., 138–39, 155

school districts, 198–99, 216

Schwartz, Speaker Ramon, 135

Scotch-Irish, 5, 15, 18

secession, 4, 33, 156

secretary of state, 97, 144, 176, 205

sectionalism, xxiv-xxvi

Senate members, demography, state, 123–24

Senate Rule, 19 128

seniority, 126, 128–29, 134

Setzler, Senator Nikki, 107

Sharkansky, Ira 15

Sheehen, Speaker Robert J., 107, 112–13, 118, 134–35, 154, 214

Shorey, Greg D., 82

Simon, Paul, 77

Sinking Fund Commission, 145

slavery, xxxi, 4, 7, 9, 19, 21, 31–36, 46–47; abolitionists, 49

Smith, U.S. Senator Ellison D. "Cotton Ed," 65

Smith, Stephen H., 109

Smith, Winchester, 120

Smith v. Allwright, 65

social policy: conditions, 6, 14–20, 217–20, 224, 225; policy, 163–64; services, 173–75; structure, 4; variables, 16–20

South Carolina Bar, 184, 191–92

southern contractual constitutions, xx

southern Republicans, 68–69; southern strategy, 83

Spartanburg: city, 13, 98, 160, 169, 219; county, 13, 91, 94, 96, 98, 183

special-purpose districts, 198–99, 202–4, 209, 210, 215–16

Spence, Congressman Floyd, 88, 90

Spratt, Congressman John, Jr., 90–91

state agencies and boards: 104, 142–44, 175–81; Advisory Commission on state agencies and boards (*continued*) Intergovernmental Relations, 207, 214–15; Aging, 175; Alcoholic Beverage Control Commission, 143, 177, 179, 180; Alcohol and Other Drug Abuse Services, 144, 174; blind, 174; Budget and Control Board, 55, 145–48, 154, 173, 177; Budget Commission, 119, 146; Commerce, 144; Corrections, 195; Development Board, 57, 157–59, 213, 217; Disabilities and Special Needs, 175, 177; Education, 97, 143–44, 147, 164, 166, 175–76; Ethics Commission, 115; Forestry Commission, 163; Health and Human Services Finance Commission, 172, 176; Health and Environmental Control (DHEC), 104, 171–72, 177; higher education, 104, 170–71; highways and public transportation, 104, 119, 143, 147, 180; Labor, Licensing and Regulation, 178; Law Enforcement (SLED), 144, 176–77; Mental Health, 174; Natural Resources, 177; Parks, Recreation and Tourism, 161; Ports Authority, 13, 160–61; Public Safety, 144, 177; Public Service Commission 119, 177, 189; Reorganization Commission, 148–49, 178; Revenue and Taxation, 144, 177; Social Services, 173, 175–76; Tax Commission, 143, 146–47, 177, 206; Technical and Comprehensive Education (TEC), 171; Transportation, 144, 177–78; Vocational Rehabilitation, 173–75

State Court of Appeals, 189–90
state mandates, 206–8

State Supreme Court, 182–86, 189–90, 196; office of Court Administration, 188–89
state-local fiscal relations: fragmentation, 209–10; local option sales tax, 208–9; mandates, 206–8
static counties, 16, 17, 18–20
Stevenson, Adlai, 79, 81
suffrage, 32, 37, 39, 42, 51–52, 74
Sumter, General Thomas, 30
Sumter: city, 12, 162; county, 10, 12, 19
sunbelt, xxv–xxvi
sunset act, 131

Tallon, Congressman Robin, 91–92
Target 2000, 167–69, 217
taxation, 44; incentives, 158; legislation, 58–59; protest, 215; reform, 224; sales, 167. *See also* state agencies and boards, Revenue and Taxation
technology, xxi–xxii, xxiv
Texas, xxv, xxxi, 9, 140, 145
textile industry, 14, 19, 23, 83, 101, 106, 157–58, 219
State, the (newspaper), 95, 111–12, 116–17, 136, 144
Thelen, Gil, 116
Theodore, Lieutenant Governor Nick, 95–97, 127, 140, 179, 222
Thigpen, Neal, 85
Thompson Report, 167
Thurmond, Senator J. Strom, 54, 66, 68, 73, 92, 221; as governor, 149; role in elections, 82–84, 86–87, 98–99
Tillman, Senator Benjamin R., 38, 89, 169, 181

Timmerman, Governor George Bell, 151

tourism, 161, 218. *See also* state agencies and boards, Parks, Recreation and Tourism

townships, 201

traditionalistic political culture, xxvii, xxix-xxx, 3, 6, 15, 19, 21, 33, 46–50, 64–65, 119–20, 217

Truman, Harry S., 66

turnover, legislative, 125–26

Tyer, Charlie B., 71

unified judicial system, 42, 183–84, 188–91

Union County, 13, 91

unionization: anti-union policy, 158; of new corporation, 101; right-to-work law, 158

U.S. Constitution, xix; civil rights amendments, 35; Eleventh Amendment, 60; Sixteenth Amendment, 59; Tenth Amendment, 59; Twenty-Fourth Amendment, 53

universities and colleges: Benedict, 171; Clemson, 14, 103–4, 169, 171, 213; Charleston, 169–70; Coastal Carolina, 169; Francis Marion, 170; Lander, 170; Medical University, 170; South Carolina State, 58–59, 169–71; South Carolina, 103–4, 151, 169, 179, 213; Winthrop, 169–70

Up-Country, 7–10, 18, 20, 29–33, 35, 40, 47, 95, 100, 156, 200

urban: policy, 213; population, 12–13; vote, 82; workers, 67

veto-proof minority, 122

Vines, Kenneth, 182

Virginia, xv, xxiii-xxiv, xxxi, 140, 191; as colony, 24

vocational rehabilitation. *See* state agencies and boards, Vocational Rehabilitation

voters: participation, 74–75; and party, 70–71; registration, 53–54, 74–75; white primary, 52, 65; younger voters, 69–70

voting rights, 51–54; Act of 1965, 39, 51, 53–54, 82

Waddell, Senator James, 107

Wade Hampton Hotel, 130, 137

Waites, Representative Candy, 212

Wall Street Journal, 59, 157

Wallace, David D., 32–33, 40

Wallace, George, 83–84

Waring, U.S. Judge J. Waties, 65

waste: hazardous, 103, 222–23; radioactive, 57–58

water power, 11, 13

Watson, Congressman Albert, 68, 82, 88–89, 92–93

Webster, Daniel, 48

Wedlock, Eldon, 118

West, Governor John, 51, 92–93, 147, 152, 159, 170

Westmoreland, General William, 93

westward population migration, xv

Whig ideas, xix-xx

White, Knox, 91

White supremacy, general, 23, 38–40, 46–47; white primary, 52, 65

Wilkes, Representative Tim, 107

Wilkins, Representative David, 114, 179

Williams, Senator Marshall, 126, 133

Williamsburg County, 12

Wilson, Woodrow, 149
women: rights, 40; in legislature, 122–24
Workers' Compensation Commission, 113
working class, 72; as voters, 83
Workman, W. D., III, 91
Workman, W. D., Jr., 86–87, 93, 95, 117

Wright, Fielding, 66

York County, 100, 159, 206
Young, Congressman Edward, 89, 93–94
Young Turks, 132

Zeigler, Senator Eugene, 86

In the Politics and Governments of the American States series

Alabama Government and Politics
By James D. Thomas and William H. Stewart

Alaska Politics and Government
By Gerald A. McBeath and Thomas A. Morehouse

Arkansas Politics and Government: Do the People Rule?
By Diane D. Blair

Colorado Politics and Government: Governing the Centennial State
By Thomas E. Cronin and Robert D. Loevy

Kentucky Politics and Government: Do We Stand United?
By Penny M. Miller

Maine Politics and Government
By Kenneth T. Palmer, G. Thomas Taylor, and Marcus A. LiBrizzi

Mississippi Government and Politics: Modernizers versus Traditionalists
By Dale Krane and Stephen D. Shaffer

Nebraska Government and Politics
Edited by Robert D. Miewald

New Jersey Politics and Government: Suburban Politics Comes of Age
By Barbara G. Salmore and Stephen A. Salmore

North Carolina Government and Politics
By Jack D. Fleer

Oklahoma Politics and Policies: Governing the Sooner State
By David R. Morgan, Robert E. England, and George G. Humphreys

South Carolina Politics and Government
By Cole Blease Graham Jr. and William V. Moore